OPERATIONS RESEARCH SOCIETY OF AMERICA

Publications in Operations Research
Number 14

PUBLICATIONS IN OPERATIONS RESEARCH

Operations Research Society of America

Editor for Publications in Operations Research

DAVID B. HERTZ

No. 1. QUEUES, INVENTORIES AND MAINTENANCE
Philip M. Morse

No. 2. FINITE QUEUING TABLES
L. G. Peck and R. N. Hazelwood

No. 3. EFFICIENCY IN GOVERNMENT THROUGH SYSTEMS ANALYSIS
Roland N. McKean

No. 4. A COMPREHENSIVE BIBLIOGRAPHY ON OPERATIONS RESEARCH
Operations Research Group, Case Institute

No. 5. PROGRESS IN OPERATIONS RESEARCH, VOLUME I
Edited by Russell L. Ackoff

No. 6. STATISTICAL MANAGEMENT OF INVENTORY SYSTEMS
Harvey M. Wagner

No. 7. PRICE, OUTPUT, AND INVENTORY POLICY
Edwin S. Mills

No. 8. A COMPREHENSIVE BIBLIOGRAPHY ON OPERATIONS RESEARCH, 1957–1958
Operations Research Group, Case Institute

No. 9. PROGRESS IN OPERATIONS RESEARCH, VOLUME II
David B. Hertz and Roger T. Eddison

No. 10. DECISION AND VALUE THEORY
Peter C. Fishburn

No. 11. HANDBOOK OF THE POISSON DISTRIBUTION
Frank A. Haight

No. 12. OPERATIONS RESEARCH IN SELLER'S COMPETITION: A STOCHASTIC MICROTHEORY
S. Sankar Sengupta

No. 13. BAYESIAN DECISION PROBLEMS & MARKOV CHAINS
J. J. Martin

No. 14. MATHEMATICAL MODELS OF ARMS CONTROL AND DISARMAMENT: APPLICATION OF MATHEMATICAL STRUCTURES IN POLITICS
Thomas L. Saaty

MATHEMATICAL MODELS OF ARMS CONTROL AND DISARMAMENT

Application of Mathematical Structures in Politics

THOMAS L. SAATY

United States Arms Control and Disarmament Agency

John Wiley & Sons, Inc.

New York • London • Sydney • Toronto

The opinions expressed here are those of the author. In no case are they to be construed as those of the U.S. Arms Control & Disarmament Agency or of the U.S. Government.

Library of Congress Catalog Card Number: 68-9248
SBN 471 74810 2
Printed in the United States of America

To
George G. O'Brien

QUAERENS PACEM

PREFACE

"Not for another thousand years will mathematics be of any use to history," said a historian friend. Undoubtedly there lived in ancient times people who worshiped the objects of the solar system in anthropomorphic reflection and would have ridiculed orbital motion as the essence of what may be of interest to a distant observer. What really mattered to them was that these objects were the dwelling places of the gods. The movement of these celestial bodies was only a small incidental part of their total activity.

It is difficult to ask the right question that relates an object to an involved observer and to consider only those *observed* properties of the object that affect the knowledge and understanding of the observer. After all, the object may have an infinite number of properties with which we need not be concerned. How to focus concern is a matter of ingenuity and pragmatism.

Mathematics is a tool that forces precision on the imagination and focuses attention on central issues without the undue embellishment of extraneous ideas. It provides a sound basis for analysis wherever its usefulness is established.

Politics needs a unifying language to cope with its fantastically complex problems. Esperanto is not the kind of language we have in mind, helpful as it may be in inducing communication among the peoples of the world. What is needed is a coherent universal logic aided by sensitive techniques to assess the impact of policies on the fulfillment of objectives. Complex structures must be represented unambiguously so that they may be grasped with clarity and the right decisions made.

The notion of equilibrium plays a central role in mathematical analyses. In politics equilibrium may be defined as a state between two or more parties in which each side considers his position as being the best that he can get in the event that his opponents adhere to their equilibrium strategy. In a sense this amounts to the requirement that each party do what the other would do in his place. Conflict has been defined by Boulding as competition with incompatible potential future positions in which each party's objective is to occupy such a position. The cultivation of an international environment for peaceful settlement of conflict among adversaries calls for a better understanding of the processes that give rise to conflict. One objective of research on arms control is to determine the effect of arms on the probability of the outbreak and escalation of war. We may not understand the effect of arms on conflict because we lack the tools for abstracting and adequately articulating a conflict process. Such tools would be used to build new structures to give a fresh look at the recurring problem of war. Their development is not a simple matter of reinterpreting the known or even of changing human nature, for no matter how peaceful people may wish to be they will always have opinions on which they will disagree. Yet decisions must be made and therefore reconciliation is essential.

The dual warring and arms-controlling efforts of man demand long-range interest in research and understanding, but the present urgent need is to buy time by halting the spread and use of nuclear weapons and to use it in a profitable search for permanent solutions.

I believe that mathematics is a useful tool for constructing models in arms control, and examples of these models are provided. I feel that problems of war and peace, which have not been adequately understood over a period of several thousand years, require new tools that have been developed with ingenuity and patient research. This book points out basic problems and some progress toward their solution.

I have not been concerned with weapon systems, their technical nature, the peaceful use of nuclear power, and similar questions that occupy the energy and attention of many able scientists throughout the world and are documented in the literature.

Arms control is not an end in itself. As Public Law 87-297, which established the Arms Control and Disarmament Agency, states: "Arms control and disarmament policy, being an important aspect of foreign policy, must be consistent with national security policy as a whole."

Although this book concentrates on arms control, it is inevitable that the broad political framework in which it takes place must also be considered.

I am indebted to several people for help and encouragement in preparing the manuscript. In particular, my thanks go to Russell Ackoff, Eric Anschutz, Bowman Cutter, André Ducamp, J. E. I. Heller, John Harsanyi, David Hertz, Nigel Howard, Michael Intriligator, Paul J. Long, Michael Maschler, Martin McGuire, Frederick J. Perry, Wyman Richardson, Herbert Scoville Jr., Jeffrey Smith, Sylvia Waller, and especially my wife Rozann for their reading, editing, and valuable suggestions.

THOMAS L. SAATY

Bethesda, Maryland
April, 1968

CONTENTS

MATHEMATICAL MODELS OF ARMS CONTROL AND DISARMAMENT

Part I

ON THE DEFINITION OF OBJECTIVES

In any area of human relations, including arms control, the process of decision making by people or governments may be analyzed according to

1. The selection of objectives and their consistency.
2. The adoption of stable policies (perhaps the most important topic discussed extensively here).
3. The choice of effective actions to carry out the policies and fulfill the objectives.

Actions may lead to a modification of objectives, giving the cycle in Figure 1.

Figure 1

Chapter 1

THE FRAMEWORK OF ARMS CONTROL

1.1. INTRODUCTION

Three major problems face our world. They are, in order of urgency:

1. The survival and security or peace problem.
2. The food and population problem.
3. The profitable and enjoyable preoccupation of the population in productive activities.

The subject that concerns us in this book is the first, that is, how to improve our chances of survival and attain greater peace and security.

Its opening statement, Public Law 87-297, September 26, 1961, known as the Arms Control and Disarmament Act, eloquently outlines the broad purpose of the Arms Control and Disarmament Agency, established according to this Congressional Act. It states, in part: "An ultimate goal of the United States is a world which is free from the scourge of war and the dangers and burdens of armaments; in which the use of force has been subordinated to the rule of law; and in which international adjustments to a changing world are achieved peacefully. It is the purpose of this Act to provide impetus toward this goal by creating a new agency of peace to deal with the problem of reduction and control of armaments looking toward ultimate world disarmament."

The primary functions of the Agency are

"(*a*) the conduct, support, and coordination of research for arms control and disarmament policy formulation;

(*b*) the preparation for and management of United States participation in international negotiations in the arms control and disarmament field;

(*c*) the dissemination and coordination of public information concerning arms control and disarmament; and (*d*) the preparation for, operation of, or as appropriate, direction of United States participation in such control systems as may become part of United States arms control and disarmament activities."

The pursuit of arms control may be outlined in the following steps:

1. The consideration of national objectives and how they relate to arms control.
2. The development of arms control policies.
3. The coordination and adoption of these policies within each government concerned.
4. Negotiations to bring about multination agreements: this entails evolution of policy to give such measures wider acceptance; and the signing of treaties.
5. The application of agreements and their enforcement.

These steps guide the organization of this book.

The purpose of the book is to explore some basic problems of arms control through mathematical models and to show that such models might be used to study idealizations of problems arising in the arms control area. In this analysis of theoretical concepts one learns to look for underlying basic concepts that occur in the real situation such as the idea of equilibrium and stability; the effect of cooperation versus threats and noncooperation; the value and use of information in negotiations, and so on. Our models are not constructed as a ritual to prove some immediate point in arms control negotiations. Major useful theories are rarely constructed in a single flash of genius. Previous analyses and data serve as illuminating guidelines in this process.

1.2. WHAT IS ARMS CONTROL?

Arms control has been defined as [3] *the attempt of nations to impose arbitrary limits on the instruments and consequences of conflict.* Note that this does not mean minimizing the consequence of conflict, because it would entail simultaneous minimization of the probability of outbreak of armed conflict and the resulting damage. The joint probability of these two events cannot be adequately estimated.

A more restrictive definition requires the minimization of the probability of starting armed conflict (a special type of conflict), after having imposed limits on its consequences. This definition assumes the presence of a method of enforcing agreements.

No longer is it feasible to use unlimited force to coerce other nations to capitulate or yield advantage. In doing so a country may bring about its own destruction. If we accept this danger of using nuclear weapons as the major problem of our generation, we must accept the corollary of increased danger from the proliferation of such weapons. The more nuclear powers there are, the greater is the opportunity for miscalculation and error, or deliberate nuclear attack.

Widespread ownership of nuclear weapons can pose a great threat to a secure environment. Therefore the present concern of arms control is to harness and freeze the increase of these weapons and their delivery systems. Arms control has a far more extensive concern, however, with how nations resolve their differences and thus has a long-range interest in addition to the immediate concern with nuclear weapons. To the extent that a secure environment contributes to the fulfillment of a nation's objectives, the control of arms is a method that complements armament and national defense.

Rarely is a major problem solved in one stroke and this most serious problem is no exception. We must go at it little by little, diligently and with patience.

Time may be used as a device to divide disarmament problems into three classes: immediate, intermediate, and long-range problems.

The immediate objective is to control arms by reducing weapons in order to decrease the probability of the occurrence of a conflict, and also to decrease its intensity if it breaks out. Of course, this objective will be there for a long time to come and will always be immediate. Intermediate problems of arms control and disarmament require a thorough understanding of the consequences of war, methods for de-escalating conflicts when they occur, and an awareness of the dangers and consequences of intensifying hostilities to the parties involved, through a well-predicted outcome. Less reliance on weapons is a consequence of this approach. The solution of long-range problems requires developing the art of peacefully settling issues in a council with give and take. Sufficient authority such as an international legislature must be available to channel the parties involved into positive and responsible action. Sometimes postponement leaves it to time to obviate the necessity for a solution. Policies and agreements of bargaining are only the beginning.

It was pointed out in the definition of arms control that methods for enforcing agreements must also be found. Enforcement itself involves a number of problems. Thus whereas agreement on limits may require understanding of the balance of power and national securities of various countries together with the role of weapons in providing security, enforcing agreements requires monitoring, inspection and verification of possible violations, imposing sanctions, and taking corrective action. Each of these measures is itself a subject requiring substantial development as an engineering aspect of arms control.

Research in arms control is needed to develop understanding of the causes of outbreak of hostilities; the development and buildup of weapons preceding war; the effect of weapon buildup on the risk of outbreak of hostilities; and how political settlements, be they territorial, military, or other, affect the nature of war. An aim of arms control negotiations may even be the limitation of arms for economic reasons.

To effect arms control measures nations proceed by considering the objectives and the limitations within which these objectives are to be attained; then they negotiate with other nations to attain a degree of fulfillment of those objectives. Negotiation is a successive approximation process requiring adaptation within accepted national goals.

The definition of objectives requires some knowledge of the utility of certain policies. Thus utility is an important concept in arms control. As the fulfillment of objectives comes in conflict with those of other nations, the notion of strategy is used. The theory of games is a mathematical theory which deals with the analysis of strategies of this type. A central concept of this theory is that of identifying strategies that lead to equilibrium. The object of the theory would then be to point out to the parties the various equilibria and recommend that the only actions to be taken should be those which lead to equilibrium.

1.3. SOME CURRENT INTERESTS OF ARMS CONTROL [17]

1. Destruction of specified obsolete (or other) weapons.
2. Verification that fissionable materials from peaceful programs are not being diverted to weapons.
3. Transfer of fissionable material for peaceful use under control of the International Atomic Energy Agency by both the United States and the U.S.S.R.
4. Exploration of a verified freeze of the number and characteristics of strategic nuclear offensive and defensive vehicles.
5. Prevention of further proliferation of nuclear weapons.
6. A comprehensive test-ban treaty.
7. Establishment of observation posts to prevent or reduce the likelihood of surprise attack (not a current pursuit).

This partial list points to the concrete objective of arms control from which indications are derived as to where theoretical developments may be useful. Each of these topics has a number of papers and ideas associated with it explaining the position to be taken.

Some of the recent achievements of arms control have been:

1. The partial nuclear weapons test-ban treaty.

2. The establishment of a hot line between Washington and Moscow to cope with emergency crises, averting miscalculation leading to war.
3. The Antarctic Treaty to the effect that the area is not to be used for military purposes.
4. Outer space agreement banning its use to satellites carrying nuclear weapons.
5. The Treaty on the Nonproliferation of Nuclear Weapons.

1.4. THE ROLE OF MATHEMATICAL MODELS

The techniques of mathematics may be divided into three closely related areas:

1. Deterministic models given in the form of equations and inequalities describing the behavior of a system such as is done by a differential equation of motion or by the constraints in an input-output model. These are known as descriptive models.
2. Optimization models that superimpose an expression to be maximized or minimized subject to constraints as described in (1). The expressions may be given in algebraic or integral form or in any of the standard forms in which algebraic operations of integration or differentiation are performed. Optimization problems concerned with conflict utilize a separate theory—the theory of games. Since optimization prescribes best modes of action, its models are called normative.
3. Probability models which also occur in the form of equations and inequalities but with a probability statement such as may be applied to expectations, for example. Decision theory, which is a field of optimization, is concerned with *expected* utility maximization. Thus probability expressions and constraints also occur in the framework of optimization.

These three areas may now be represented by a triangle that depicts their interrelations (Figure 2). Most mathematical representations of a real-life phenomenon encounter their greatest obstacle at the earliest step

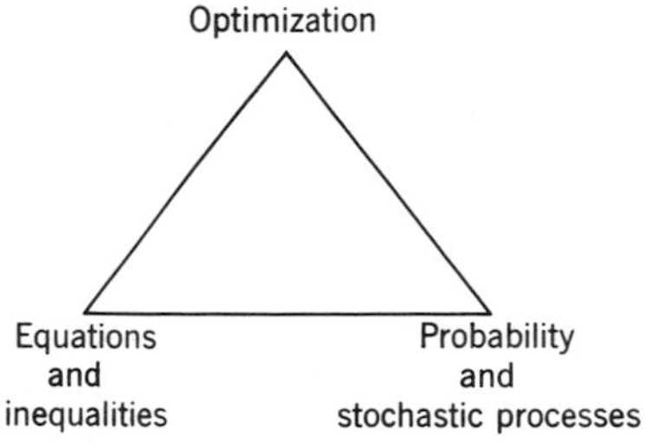

Figure 2

of turning ideas into expressions, equations, and inequalities, that is, correctly formulating the problem and asking the right kind of questions about this representation. The mathematical quest for existence and uniqueness of solutions, characterization of their properties, their construction, and the convergence of the algorithm used come later. In the political field formal tools and a framework which facilitate a mathematical approach do not exist yet. Thus for broad familiarity concepts should be our primary concern.

A model approach to political problems on whose solution even the opinions of reasonable men radically differ cannot be a panacea. It is helpful, however, to discover those areas where mathematical formulation can aid rational decision making.

In very brief terms mathematical formulations of a complex problem point out possible outcomes and improve the selection of an optimum strategy of action.

In general, logically precise statements and their manipulation can be programmed for a computer. Statements involving unspecified uncertainty or vagueness cannot. A problem may not have a mathematical formulation because:

1. It has a complex structure which is inadequately understood.
2. The structure is understood, but it involves uncertainty whose relevant probabilities cannot be estimated.
3. The phenomenon appears to be well understood empirically, but there is no known theoretical structure for its representation.
4. The structure is known and well understood but not solvable even by approximation methods.

We must distinguish between vagueness and uncertainty. Uncertainty indicates that quantities are known only probabilistically and the structure itself must portray this property. The answers would take into consideration variability due to uncertainty. Vagueness, however, refers to lack of adequate understanding of the problem to be represented.

Considerable difference in attitude and ability to discriminate are required in viewing the use of quantification in the social sciences as opposed to its use in the physical sciences. Quantification in the physical sciences is a tool of explanation and prediction used to construct theoretical models from which exact or approximate numerical answers can be obtained. The absolute magnitude of the numbers is essential because there is usually a scale of measurement used such as the centimeter-gram-second system of physics. Simply stated, quantification in science generally leads to solving equations for exact numerical answers.

As a tool for interpretation in politics, quantification plays a different role. It provides criteria to test for the existence of certain qualitative concepts. Examples of such concepts are stability and consistency, which are basic to the interpretation of various configurations in human relations. Since configurations are relative in time, place, and people, the notions themselves are also relative. Only in the future could such ideas as the absolute stability of policies and the absolute consistency of a set of objectives be defined. Basic scales for measuring the magnitude or value of actions and degree of fulfillment of objectives must come first if their probabilistic nature could ever be more usefully quantified. Deriving the odds for a certain game of chance, for example, does not assure one of winning or losing. It only aids him in the selection of a strategy for betting in repeated plays. He understands the situation but cannot bend it to advantage in any single play. If he knows that the odds are against him and he has no way of improving his chances then even long-range considerations will not help. It is useful to have this type of information.

What follows is a report on progress in preliminary research on a difficult subject. Applications to the settlement of international problems are ultimate objectives.

1.5. ON OBJECTIVES AND THEIR CONSISTENCY; AN EXAMPLE

It is not the purpose of this book to define the national objectives of any country but merely to point out the importance of defining and using some objectives for scientific evaluation of policies. This short section gives an example of a scientific approach in the analysis of the consistency of objectives.

Tradition, geography, economics, politics, international relations, and form of government of a nation suggest to its people and particularly to its government and leaders the objectives or ends to pursue. Such objectives may deal with the way an individual is to be treated, and how much liberty and freedom he is to be allowed. They may also involve ideas regarding the degree of control that the government exercises over an individual's choice and activity. Other objectives may be concerned with influencing other nations and their people through diplomacy. Some objectives of a nation may be established in its constitution and other legal documents. Others may remain unwritten but implicitly understood. Some objectives start out as beliefs and gradually become ends for action.

The policies of a nation are the means it adopts in various areas of activity to attempt to achieve a measure of fulfillment of its objectives. A policy may be concerned with the amount of defense forces a nation should have in order to deter aggression and maintain security. Another policy may outline the approach to be taken in an international negotiation. A third may even pursue aggression on a planned basis as Hitler did.

Policies are subject to change and evolution according to the circumstances. Thus the attainment of objectives may vary according to the emphasis a government puts on the pursuit of its policies. An objective is a goal. A policy is a plan of action. The only way that the attainment of an objective can be measured is through the success of a policy relating to it. Thus the adoption of policies requires a thorough understanding of objectives and careful measured judgment supported by experience of a pragmatic nature. The task of selecting objectives requires perception of man's nature and set of values. It is not a mathematical pursuit. Whether objectives are consistent or lead to contradictions can be determined by logical analysis. Assigning priorities to objectives and distributing the available effort accordingly is another important pursuit which requires sound judgement and broad experience.

We now consider an interesting scheme, utilizing logic relations to analyze the consistency of the objectives of a nation as they come under the influence of objectives of other countries. This is the method of A. Joxe [32] who uses West Germany for his illustration. Starting with four goals or motivations he relates them to a set of five political objectives. It is on the level of political objectives that logical contradictions occur. Both objectives and motivations may come into conflict with those of another country. It is important to note that the analysis applies to the period in which the motivations and objectives are held. We start with the motivations and objectives:

	Motivation		Political Objectives
A	Peace and prosperity	$\rightarrow a$	Security through the status quo
B	Political equality	$\rightarrow b$	Indirect access to nuclear weapons
C	Reunification	$\rightarrow c$	Absorption of the GDR (German Democratic Republic)
D	Anticommunism	$\rightarrow d$	Alliance with the U.S.; Atlantism
$A + B$	Political equality; Peace and prosperity	$\rightarrow e$	European integration

Next rearrange the objectives on an "aggressiveness" scale ranging from plus indicating aggressiveness to zero indicating neutrality and finally to minus indicating cooperation. Now consider the effect of each objective on every other one regarding whether it affects the other's fulfillment, whether it contradicts it, or whether it is meaningless to ask for a relation between them. For example, objective a contradicts objective b since in this case strengthening security through the status quo does not promote access to nuclear weapons. However, the converse can be true. Thus $a \not\rightarrow b$ (i.e., a does not imply b) but $b \rightarrow a$. (Someone else may apply the same method using his own assumptions and reasoning. Since our purpose is to convey the method, we shall not stop to give detailed arguments justifying each relation.) Similarly, $a \not\rightarrow c$ since security and status quo favor increased differentiation between the two Germanies. Also $c \not\rightarrow a$ *unless* c is interpreted as security of the two Germanies together. We have $a \rightarrow d$; $d \rightarrow a$; $a \rightarrow e$; $e \rightarrow a$; $b \rightarrow c$; $c \not\rightarrow b$; $d \rightarrow b$; $b \not\rightarrow d$ *unless* the Atlantic Alliance is considered by the U.S. as compatible with sharing nuclear weapons; $b \not\rightarrow e$; $e \rightarrow b$; $c \not\rightarrow e$; $e \not\rightarrow c$; $e \not\rightarrow d$; $d \not\rightarrow e$; $c \not\rightarrow d$ *unless* there is a strategy to force the East German regime out; $d \rightarrow c$. This leads to the following table, which indicates when relations are possible and also those with "unless" (that is, yes there is an implication if) type of condition. It also indicates whether one can say that the row objective favors the column objective. Obviously we are matching the objectives against themselves. A graph of the system of possible discourse is shown in Figure 3.

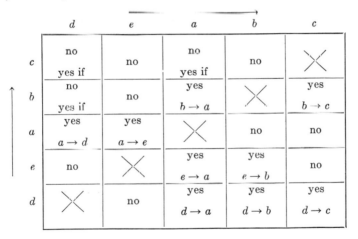

	d	e	a	b	c
c	no yes if	no	no yes if	no	X
b	no yes if	no	yes $b \rightarrow a$	X	yes $b \rightarrow c$
a	yes $a \rightarrow d$	yes $a \rightarrow e$	X	no	no
e	no	X	yes $e \rightarrow a$	yes $e \rightarrow b$	no
d	X	no	yes $d \rightarrow a$	yes $d \rightarrow b$	yes $d \rightarrow c$

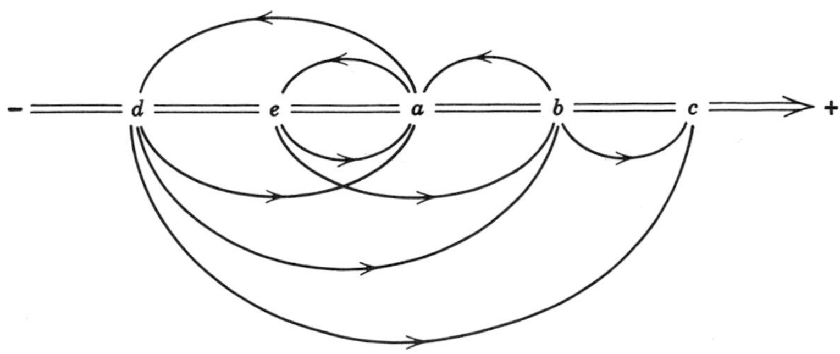

Figure 3

The graph in Figure 4 gives the impossible relations (the continuous lines) and those which are impossible "unless" (the dotted lines). It is followed by a graph (Figure 5) that gives in bold drawing the most economical route of possible relations in the previous graph. It is given by $d \rightarrow a \rightarrow e \rightarrow b \rightarrow c$. This route corresponds to the following justifying discourse which, of course, has never been held and does not correspond to any definition of Bonn's policy. The Atlantic Alliance promotes stability and the status quo, which in turn favor European integration, which in turn favors the accession of West Germany to nuclear coresponsibility (by sharing in European policy making), which promotes the chances for a political success permitting the absorption of the GDR.

Note that additional relations must be suppressed because they may contradict other relations; for example, $b \rightarrow c$ and $b \rightarrow a$ are contra-

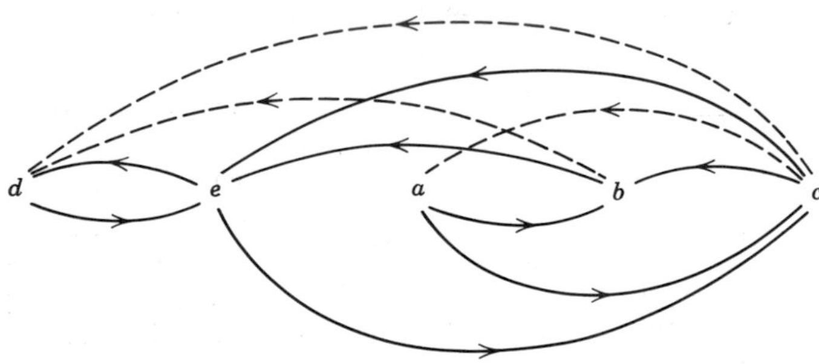

Figure 4

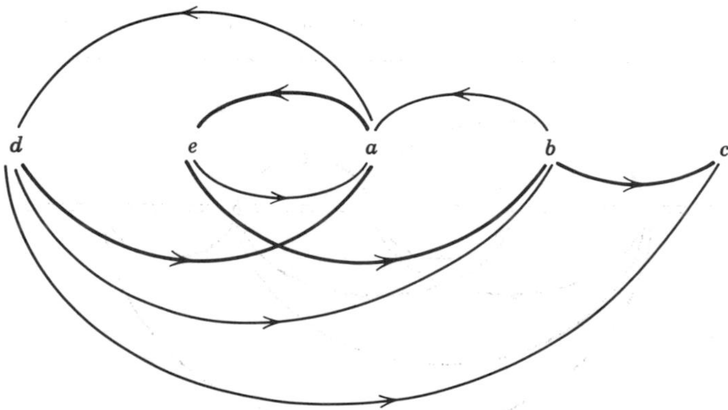

Figure 5

dictory, hence $b \rightarrow c$ is suppressed in official declaration (because the U.S.S.R. may react) to acquire nuclears can facilitate the annexation of the GDR and also that it can assure security in the status quo.

Another type of suppressed relation is $e \rightarrow b$ (hope for a European bomb) which contradicts French and British attitudes. This gives a graph (Figure 6) in which a single arrow indicates contradictory relations and a double arrow indicates a suppressed relation because a contradiction with objectives of other nations can be perceived that must be considered.

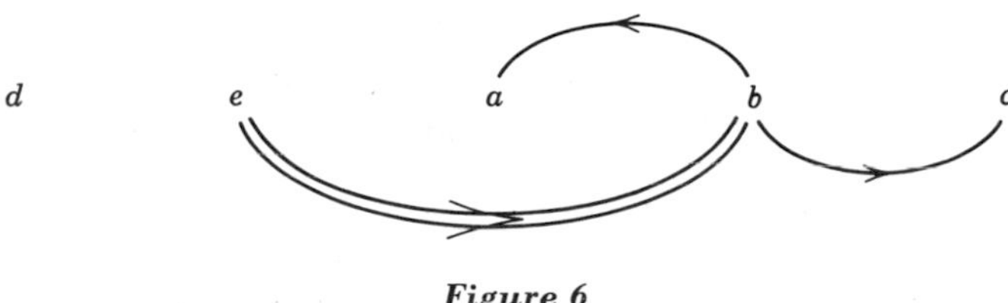

Figure 6

When the last graph is suppressed from the initial graph of possible relations, the graph in Figure 7 remains.

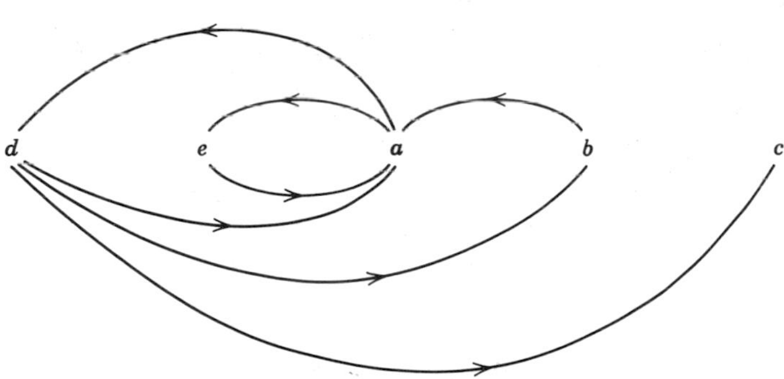

Figure 7

In this graph we no longer have the connected economical route of the initial graph that makes it impossible to have a route which at the same time does not pass through the same point twice and which connects the political to the strategic objectives. Consequently nations use rhetoric to fill in the missing links: for example, the following statements may be made:

$d \Leftrightarrow c$	1. We refuse to choose between Europe and Atlantism; both of them are indispensable to our security.
$c \Rightarrow c$, $c \Rightarrow a$	2. Only reunification would bring true security to both Europe and West Germany because there is no status quo possible without German reunification.
$a \Rightarrow c$	3. Peaceful development will inevitably draw the GDR into the orbit of West Germany.

They lead to the graph in Figure 8, with double-arrow insertions for using rhetoric to obtain a most economic route. This graph may first be used to search for a shortest discourse that includes all the objectives but without rhetorical connections; we have $d \rightarrow b \rightarrow a \rightarrow e$ supplemented by $d \rightarrow c$ and represented by Figure 9. This route leaves

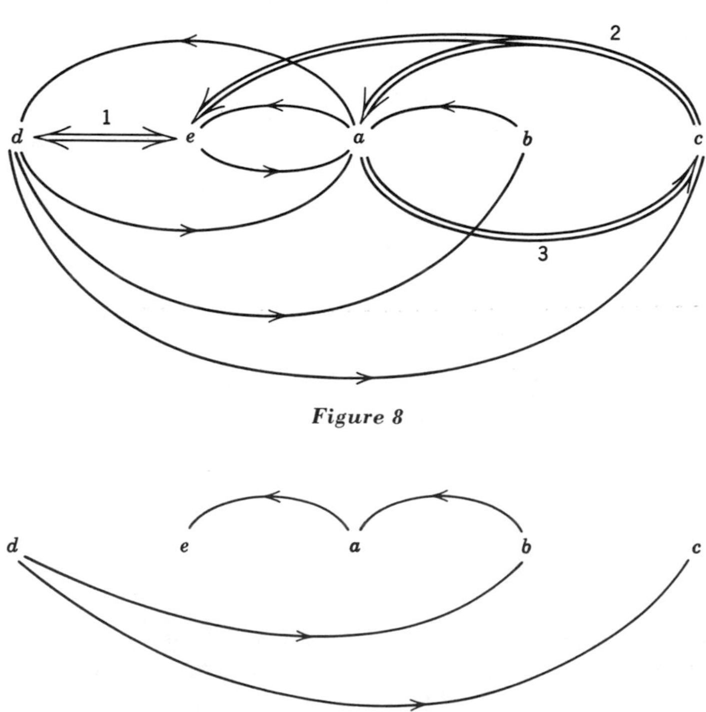

Figure 8

Figure 9

reunification aside, with the only support possible through Atlantism. It gives the image of a West Germany provided with nuclear weapons, with the support of the United States, tending toward security and the status quo for the integration of Europe. It explains the need for using rhetorical tie-ins and for breaking up the discourse into several sections.

The following are examples of this type of rhetoric:

1. Only reunification by the absorption of the GDR can assure a truly safe status quo for Germany; hence this is the only way to obtain a true European integration constituting the foundation for German security.
2. European integration is not contradictory to Atlantism, which alone will lead to reunification.
3. Reunification is the only form of a true status quo.
4. A true status quo will finally permit true integration so far blocked by the question of reunification.

One method of modifying the system is to renounce certain objectives, but this would entail the danger of leaving out a method to satisfy those motivations that use these objectives as an outlet. If nuclear weapon access is renounced, return to nationalism may be a substitute for the desired status, thus renouncing a united Europe. Alternatively, the meaning of "reunification" may be altered and so on.

Part II

THE STABILITY OF POLICIES

Chapter 2

MODELS OF ARMS RACES: EQUILIBRIUM AND STABILITY

2.1. INTRODUCTION

Objectives require consistency, whereas policies must be tested for effectiveness. A policy may aim at achieving an objective but when applied actually lead to diminishing the fulfillment of that objective. A useful criterion for testing the effectiveness of a policy is its stability. A policy that is stable and is preferred to an existing policy in the fulfillment of an objective is considered a feasible course of action.

2.2. EQUILIBRIUM AND STABILITY

It has been well recognized in the development of scientific theories that to construct a useful model, one must adopt notions around which it is possible to analyze equilibrium and stability. These two ideas are pivots on which analysis revolves. A system is said to be in stable equilibrium if after a small disturbance it tends to return to its original state. It is unstable when a small disturbance tends to move it further and further away from its original state. A ball at the bottom of a salad bowl is in stable equilibrium, but a ball precariously balanced on the top of an upside-down spherically shaped bowl is unstable. In many social affairs stable equilibria are desirable situations and unstable equilibria are undesirable. For instance, an economic system violently fluctuating between boom and depression is undesirable, whereas one remaining in a well-balanced intermediate position is desirable. There have been several different approaches to political problems utilizing models based on stable equilibria. We will examine some later in this chapter.

Le Chatelier and Gibbs gave mathematical conditions for deciding whether an equilibrium position would be stable or unstable in such a complicated discipline as physics.

There are instances in which stability is a bad thing and an unstable equilibrium is a good thing. To illustrate the first, consider the case of a person caught running between two tigers and the only way to escape is to get closer to one of the tigers. His momentary optimum position is half-way between. It is extremely dangerous for him to stay there, however, so he should make up his mind to escape in the direction of one of the tigers before they close in on him. He needs some extra psychological energy (that is, courage) to escape from this momentarily stable equilibrium.

An example illustrating the desirability of unstable equilibria is a small child placed between two chocolate bars and offered and constrained to take only one of them. For a moment he may be in a state of suspended equilibrium, unable to decide on which to choose, but he will soon rush to one of them and escape from this unstable equilibrium situation of indecision by a minimal disturbance which attracts his attention to that one. More generally, choosing between two good things is usually easy (unstable equilibrium), but choosing between two evils may be very difficult even if indecision is disastrous (undesirable stable equilibrium).

The word equilibrium is derived from the latin phrase *aequa libra,* which means a poised balance signifying a "balance" of forces whose resultant is zero. The idea of equilibrium may be applied to systems whose mathematical representation is given by means of equations, particularly differential equations.

Thus a moving system is in a stationary state when its velocity vanishes. It is then said to be in equilibrium. The term is also applied to a system with a continuous expenditure of free energy. This type of equilibrium is also referred to as quasi-equilibrium. A situation in which a minimum (or a maximum) is attained is also an equilibrium; a sphere placed in a salad bowl reaches equilibrium when its potential energy attains a minimum compatible with the geometry of the bowl. A small perturbation would disturb its equilibrium, but it must be given sufficient energy from the outside, for example, a strong push, to knock it out of the bowl and permanently destroy its present equilibrium.

A further generalization of the idea is applied to a conflict and competition situation involving several parties. In game theory the concept of equilibrium point refers to a situation in which none of the parties have an incentive to change their actual strategies as long as the other parties stick to theirs. These strategies are called equilibrium strategies. It is possible to classify equilibrium points particularly according to whether they have short-sighted or long-range characteristics.

The conditions for equilibrium in the case of differential equations are generally obtained by equating to zero the velocity components of the system. (The case when the coefficients are also functions of time is a more difficult one and gives rise to the idea of dynamic equilibrium.) The mode of approaching the equilibrium depends on the roots of the characteristic equation of the system. It is this analysis of the existence and character of the equilibrium that provides understanding of the long-run behavior of a system.

An example of static equilibrium is illustrated by a cold car engine which is slow to get started and takes some time to warm up. During this time it vibrates, coughs, and is exceedingly reluctant to go. After awhile this type of activity levels off as the engine warms up. One could never tell that the car had been so negative in getting out of its state of inertia, which is one type of static equilibrium, into another state of static equilibrium, the steady state of operation.

An example of a dynamic equilibrium is illustrated by an individual standing on a small platform on the sloping part of the hood of his car. As long as the car accelerates the individual can remain standing. Once it slows down, however, the individual falls down and the car runs over him.

Some have argued against equilibrium as a goal in the analysis of political situations, saying that nations seek to resist changes or disturbances. However, establishing a power equilibrium between nations, for example, may release resources in a country which would enable it to pursue economic change. Thus the notion of equilibrium need not be interpreted as an ultimate goal but rather as a pause to integrate energies and resources in new directions which may lead away from the initial equilibrium and serve as an incentive toward a new equilibrium. Essentially we have a path up a mountain with resting places. The rest itself is an impetus for taking short cuts toward the top.

Most theories using the concept of equilibrium are static. The concept of static equilibrium, very useful for many purposes, for example, in economics, also has severe limitations. First, even if we have a stable system, it will be in or near its equilibrium position only if the speed with which it tends to return to its equilibrium position is very high and the number of disturbances affecting it per unit of time is low. Second, many systems cannot be properly represented by a stable equilibrium model because their present state depends not only on the present values of the independent variables determining the system but also on the past values of these variables (time lags) and/or on the rate of change. In dealing with such systems, static theories have to be replaced by very complicated dynamic theories.

Remark. Another useful idea in mathematics is that of a property which remains invariant to change and hence has the general characteristics of stability. In this connection mathematicians have used the general notion of a fixed point. If T is a transformation mapping a set X into X, then a solution $\bar{x}$ of the equation $Tx = x$ for x belonging to X is known as a fixed point. The idea of a fixed point has its origins in topology and is amenable to wide interpretation when sets are transformed into themselves or into other sets. The idea is being used with a measure of success in looking for invariant properties in the social sciences [27a].

2.3. THE EFFECT OF MULTIPLE WARHEADS ON THE REGION OF STABILITY—A GEOMETRIC APPROACH

Let us illustrate the use of the notion of stability in a real situation using simple geometric arguments. Our mathematical development was done jointly with N. Dalkey who provided the basic idea.

Consider a simplified illustrative model (with no claim for applicability) involving the threatened use of missiles by two competitors, I and II, to deter each other. I assumes that II will attempt to destroy his missile system and vice versa. To each competitor the value of his missiles is measured by the amount of damage they might be expected to inflict upon his opponent's cities if they engage in war. This value depends not only on the size of his and of his opponent's forces but on their reliability. Other factors are suppressed in this discussion in order not to stray from the main idea of how to use geometry as an aid to general qualitative thinking about problems of arms control. The value function is likely to be obtained by qualitative logical arguments supported by quantitative analysis. The purpose is to show that with multiple warhead missiles, a stable situation is harder to attain. This means that both sides will need more missiles, hence will spend more money. It also means that the period of time in which one goes from the stable situation of single warheads to that of multiple warheads can be a period of tension. Each side may fear an attack by the other during the time he is preparing a defense against the new system.

Let us see if there is a region of stability for the problem of single warhead missiles. When each side has built enough missiles so that he feels he has enough to assure himself an acceptable level for destroying his opponent, there is a possibility of stability.

Let us denote the number of missiles of I and II respectively by f_{I} and f_{II} and use these to represent axes in the plane (see Figure 10). At the 45° line (of parity) the forces of both sides are equal. Competitor I does not feel that a 1 for 1 trade-off is essential because all he is concerned with is to destroy a certain fraction of II's cities. His thinking con-

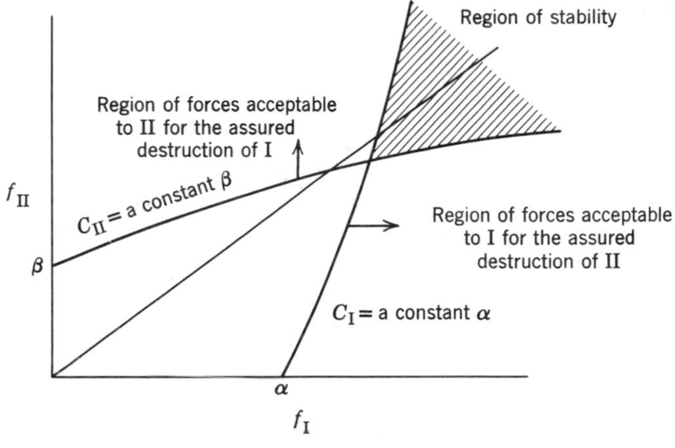

Figure 10

cerning deterrence is partly guided by a "value" contour C_I = constant, developed according to his estimates of the number of missiles of II, their reliability, and the reliability of his own missiles, and so on. This is a typical contour taken from the value surface defined over the f_I, f_{II} plane which gives I the number of missiles that survive an attack by II because (by assumption) from I's point of view, for deterrence he does not intend to attack II but only II's cities after II attacks his missiles. The way I would use the surface is to draw the contour in the plane corresponding to a desired $C_I = \alpha$ counter-value (i.e., the damage he can still do to his opponent's cities). From the C_I contour I can estimate the number of missiles he must have for any given number of II's missiles in order to have C_I left after an attack by II (calculations will follow). To the right of the contour $C_I = \alpha$ is I's area of assured destruction of II if α is chosen large enough for this purpose.

To see how this curve is generated in I's thinking, note that below the 45° line II will allocate one missile to destroy each of I's missiles. When II has zero missiles I has α missiles to assure II's destruction after an attack by II. If II has few missiles, I needs a few more than α to bring about assured destruction and so on; when II has a large number of missiles, then beyond the 45° line I does not need to increase his forces proportionately because II will allocate more missiles for each missile of I and so the effectiveness of allocations of II's missiles is lower at this level. Similarly, II constructs his own assured destruction contour $C_{II} = \beta$. The region of stability is the area common to the assured destruction regions of I and II.

Now suppose that a complicating idea enters the picture. Each side decides to put several warheads on each of his missiles. The result is that the region of stability is farther out.

Suppose I has M missiles and II has N missiles. Let t be the number of warheads on each missile of I and II. The total number of warheads of II is tN and the fraction assigned to each of I's missiles is tN/M.

Let u be the probability that a missile of II's is destroyed by an attacking missile of I's and let v be the corresponding probability for I's missiles. The probabilities of destruction by one of t independently-targeted multiple warheads are $u/\sqrt[3]{t}$ and $v/\sqrt[3]{t}$ respectively. To see this, note that approximately the intensity of damage from a blast (not including thermal damage) is measured by the radius of the sphere (or spherical cap) of the blast. The volume of this sphere is proportional to the yield of the warhead which distributes the blast effect uniformly in the sphere. Therefore, the radius is proportional to the cube root of the warhead yield. If a single warhead of I's is equivalently divided into t equal-yield multiple warheads, the blast effect of each component is proportional to $\sqrt[3]{1/t}$ of the original warhead. Then the probability that a missile of II's is destroyed by one of I's multiple warheads is $u/\sqrt[3]{t}$. A similar argument gives $v/\sqrt[3]{t}$.

The probability that a missile of I's survives an attack by one warhead is $1 - v/\sqrt[3]{t}$. The probability that a missile of I's survives an attack by tN/M warheads is the product $(1 - v/\sqrt[3]{t}) \cdots (1 - v/\sqrt[3]{t})$ taken tN/M times; that is, $(1 - v/\sqrt[3]{t})^{tN/M}$. Thus the value to I is the amount he can destroy with his surviving missiles and we have

$$\alpha = M(1 - v/\sqrt[3]{t})^{tN/M}.$$

Similarly,

$$\beta = N(1 - u/\sqrt[3]{t})^{tM/N}.$$

This gives Figure 11, in which the slopes are more sluggish than those of $t = 1$, hence their point of intersection is farther out. This indicates that the region of stability itself is also farther out.

To see how much farther out the stability region is than before we assume symmetry in the forces and equate M and N, and also equate $u/\sqrt[3]{t}$ and $v/\sqrt[3]{t}$. We obtain from either formula

$$M = \frac{\alpha}{(1 - u/\sqrt[3]{t})^{t}}.$$

If $\alpha = 400$, which is reasonable for assured destruction, $u = 0.6$ and $t = 1$, we have $M = 1000$. On the other hand, if $t = 8$ then to maintain the same level of assured destruction after a first-strike by the

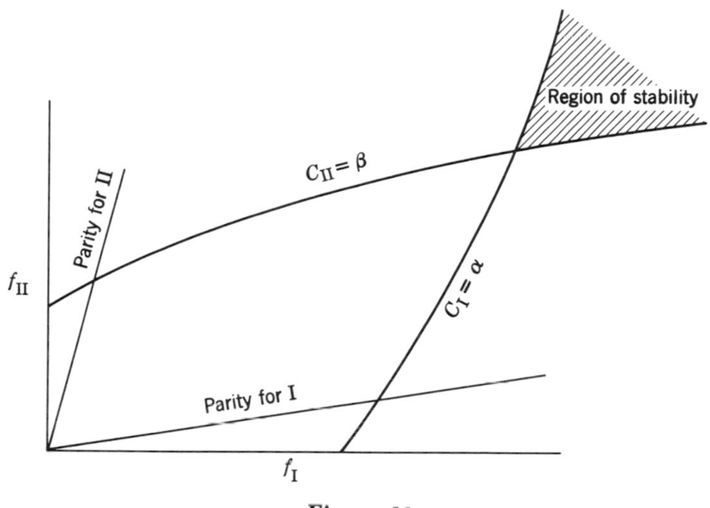

Figure 11

opponent, approximately $M = 6900$ missiles are needed. The difference between these two values is great and implies with this crude analysis that the transition to the complex system may require a long period to lapse before stability is reached again. Stability in the real world may not depend on a single weapon system. The seeming instability may be offset by other weapon systems belonging to each side. It may also happen that the new system is developed at a sufficiently low rate that stability is not drastically affected. Thus we cannot imply from this simple example that multiple warheads are destabilizing.

2.4. ON THE STABILITY OF DETERRENCE*

Here we propose to treat two situations. The first is concerned with the stability of deterrence, that is, the presence of sufficient power in the hands of each of two competitors to inhibit his opponent's pursuit of political, economic, or other gain through the use of force. We give a rationale for this situation and examine its consequences. Deterrence means the existence of effective means and willingness to use them to inhibit gains by an opponent pursued through the use of force or by subtler means. These gains are assumed to be unfavorable to the deterring side. In a restricted sense, deterrence also means making an attack by the opponent unprofitable. The other problem requires finding a cri-

* I am grateful to Colonel Paul J. Long for his help in writing this section.

terion to partially answer the following question: In a two-nation situation, if nation A has sufficient power to destroy nation B and if this capability is invulnerable to an attack by B, why should A continue to acquire more weapons?

In analyzing both problems four factors seem to dominate:

1. The gain that each side threatens to make which would be regarded with suspicion and disfavor by the opponent. Gain of a competitive nature such as seeking world markets for trade, forming alliances, and the like is a challenge to an opponent and may invite him to participate in peaceful competition. Through negotiations and treaties nations may obtain the cooperation of other nations in pursuit of mutual gains. On the other hand a gain may be a direct threat to the policies of the opponent or an indirect threat if, for example, it involves other countries, such as taking these countries by force or overthrowing their governments in favor of governments sympathetic to its own ambitions and idealogy. Such gains would be regarded with disfavor by the opponent who would naturally seek to deter them.

2. The conditional probability that either side would attain the possible gain through its policies. There may be many obstacles in attaining a desired level of gain. To effect a gain involves paying the price of the effort involved in addition to suffering possible damage by the opponent. Thus among other factors on which it depends, the probability of attaining a gain unfavorable to an opponent is a function of the perceived capability and will of the opponent to resist by force (see 3 and 4). Where possible gains are of an acceptable kind involving give and take of a normal commercial nature, there is no reason for the other side to oppose or deter them, and hence they are not involved in this problem. Note that gain may be derived from a third country and may imply commitment (by the deterring country) to defend it against attack.

3. The amount of destructive power possessed by each side to prevent unfavorable gain sought by the opposite side. This destructive power is measured according to the manner in which it is perceived and evaluated by the other nation.

4. The unconditional probability that either side would bring about possible damage by actually applying its destructive power (by initiating war) if the other side pursues its gains. This probability is known as the risk-of-war probability or bellicosity factor. For some countries this factor would be set at a high value because of the ambitions and belligerence of their leaders. In other countries the national laws, customs, and form of government discourage policies with a high risk-of-war probability.

The Model. We will now develop a quantitative framework for combining these ideas and then use it to examine the situations posed earlier. Although this model is given in quantitative terms, it will serve the purpose of constructing general explanations using order-of-magnitude comparisons rather than absolute numbers.

Let G denote the quantity of gain associated with country A and let P be its conditional probability of attainment; the "condition" in this case is that B does not respond with force to stop it. Then PG is the expected gain for A if there is no opposition from B (see later if expected gains against forceful opposition are included).

Let D and Q be the destruction capability of A and the unconditional probability of its being applied to prevent gain by B. Thus A's expected damage to B in case of war is QD. Let g, p, d, q be the corresponding quantities for B.

If we assume that risking war has bearable consequence we may let $\tilde{P}$ be the probability that A attain gain $\tilde{G}$ in the case of war and let $\tilde{p}$ and $\tilde{g}$ be the corresponding quantities for B. We may now associate with A and B, respectively, the gain-loss or gain-deterrence ratios

$$R = \frac{(1 - Q)pg + Q\tilde{p}\tilde{g}}{QD} \qquad r = \frac{(1 - q)PG + q\tilde{P}\tilde{G}}{qd}.$$

Here R represents the expected gain of B and the price A could make him pay for it and r the expected gain of A and the price B could make him pay for it.

If the probabilities Q and q are small the foregoing expressions may be approximated by

$$\bar{R} = \frac{pg}{QD} \qquad \text{and} \qquad \bar{r} = \frac{PG}{qd}.$$

We shall now analyze the stability of deterrence. Stability here does not mean the mere absence of war but the ability of opponents to negotiate problems without the use of force by either side but in the presence of the threat of force to cancel unilateral gain. On the other hand instability also does not mean the presence of a state of war. Rather it means that one side cannot deter or sway his opponent by any means (including use of force) from pursuing gains of which he does not approve. Instability turns into war when one side decides to resist in any case. We have three essentially different cases to consider.

1. $R \ll 1, \quad r \ll 1.$
2. $R \ll 1, \quad r \geq 1.$
3. $R \geq 1, \quad r \geq 1.$

In the first case both A and B are deterred by each other. At any specified time, however, D and d are constant, but Q and q can be varied over a small interval of time. It is clear that if deterrence is obtained for $\bar{R} \ll 1$ and $\bar{r} \ll 1$ then it should also obtain for $R \ll 1$ and $r \ll 1$. The converse need not hold since by lowering Q or q the expected deterrence values QD and qd may change the status of stability.

To make deterrence credible A will reason that he must make R as small as possible by increasing QD. By increasing D (and making this power invulnerable) he decreases q since B knows that if war ensues he would be destroyed, which is unacceptable to B. Side B may also decrease or abandon his expected gain so as not to provoke A to go to war. Thus A may succeed in blocking B from making gains. Similarly, B will try to do the same. Thus a stable situation would prevail if both R and r are less than unity.

A problem arises as to how either side can make its deterrence credible and still minimize the risk of its own destruction. If the deterring forces on both sides are vulnerable, the side that strikes first at his opponent's weapons would remove the deterrence of the opponent, reducing the problem to the second case. A first strike, however, may be discouraged in two ways: (a) by building weapons to destroy the enemy's attacking weapons (which may be a formidable task) and (b) by making the deterring forces invulnerable and hence developing the capability to retaliate against a first strike, producing such damage that the idea of striking first becomes unattractive to the opponent.

If each side can destroy the other, stability of deterrence is attained. The problem, however, now becomes one of how much gain can either pursue before the other side decides that mutual destruction would be preferred? By raising its risk-of-war against unfavorable gains made by its opponent, each side gives its opponent a signal of possible consequences if such gains are continued. Either the situation is brought under control through negotiations and through mutual cooperation or a threshold is reached when one side decides to apply the forces used for deterrence. Thus stability requires that (a) the parties abandon the pursuit of unfavorable gains and (b) negotiate their differences or (c) destroy each other. If both sides have invulnerable deterrent forces, it is advisable to follow the principle: Do not apply large expected destruction except against correspondingly large expected gains by the opponent.

If $R \ll 1$ but $r \geq 1$ then A may not be deterred by B, particularly if B does not have sufficient destructive power to make A's pursuit of gain unattractive to A. This situation is unstable and A may attempt to dictate or block the expected gains of B.

Since qd is small, B's immediate recourse is to resort to threats and possibly bring about internal instability to indicate carelessness and willingness to go to war, thereby increasing the value of q in A's estimates so that qd may seem great to A (if he believes it). In that case A would use r to determine whether his expected gain would justify pursuing his policy and risking war or whether to acquiesce to B's high risk of war. If he is blocked, B would achieve deterrence of A.

If $R \geq 1$ and $r \geq 1$, conflict tends to occur when one party judges a low damage expectancy for his opponent and pursues his gains. Sometimes, as indicated in the previous paragraph, his calculations show that gain even with war is high and he takes the risk. Examples of this type of instability (underestimating the risk of war) are illustrated by World War II.

If A and B cooperate economically, culturally, and by other means, increased expected gains to either may result in an increase to the other, hence deterrence would not be as meaningful.

Remark 1. The expected gain and expected deterrence may be written as sums of smaller expected gains and deterrences as follows

$$pg = \Sigma p_i g_i; \qquad QD = \Sigma Q_i D_i$$

and the analysis may be applied to the allocation of the smaller deterrence $Q_i D_i$ to the smaller gain $p_i g_i$ and the overall effect then deduced.

Let us now examine the second, and perhaps more difficult, problem which essentially asks: Under what conditions are more weapons desirable if a complete destruction potential is already possessed by both sides? It is sufficient to discuss this problem in the context of no war since by assumption war brings no gain to both sides.

Suppose that A wishes to compare the desirability of the ratios

$$\bar{R}_1 = \frac{p_1 g_1}{Q_1 D_1} \quad \text{and} \quad \bar{R}_2 = \frac{p_2 g_2}{Q_2 D_2},$$

assuming that $D_2 > D_1$. Let B have corresponding quantities $\bar{r}_1$ and $\bar{r}_2$ with $d_2 > d_1$. We consider the following criterion for deciding the preference of D_2 to D_1 by A:

$$\left(\frac{\bar{R}_2}{\bar{R}_1}\right)^\alpha < \left(\frac{\bar{r}_2}{\bar{r}_1}\right)^\beta$$

where α is the weight A places on his relative deterrence and β is the corresponding weight for B. In analyzing this criterion four expected gains and four expected losses or expected destructions must be considered. If we regard the expected gains as constants the foregoing simplifies to

$$k\left(\frac{Q_1D_1}{Q_2D_2}\right)^{\alpha} < \left(\frac{q_1d_1}{q_2d_2}\right)^{\beta}$$

where k is the constant

$$\left(\frac{P_2G_2}{P_1G_1}\right)^{\alpha}\left(\frac{p_1g_1}{p_2g_2}\right)^{\beta}$$

Damage may be directed against the gains (or values) of the opponent or against his forces which serve as a deterrent. The way to satisfy the criterion is to make Q_2D_2 large and q_2d_2 small. Destruction of B's forces increases the opportunity for A to make the gains he desires. If D_1 is adequate to destroy the value targets of B, then the justification for adopting a new force level D_2 must lie in its effect on both q_2 and d_2, that is, on his likelihood to fight and on his forces. First D_2 may help decrease the probability of a war being started by B. This yields $q_2 < q_1$. Such an effect on q_2 cannot be known exactly but must be the result of prediction based on previous observation about B's behavior. Since human judgment has a limited accuracy when expressed in terms of numbers, it is sufficient to observe that ultimately a threshold is reached beyond which q_2 cannot be made smaller. A nonzero value of q_2, for example, discourages errors by A that inflict some damage on B. It may be safely argued that B could not tolerate many errors whose total effect is unacceptable to B. The fact that small-scale conflicts may escalate to a large war also shows that q_2 can never be forced to zero. Thus at some point where nations A and B attempt to force $q_2 < q_1$ and $Q_2 < Q_1$ respectively, the law of diminishing economic and deterrence returns must operate. At that point the effort must be directed to weapons which cannot be the cause of error and to explicit or implicit agreements which bind both sides not to escalate into the full war framework.

Alternatively, A may partly intend D_2 to make d_2 smaller by using D_2 to counter the forces of B (e.g., using antiballistic missiles, or by targeting against the destructive potential d_2). This again could make the right side of the inequality large. However, B may now attempt to protect the value of d_2 and apportion some of it to counter-balance D_2. Since it takes time to achieve the desired results, each side is seen to develop more and sometimes new weapons.

Although zero is a lower bound and unity is an upper bound for the values of Q and q there are no noneconomic bounds for D and d. Each time one of the opponents finds that his potential destructive power is decreased through the development of more weapons by the other side, he attempts to build more weapons himself constrained by his economics. The only way to stop such buildup is through mutual agreement.

Generalization. We extend the foregoing analysis to n countries. Let $P_{ij}G_{ij}$ and $\tilde{P}_{ij}\tilde{G}_{ij}$ be the expected gain without and with war respectively that country i pursues against country j. Let $q_{ij}d_i$ be the expected damage that country i can inflict on country j if war breaks out.

If d_i is large it may be divided into parts d_{ij}, each directed against a different opponent or alliance of opponents. In a limited war only a portion of the forces of at least one side is used. If no alliances are involved the analysis of stability between nations proceeds as before using the ratios

$$R_{ij} = \frac{(1 - q_{ij})P_{ji}G_{ji} + q_{ij}\tilde{P}_{ji}\tilde{G}_{ji}}{q_{ij}d_i}.$$

In the case of alliances different possibilities exist.

If two nations cannot deter a third one separately, they may be able to do so jointly. In this case their forces are pooled together, but their risk-of-war may be scaled according to their joint determination to resist unfavorable gains by their common opponent. If $P_{12}G_{12}$ and $P_{13}G_{13}$ are the expected gains of country 1 from countries 2 and 3 respectively and if their responses to this gain are $q_{21}d_2$, $q_{31}d_3$ respectively then an alliance of 2 and 3 would improve their joint deterrence of 1 since

$$\frac{P_{12}G_{12} + P_{13}G_{13}}{q_{21}d_2 + q_{31}d_3} < \frac{P_{12}G_{12}}{q_{21}d_2} + \frac{P_{13}G_{13}}{q_{31}d_3}.$$

This conforms to the well-known arithmetic relationship that

$$\frac{a + c}{b + d} < \frac{a}{b} + \frac{c}{d}$$

which holds if b and d are positive. Country 1 would prefer the "divide and conquer" idea expressed on the right because it is less deterred by 2 and 3 separately. On this basis the notion of stability for alliances may also be developed.

Applications. Wars generally occur between nations whose gain-deterrence ratios are ≥ 1. Those who resort to war find from their calculations, if they are behaving rationally, that their net expected gain $q\tilde{P}\tilde{G} - qd$ is positive. Occasionally, one nation underestimates the destructive power of its opponent or his dynamic capacity to develop this power, and thus loses a war that it provokes. Two ways in which two nations acting rationally, whose ratios are $\ll 1$, may be drawn into major wars are through alliances and through the escalation of minor conflicts. The first occurs when one or both of them are involved in alliances whose comparative ratios are either both ≥ 1 or only one of them is ≥ 1 and decides to resist. The second and more frequent way arises from the pursuit of small expected gains from which it is unable to retreat when greater than anticipated resistance occurs. The object of each side would be to accumulate gain little by little without provoking forceful opposition. This situation may escalate to a higher level of conflict if at some point one of the sides decides to use force to prevent the other from making a small expected gain.

Let us examine the United States–Communist Chinese deterrence situation. If the ratios are R and r for the United States and China respectively, allowing for high Q and q and using the corresponding expressions, we have $R \ll 1$ and $r < 1$ (but r is not $\ll 1$). This follows from the following assessment of the situation:

U.S.: G = small, P = high, Q = high, D = large, $\tilde{G}$ = small, $\tilde{P}$ = low.

China: g = large, p = low, q = high, d = small (large if Russia is included), $\tilde{g}$ = small, $\tilde{p}$ = low.

$$R = \frac{\text{low} \cdot \text{low} \cdot \text{large} + \text{high} \cdot \text{low} \cdot \text{small}}{\text{high} \cdot \text{large}},$$

$$r = \frac{\text{low} \cdot \text{high} \cdot \text{small} + \text{high} \cdot \text{low} \cdot \text{small}}{\text{high} \cdot \text{small}}.$$

Thus China is more deterred by the United States than the United States is deterred by China.

Nuclear capability in the United States diminishes the potential of Chinese manpower to the extent that China does not feel it has Russia as an ally against nuclear threat. In that case China's manpower may be effectively deterred with nuclear weapons if China acts rationally. China has avoided risking direct action by the United States through restraint in its own actions. However, China has assumed a belligerent attitude (not action), which is essential for increasing the credibility of a higher probability of applying force. This antagonistic attitude, unless matched by a similar attitude by the United States, tends to alter and diminish the pressure applied by the United States. Even the internal instability of China may tend to increase the credence of a high risk-of-war level. It is not easy to say whether or not this instability is partly caused by external pressures. Internal instability in a large country which is not entirely helpless contributes to easing external pressures since its risk-of-war is less predictable.

China has been seeking stability with the United States and the U.S.S.R. by building its own nuclear arsenal. The alternative to the present course of building a nuclear arsenal would have been to establish friendly relations with the powers which can affect China's future. In the absence of friendly relations China doubtless considers that it needs power to give it external stability. It can then look at problems more objectively. With stability it may expect to gain in world influence. The United States, anticipating the emergence of a stronger China, has taken steps to inhibit future Chinese gain in Southeast Asia.

One way for a weaker country to make its opponent's massive deterrence less effective is to break down its own overall expected gain into small units and pursue those smaller expected gains that are the most likely to succeed without activating the opponent's deterrent forces.

To achieve its expected gains as a communist society, China has divided its total expected gain into smaller components consisting of liberation fronts in different countries. The total deterrent of the United States must now be divided into comparable components, each intended to cancel a small Chinese gain. Thus a Chinese strategy could be to divide its gain into such small parts that the task of deterring each one may be so expensive that from the standpoint of the United States the deterrence cost exceeds the gain to China.

In any future relations between India and China, India will seek to stabilize its external relations with China by increasing its deterrent position either through its own means or through great power support. Pakistan will then need to stabilize with India. This stability is sought not necessarily from fear of war but for a stronger position in negotiations on any significant political matter. Japan will seek relations with China which are more stabilizing. Acquiring deterrence has the primary purpose of inhibiting undesirable gains sought by the opponent. Sometimes what deters an opponent may be threatened damage to a third party that is an ally of the opponent.

The escalation of nuclear weapon buildup may also be interpreted within this model. In the presence of nuclear stability with the U.S.S.R., the United States has had to formulate its policies in the framework of conventional war in order to avoid nuclear collision. It is the continued threat of communist expected gain that has forced the United States to keep its risk-of-war (determination to resist communism) high and its weapon arsenal large. The United States acts to keep its deterrent credible and alter the communist goal. One method of inhibiting gains by the opponent is to compete with him or threaten him with greater gain so that his energy may be diverted more to frustrating or deterring such a gain than to pursuing his own gain. The capability for making gain and for developing deterrence depends on the economics, total manpower, and intellectual resources of a nation. It follows that if it is desired to diminish an opponent's ability to make external political gains, that nation could be driven to armament (by another nation whose resources are greater) thus taking a major portion of its resources away from making gains.

It may be useful to point out that even though deterrence is designed to inhibit unfavorable gains, war has the dual effect of blocking gains and destroying the existing values of a country. Each country has an existing value V to which it hopes to add gains. Deterrence against a country with a small value of V is not as effective as it would be against a country with a large value of V. The latter has more to lose in case of war and its expected gains may be relatively small compared to its total value. A powerful nation with a small value of V would tend to seek relatively large expected gains. This implies the pursuit of policies with a high risk-of-war.

Thus when responsive forced armament is associated with greater levels of richness, the nation assumes greater responsibility for its own actions because it understands the effect of power (of which it has some) and values its internal wealth V. It is in a situation of being able to deter and be deterred in pursuit of its values. With increased responsibility stability becomes more desirable.

France pursues an interesting course. It seeks its gains partly by establishing friendly relations and partly by acquiring (increasingly viable) deterrence. Theoretically, this should be the ideal form in which each nation can hope to attain its gains. Such a policy may be less effective in the long run if France discriminates with strong bias between those countries which it will befriend and those which it will oppose. Such bias may be damaging to France and to the rest of the world.

Consider now the situation of three countries, the United States, U.S.S.R., and China. The situation is stable if each country can effectively deter an alliance of the other two. It is otherwise unstable. If China develops a nuclear capability and thereby attains nuclear stability, its large manpower superiority requires a counter nonnuclear capability by the United States and the U.S.S.R. to produce stability in situations in which nuclear weapons may not be suitable, for example, "wars of liberation." Without a rich society China is likely to exert pressure when it acquires a credible deterrent. This follows from the fact that if conflict occurs, China's losses relative to its opponent's losses are small. If China's opponents act rationally, they would carefully consider each issue before forcing a showdown.

In the set of three countries, instability may exist between every pair and even between any single one and an alliance of the other two. More conducive toward stability is an alliance of China with either the United States or the U.S.S.R., for then the partnership has a member who has large values. The opponent of the alliance also has large values and hence a conflict situation is likely to be negotiable. The greatest instability is that of an alliance of the United States and the U.S.S.R. against China with strong deterrent but without large values. It seems that the most favorable way to correct this type of instability is an industrially developed China. An alliance of China with the United States is a greater threat to the U.S.S.R. because of the presence of Chinese manpower near its borders and the possible immediate gain to China there rather than in any other sector of Asia where the population burden is great. Thus an alliance of China with the United States is less stable than a China-U.S.S.R. alliance, and it poses a direct threat to Russia. Chinese manpower may hurt American interests but cannot be considered as a direct threat from across the Pacific.

2.5. A QUANTITATIVE APPROACH TO ARMS REDUCTION [58]

When we think of disarmament, or simply of arms reduction jointly agreed to by two nations, we have in mind different weapon systems such as missiles and airplanes and the numbers of each owned by both sides. We also have in mind a collection of negotiated rules which say that the existing arms must be reduced to some new level agreed to by both sides. We may think of additional future reductions. In order to have an explicit quantitative view of this process, we need to formalize the idea of a level of arms and the process of reducing arms from an initial level to a negotiated level.

We illustrate here the general technique of reduction with a specific example showing the mechanics. This example, not related to the arms control field, is based on tools from graph theory. In the next section and in Sections 3.6–3.7 we take more pertinent examples and show how the judgment of leaders in each nation enters into the determination of acceptable policies and how the results of the subsequent analysis for all nations involved may be combined to select a policy acceptable to all.

We begin by defining a set Σ consisting of a finite number of conditions, or states of being, where each state represents a level of arms available to two competitive opponents X and Y under conditions of stability. Stability, balance, or equilibrium is an essential criterion in this formulation. It requires that neither opponent judges his position, that is, his condition or state of being (defined below), to be weaker than his opponent's.

The elements E_j $(j = 1, \ldots, p)$ of Σ, representing these states, are vectors:

$$E_j = (a_{1j}, \ldots, a_{nj}; \quad b_{1j}, \ldots, b_{nj}),$$

where a_{kj} denotes the number of weapons of type k (that is, a specific type of gun, or an amount of information, or a method of obtaining a specific commodity, or an economic factor, etc.) available to X at step j of the disarmament process, and b_{kj} is the quantity of a similar commodity simultaneously available to Y. X and Y will each select a set of rules to be applied to an initial state of arms to produce a new state. The same rules, or different rules, may be applied to the new state to obtain a third state, etc. X's total scheme of arms reduction will produce a set of states, any one of which need not be acceptable to Y. The object is to find those states on which there can be mutual agreement and then establish rules for reducing arms to those states. It is assumed that the initial state to which the rules are applied will be considered as an equilibrium state by both sides, not necessarily for military reasons only but also for political, economic, or other reasons. Our subsequent discussion will show the dependence of the entire process on compensating factors used by the competitors. Our purpose now is to show how to obtain Σ.

An equilibrium state is one that is admissible and can be attained by both sides. A natural criterion for selecting admissible states is for X to take $a_{kj} = \alpha_{kj} b_{kj}$ where α_{kj} is known as an acceptable compensating factor.

It is clear that a common denominator for units of arms reduction is essential to this formulation. Thus, if there is a numerical superiority of one weapon type, this may be compensated for by superiority in the reverse order of another weapon. The deficiency (or advantage) α_{kj} must be measured in the basic unit of both weapons. Indeed the compensation may be on the basis of several rather than one other weapon type; hence a unit of common measurement is required.

A single judgment factor may not be adequate to determine whether a state is admissible; hence we define a state E_j to be admissible as a candidate for the set Σ_x of X's states if $\|\alpha_j\|$, called the norm of $\alpha_j = (\alpha_{1j}, \ldots, \alpha_{nj})$—the vector of compensating factors—is not less than a specified value, α, selected by X. The norm $\|\alpha_j\|$ is a measure of all α_{kj} $(k = 1, \ldots, n)$. Since the importance of weapons will differ from one type to another, a useful norm to take for α_j is

$$\|\alpha_j\| = \Sigma_{k=1}^{k=n} \quad W_k \alpha_{kj},$$

where W_k is a weight of the importance of weapon type k. Similarly, β_{kj} and $\|\beta_j\|$ may be introduced for the definition of Σ_y, the set of

Y's admissible states. Note for example that the state $(0, \ldots, 0; 1, \ldots, 1)$ is admissible to Y but not to X and hence it is in Σ_y but not in Σ_x. Similarly $(1, \ldots, 1; 0, \ldots, 0)$ is in Σ_x but not in Σ_y. It is easy to assume that such states are admissible, since one side will have zero arms.

Finally, the *set* of admissible equilibrium states is $\Sigma = \Sigma_x \cap \Sigma_y$; that is, it is the common part of both.

Note that α_j and some of the other parameters of this model cannot be determined and that an alternative approach is needed in which the parameters are not absolute but are estimated in the relative setting of negotiations. There each side learns to estimate the value of weapons to the other side through the use of offers and counter offers. This idea will be examined in Chapter 4. The main purpose of the present discussion is to clarify the problem.

One problem of arms control is to prescribe rules for reducing arms. Whatever the rule, its purpose is to effect a transition from one state in Σ to another state in Σ. The rules developed by each competitor need not coincide with those of the other; for example, Σ_x will naturally contain states not in Σ_y and the converse. Thus the problem is to find those rules that provide a sequence of transitions between states of Σ without ever going into a state not in Σ.

Assume that we have a listing of all the elements of the set Σ. (Clearly this is difficult in practice, since neither side would be willing to acknowledge his compensating factors. This approach shows, however, how, by offering the other side various rules that he accepts or rejects, it is possible to guess at approximate magnitudes of his compensating factors.) These elements are obviously finite, although the escalation of weapons increases the size of Σ in time. For simplicity let us assume that the states of Σ are $E_1, \ldots, E_r$.

If the problem of finding transition rules is solved, the next problem is to find a method of applying these rules to obtain all those states that fall on a path of arms reduction from a given initial state, for example, E_1 to any intermediate state E_q, $q < r$. If there is no such path, the rules are inadequate and must be altered to make the steps possible. It is clear that the transition from the initial to a designated intermediate state can be effected in a single step; but because of the many possibly adverse effects of large reduction steps in arms, it is essential to carry out the reduction in tolerably small steps. In addition a single step need not be acceptable to both sides nor feasible as far as safety is concerned, since it takes time to effect arms reduction and to monitor its execution.

A useful outcome of this approach is that it can be used to determine whether it is impossible to reach a prescribed state from an initial state according to a given set of rules. In other words not every method that may be advanced, even a seemingly good one, is guaranteed to lead to a stable predetermined state, if it is assumed that this method is to be used over and over again.

The first problem of choosing the rules of transition is nonmathematical. It depends on several political, military, and economic factors. Its solution requires detailed information and judgment from these areas. The problem of applying the rules to determine the possible intermediate steps of disarmament can be studied mathematically, however, even if the rules are changed between the steps; for then, all that need be done is again to apply the method developed below using the state at which the rules are changed as an initial state.

Let us associate with each state E_j belonging to Σ a vertex v_j ($j = 1, \ldots, r$) of a linear graph. We then associate with the vertices v_j a vertex matrix whose entries are zero or one depending on whether there is a line incident with the two vertices or not. Thus the entry is unity if it is possible to make a transition from one corresponding state to another, and zero otherwise.

This vertex matrix V represents the effect of a single transition as prescribed by the rules. For the matrix of two successive transitions we take VV. To obtain the path of transitions from the initial state E_1 to a final state E_q we compute V^s where s is the smallest value that yields a unit entry in the $(1, q)$ position of this matrix. Matrix multiplication will introduce elements whose value is greater than unity, indicating the number of possible ways (paths) in which that transition can be made. Since all that is needed is one path, it suffices to reduce the values of all nonzero elements to one. Alternative paths between E_1 and E_q may be possible and are indicated in the final matrix by the presence of elements whose values are more than one and which correspond to vertices that are connected along different paths from E_1 to E_q. The exact transitions of the solution path are obtained by working backwards from the solution matrix. Thus the unit element in the $(1, q)$ position is the result of multiplying some unit element of the first row of V^{s-1} by a unit element in the corresponding position of the sth column of V. If we note the position of that element of V^{s-1} it corresponds to the vertex connected to v_q on the path and hence to the state from which the last transition occurs. If we again examine the row and column of the previous multiplication giving rise to this unit element we determine the state from which the next to the last transition occurred, and so on, working backwards. In this manner we determine a feasible path to follow from E_1 to E_q.

The process may be applied at each stage with a change of rules at the beginning of the next stage accompanied by its transition matrix. The new rules may not be consistent with the desire to reach a prescribed final state, but that can also be tested by means of this procedure.

Several interesting problems arise in conjunction with this model. One problem is to devise a procedure for estimating α_{kj} when either a_{kj} or b_{kj} is not known. Since knowledge of α_{kj} is essential for determining admissible states, an alternative approach would be to define Σ in terms of states that are admissible with prescribed probabilities.

The value of a weapon system as a function of the number of units in the system does not comply with a linear scale. Equal percentage reductions are unrealistic because of inherent nonlinearities. The reduction of a force in steps, for example, can leave behind an ineffective amount for one side compared to what the opposite side has. As in chess the player with the smaller number of pieces usually avoids trading off because an equal exchange works to his disadvantage.

Decisions are not easily reached between two countries for the reduction of weapons because their assessment of the value of these weapons will generally differ. Thus it is difficult to determine how many U.S. missiles or bombers can be traded off against how many Soviet missiles or bombers of a comparable type, because in the global picture each nation evaluates its weapons against threats from other powers as well as against the nation with which it is negotiating.

Economic resources and the judgment and experience of military personnel and of designers and developers of weapon systems play a significant role in determining preference among these systems. However, this preference has no established scale of measurement which scientifically and with some degree of accuracy indicates the gains or losses to national security (a notion which must also be qualified) due to the development of this or that weapon system. Within a country planners compare major weapon systems in a gross fashion using resource limitation as a major constraint. Yet even here it is not known in some precise fashion how to trade off weapons of relatively comparable properties such as two long-range bombers, since they may have a variety of distinct missions to perform. When the systems differ, for example, an interceptor aircraft and a Nike, but the missions remain about the same, the problem is still more difficult. Yet each of these systems has a certain value that depends on the total defense posture and varies at different armament levels.

How to assign utility value to weapons to enable comparisons for reduction purposes is a difficult problem. A number of attempts have been made to study weapon utility in terms of cost effectiveness, reliability, missions, targeting, future weapons, etc., for arms reduction purposes.

The most promising approach so far proposed bypasses the direct approach and seems to rest with techniques that are sophisticated generalizations of the *fair division problem.* In order for two people to divide a cake between them so that each gets what in his estimation is his rightful portion, one person divides the cake into two parts and the other makes the first choice. This can be generalized to a fair division problem between n people.

For arms reduction purposes, each side could divide its own weapons into what that side considers a number of equal parts and the opposite side studies the situation and chooses one of the piles to be destroyed.

Another alternative for bypassing the weapon utility problem is to resort to disarmament through the use of minimal annihilating forces as a safeguard for possible discrepancies in weapon exchange. An illustration of this method, which attempts to bypass the direct approach to value-assessment, is the "nuclear umbrella," which ignores the fact that the removal of this umbrella of minimum protective nuclear forces leads to difficulties no less severe than faced initially with full armament. Nevertheless, the smaller forces of the umbrella give the idea feasibility.

The problem of arms reduction is a part of the political problem of power and its use, and hence must be treated in the general context of negotiations and bargaining. So far game theory (see Chapter 3) provides the best theoretical framework available to represent this process.

The following example is offered to show that the constraints imposed on an arms control situation in one case help to carry out the plan to completion, and in another case prevent it. The difference in the answer depends on the number of parties. As this number increases beyond a certain limit, the problem becomes insoluble. The example itself is appropriately suited for disarmament purposes.

Problem: Two missionaries and two cannibals come to the left bank of a river, which they need to cross in a boat that can take only two people at a time. The boat must always be considered to be on one or the other side of the river. The crossing must be made in such a way that on neither side can there ever be more cannibals than missionaries (including those in the boat), since even after years of religious indoctrination the cannibals retain their old habits. How can the four men be transferred across—assuming that they all know how to row?

We start by listing all admissible states. Let X be the set of missionaries and let Y be the set of cannibals. A state is a pair of numbers, the first of which gives the number of missionaries and the second the number of cannibals. The states of Σ_x are (2, 2), (2, 1), (2, 0), (1, 1), (0, 2), (0, 1), (0, 0). Thus the missionaries allow all those states in which their number is equal to or more than the number of cannibals. On the other hand Σ_y is (2, 2), (2, 1), (2, 0), (1, 2), (1, 1), (1, 0), (0, 2), (0, 1), (0, 0). The states that are common to both give Σ. They are admissible to both sides. The only two states in Σ_y that are not in Σ_x are (1, 0) and (1, 2). The reason for the second state is clear, since there are more cannibals than missionaries. The state (1, 0) implies that on the opposite side of the river we have the state (1, 2) in which there are more cannibals than missionaries. Thus we have for the states of Σ:

$$E_1 = (2, 2),$$
$$E_2 = (2, 1),$$
$$E_3 = (2, 0),$$
$$E_4 = (1, 1),$$
$$E_5 = (0, 2),$$
$$E_6 = (0, 1),$$
$$E_7 = (0, 0).$$

We now associate with E_1 a point v_1, with E_2 a point v_2, and so on. If the departure of the boat always leaves behind a state that is in Σ we join the points corresponding to the states before and after the departure by a line. The graph is shown in Figure 12. With this graph we can associate a vertex matrix whose elements are zero or one, depending on whether tran-

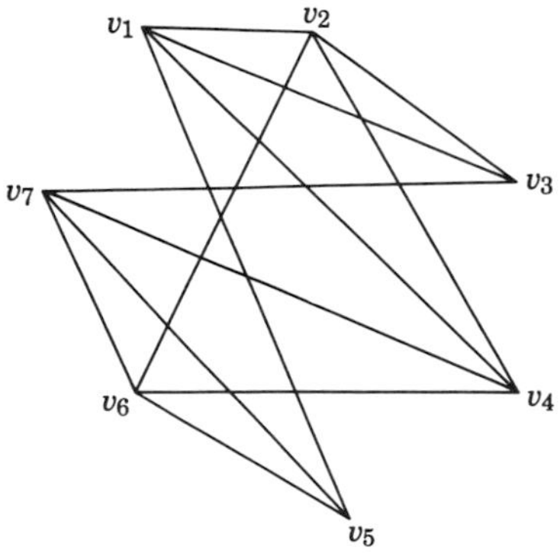

Figure 12

sitions from one state on the left bank to another also on the left bank are possible. The transitions are effected by the departure of the boat. Thus we list the vertices on the left and on top, and enter a zero or one depending on whether it is possible to go from the state represented by the vertex on the left of the matrix to another state represented by a vertex on top.

We have the vertex matrix

$$V = \begin{array}{c} \\ v_1 \\ v_2 \\ v_3 \\ v_4 \\ v_5 \\ v_6 \\ v_7 \end{array} \begin{array}{c} \begin{array}{ccccccc} v_1 & v_2 & v_3 & v_4 & v_5 & v_6 & v_7 \end{array} \\ \left\| \begin{array}{ccccccc} 0 & 1 & 1 & 1 & 1 & 0 & 0 \\ 0 & 0 & 1 & 1 & 0 & 1 & 0 \\ 0 & 0 & 0 & 0 & 0 & 0 & 1 \\ 0 & 0 & 0 & 0 & 0 & 1 & 1 \\ 0 & 0 & 0 & 0 & 0 & 1 & 1 \\ 0 & 0 & 0 & 0 & 0 & 0 & 1 \\ 0 & 0 & 0 & 0 & 0 & 0 & 0 \end{array} \right\| \end{array}.$$

On the right bank of the river there would be an identical set of states that are essentially the complementary states to those on the left bank. Their matrix would be V', the transpose of the foregoing matrix. The reader will readily verify without difficulty that to obtain the matrix of transitions after one round trip one must take the product VV'. In general for the transition matrix of n round trips we have $(VV')^n$, and since the object is to move the group to the right bank we must multiply this by V. This gives $(VV')^nV$ and the problem is to find the number of round trips n such that the element in the v_1, v_7 position of this product is one, that is, we have the transition $(2, 2) \to (0, 0)$ on the left bank. Thus the group has moved to the right bank. Note that in the successive multiplications VV', $VV'V$, $VV'VV'$, etc., elements with a value more than one will appear, indicating the number of ways in which the corresponding transition can be made. Since the object is to determine at each stage one possible transition, all nonzero elements are replaced by unity in these products. It turns out that our problem can be solved with $n = 2$ round trips and one last trip forward, that is, a unit element appears for the first time for the v_1, v_7 position of $(VV')^2V$.

The computations are as follows:

$$V' = \left\| \begin{array}{ccccccc} 0 & 0 & 0 & 0 & 0 & 0 & 0 \\ 1 & 0 & 0 & 0 & 0 & 0 & 0 \\ 1 & 1 & 0 & 0 & 0 & 0 & 0 \\ 1 & 1 & 0 & 0 & 0 & 0 & 0 \\ 1 & 0 & 0 & 0 & 0 & 0 & 0 \\ 0 & 1 & 0 & 1 & 1 & 0 & 0 \\ 0 & 0 & 1 & 1 & 1 & 1 & 0 \end{array} \right\|, \quad VV' = \left\| \begin{array}{ccccccc} 1 & 1 & 0 & 0 & 0 & 0 & 0 \\ 1 & 1 & 0 & 1 & 1 & 0 & 0 \\ 0 & 0 & 1 & 1 & 1 & 1 & 0 \\ 0 & 1 & 1 & 1 & 1 & 1 & 0 \\ 0 & 1 & 1 & 1 & 1 & 1 & 0 \\ 0 & 0 & 1 & 1 & 1 & 1 & 0 \\ 0 & 0 & 0 & 0 & 0 & 0 & 0 \end{array} \right\|,$$

$$VV'V = \left\| \begin{array}{ccccccc} 0 & 1 & 1 & 1 & 1 & 1 & 0 \\ 0 & 1 & 1 & 1 & 1 & 1 & 0 \\ 0 & 0 & 0 & 0 & 0 & 1 & 1 \\ 0 & 0 & 1 & 1 & 0 & 1 & 1 \\ 0 & 0 & 1 & 1 & 0 & 1 & 1 \\ 0 & 0 & 0 & 0 & 0 & 1 & 1 \\ 0 & 0 & 0 & 0 & 0 & 0 & 0 \end{array} \right\|, \quad (VV')^2 = \left\| \begin{array}{ccccccc} 1 & 1 & 0 & 1 & 1 & 0 & 0 \\ 1 & 1 & 0 & 1 & 1 & 0 & 0 \\ 0 & 1 & 1 & 1 & 1 & 1 & 0 \\ 1 & 1 & 1 & 1 & 1 & 1 & 0 \\ 1 & 1 & 1 & 1 & 1 & 1 & 0 \\ 0 & 1 & 1 & 1 & 1 & 1 & 0 \\ 0 & 0 & 0 & 0 & 0 & 0 & 0 \end{array} \right\|,$$

$$(VV')^2V = \left\| \begin{array}{ccccccc} 0 & 1 & 1 & 1 & 1 & 1 & 1 \\ 0 & 1 & 1 & 1 & 1 & 1 & 1 \\ 0 & 0 & 1 & 1 & 0 & 1 & 1 \\ 0 & 1 & 1 & 1 & 1 & 1 & 1 \\ 0 & 1 & 1 & 1 & 1 & 1 & 1 \\ 0 & 0 & 1 & 1 & 0 & 1 & 1 \\ 0 & 0 & 0 & 0 & 0 & 0 & 0 \end{array} \right\|.$$

The problem now is to read off the solution from the matrices. We look at the last matrix, that is, $(VV')^2V$ in the v_1, v_7 position where there is a unit element, and we ask which possible nonzero element of the first row of $(VV')^2$ could have given rise to this unit element in $(VV')^2V$ on multiplication by the seventh column of V. One possibility is the element in the 1, 4 position of $(VV')^2$ (first row, fourth column) since there is also a unit element in the 4, 7 position of V. Another possibility could be the element 1, 3 of V; but we choose the first. Thus the last transition is $v_4 \rightarrow v_7$. We next ask where this unit element in the 1, 4 position of $(VV')^2$ could have come from. By examining the first row of $(VV')V$ and the fourth column of V' we find that it came from the fact that there is a nonzero element in the position 6, 4 of V' [since the corresponding element from $(VV')V$ is also nonzero]. Thus the next to last transition is $v_6 \rightarrow v_4$. Again we ask for the origin of the unit element in the position 6, 1 of $(VV')V$ and we find that it comes from the fact that the 2, 1 element of VV' and the 2, 6 element of V are unity. Thus the third transition from the end is $v_2 \rightarrow v_6$. We similarly find that the fourth and fifth transitions from the end are respectively $v_3 \rightarrow v_2$ and $v_1 \rightarrow v_3$. Thus the transitions are given by

$$v_1 \longrightarrow v_3,\ v_3 \longrightarrow v_2,\ v_2 \longrightarrow v_6,\ v_6 \longrightarrow v_4,\ v_4 \longrightarrow v_7,$$

or simply v_1, v_3, v_2, v_6, v_4, and v_7.

We could indicate alternate transitions if we wish. To interpret the solution in words we note that since E_3 is (2, 0) both cannibals must first cross and one returns (because of v_2). Then the two missionaries must cross, in order to have E_6 on the left bank; then one missionary must return so that the next state on the left bank would be E_4. Finally both the missionary and the cannibal cross giving the final state E_7. As an exercise, the reader may attempt working out the matrix solution for the problem of three missionaries and three cannibals, all of whom can row. There are ten admissible states. The states of the problem of three missionaries and three cannibals, where all missionaries and only one cannibal can row can be represented by (m, r, c), where $0 \leqq m \leqq 3$, $0 \leqq r \leqq 1$, and $0 \leqq c \leqq 2$, where m refers to the missionaries, r to the rowing cannibal, and c to the remaining two cannibals. There are 16 possible states for this problem and again the reader should attempt writing down its transition matrix.

To determine whether a solution exists for a given problem, we argue as follows. In $(VV')^n \leqq (VV')^{n'}$, where $n < n'$ to every unit element in the i, j position in the matrix on the left corresponds a unit element in the i, j position of the matrix on the right, that is, if the vertex v_j can be reached in n round trips from v_i then it can also be reached in n' round trips. This is obviously the case since $(n' - n)$ round trips can be made with the same passenger list. Thus the sequence $(VV')^n$ $(n = 1, 2, \ldots)$ is monotone increasing and bounded above with upper bound Q, which is obtained from $Q(VV') = Q$.

If the i, j element of QV is 1, the problem is solvable, otherwise it is not. For example, the four missionary and four cannibal problem is not solvable. To see this, we have for the possible states which we now directly denote by v's:

$$\begin{aligned}
v_1 &= (4, 4), & v_5 &= (4, 0), & v_8 &= (1, 1), & v_{11} &= (0, 2),\\
v_2 &= (4, 3), & v_6 &= (3, 3), & v_9 &= (0, 4), & v_{12} &= (0, 1),\\
v_3 &= (4, 2), & v_7 &= (2, 2), & v_{10} &= (0, 3), & v_{13} &= (0, 0).\\
v_4 &= (4, 1), & & & & & &
\end{aligned}$$

The problem is to get from v_1 to v_{13}.

$$V = \begin{array}{c|ccccccccccccc|}
 & v_1 & v_2 & v_3 & v_4 & v_5 & v_6 & v_7 & v_8 & v_9 & v_{10} & v_{11} & v_{12} & v_{13}\\
v_1 & 0 & 1 & 1 & 0 & 0 & 1 & 0 & 0 & 0 & 0 & 0 & 0 & 0\\
v_2 & 0 & 0 & 1 & 1 & 0 & 1 & 0 & 0 & 0 & 0 & 0 & 0 & 0\\
v_3 & 0 & 0 & 0 & 1 & 1 & 0 & 1 & 0 & 0 & 0 & 0 & 0 & 0\\
v_4 & 0 & 0 & 0 & 0 & 1 & 0 & 0 & 0 & 0 & 0 & 0 & 0 & 0\\
v_5 & 0 & 0 & 0 & 0 & 0 & 0 & 0 & 0 & 0 & 0 & 0 & 0 & 0\\
v_6 & 0 & 0 & 0 & 0 & 0 & 0 & 1 & 0 & 0 & 0 & 0 & 0 & 0\\
v_7 & 0 & 0 & 0 & 0 & 0 & 0 & 0 & 1 & 0 & 0 & 1 & 0 & 0\\
v_8 & 0 & 0 & 0 & 0 & 0 & 0 & 0 & 0 & 0 & 0 & 0 & 1 & 1\\
v_9 & 0 & 0 & 0 & 0 & 0 & 0 & 0 & 0 & 0 & 1 & 1 & 0 & 0\\
v_{10} & 0 & 0 & 0 & 0 & 0 & 0 & 0 & 0 & 0 & 0 & 1 & 1 & 0\\
v_{11} & 0 & 0 & 0 & 0 & 0 & 0 & 0 & 0 & 0 & 0 & 0 & 1 & 1\\
v_{12} & 0 & 0 & 0 & 0 & 0 & 0 & 0 & 0 & 0 & 0 & 0 & 0 & 1\\
v_{13} & 0 & 0 & 0 & 0 & 0 & 0 & 0 & 0 & 0 & 0 & 0 & 0 & 0
\end{array}.$$

In column 13, v_8, v_{11}, and v_{12} are nonzero. Therefore if this problem has a solution $(VV')^m$ must have a nonzero element in the first row at v_8, v_{11}, or v_{12}.

$$VV' = \begin{array}{c} \\ v_1 \\ v_2 \\ v_3 \\ v_4 \\ v_5 \\ v_6 \\ v_7 \\ v_8 \\ v_9 \\ v_{10} \\ v_{11} \\ v_{12} \\ v_{13} \end{array} \!\!\begin{array}{c} \begin{array}{ccccccccccccc} v_1 & v_2 & v_3 & v_4 & v_5 & v_6 & v_7 & v_8 & v_9 & v_{10} & v_{11} & v_{12} & v_{13} \end{array} \\ \begin{pmatrix} 1 & 1 & 0 & 0 & 0 & 0 & 0 & 0 & 0 & 0 & 0 & 0 & 0 \\ 1 & 1 & 1 & 0 & 0 & 0 & 0 & 0 & 0 & 0 & 0 & 0 & 0 \\ 0 & 1 & 1 & 1 & 0 & 1 & 0 & 0 & 0 & 0 & 0 & 0 & 0 \\ 0 & 0 & 1 & 1 & 0 & 0 & 0 & 0 & 0 & 0 & 0 & 0 & 0 \\ 0 & 0 & 0 & 0 & 0 & 0 & 0 & 0 & 0 & 0 & 0 & 0 & 0 \\ 0 & 0 & 1 & 0 & 0 & 1 & 0 & 0 & 0 & 0 & 0 & 0 & 0 \\ 0 & 0 & 0 & 0 & 0 & 0 & 1 & 0 & 1 & 1 & 0 & 0 & 0 \\ 0 & 0 & 0 & 0 & 0 & 0 & 0 & 1 & 0 & 1 & 1 & 1 & 0 \\ 0 & 0 & 0 & 0 & 0 & 0 & 1 & 0 & 1 & 1 & 0 & 0 & 0 \\ 0 & 0 & 0 & 0 & 0 & 0 & 1 & 1 & 1 & 1 & 1 & 0 & 0 \\ 0 & 0 & 0 & 0 & 0 & 0 & 0 & 1 & 0 & 1 & 1 & 1 & 0 \\ 0 & 0 & 0 & 0 & 0 & 0 & 0 & 1 & 0 & 0 & 1 & 1 & 0 \\ 0 & 0 & 0 & 0 & 0 & 0 & 0 & 0 & 0 & 0 & 0 & 0 & 0 \end{pmatrix} \end{array}.$$

The set of vertices that can be reached from v_1 consists of $\{v_1, v_2\}$. v_2 can reach v_1, v_2, and v_3; so add v_3 to the set, giving $\{v_1, v_2, v_3\}$. v_3 can reach v_2, v_3, v_4, and v_6; so add v_4 and v_6, giving $\{v_1, v_2, v_3, v_4, v_6\}$. v_4 reaches v_3 and v_4, which adds nothing new to the set. v_6 reaches v_3 and v_6, which also adds nothing new to the set. We have now exhausted the possibilities. Therefore v_1 can reach only v_1, v_2, v_3, v_4, and v_6. It cannot reach v_5, v_7, v_8, v_9, v_{10}, v_{11}, v_{12}, or v_{13} in any number of round trips But in column 13 of V only v_8, v_{11}, and v_{12} are nonzero. Since none of these are included in the set, the problem is unsolvable.

If the vector giving the number of weapons for both sides could be translated into a new vector whose components have values which are comparable on some scale, then one may be able to work with those vectors corresponding to equilibrium states and apply an approach similar to that outlined in the foregoing examples to show a feasible path for carrying out any reductions. This would be a very natural and perhaps desirable way to approach the subject. There is no common measurement scale for weapons, however, not even in one country, and hence the problem is best tackled at present in the context of game theory (Chapter 3). This does not preclude continued research to develop such a scale. In addition the world consists of many powers and arms reduction must consider this, and the model generalized to accommodate more than two powers.

2.6. RICHARDSON'S MODEL

Lewis Richardson (1881–1953) developed a model to describe armament buildups between two countries. He made the following assumptions [54, 55]:

1. In an armament race between two countries, each country would attempt to increase its armament proportionately to the size of the armament of the other.
2. Economics is a constraint on armament that tends to diminish the rate of armament by an amount proportional to the size of existing forces.
3. A nation would build arms guided by ambition, grievances, and hostilities even if another nation poses no threat to it.

If the armament levels of the two sides are $N_1(t)$ and $N_2(t)$ respectively and t stands for time, then the foregoing three conditions are expressed for each side as follows:

$$\frac{dN_1}{dt} = kN_2 - aN_1 + g$$

$$\frac{dN_2}{dt} = lN_1 - bN_2 + h$$

where k, a, g, l, b, and h are positive constants.

Sometimes the constants in this model are referred to using the following terminology:

k, l are called defense or reaction coefficients

a, b are called fatigue or expense coefficients

g, h are called grievance coefficients when positive and good will coefficients when negative. They are usually assumed to be positive as done previously.

In this model the balance of power is attained when a stable equilibrium at a constant level of expenditure is reached. Stability is obtained when $kl < ab$, that is, the product of the coefficients of reaction to the other side must be less than the product of the coefficients corresponding to the expense of armament.

An unstable equilibrium occurs when $ab < kl$ and indicates a runaway arms race.

The foregoing equations describe surprisingly well the arms race of 1909–1913; Austria-Hungary and Germany were on one side, France and

Russia on the other side. Let A and B denote respective expenditure of the blocks for arms preparation and let A_0 and B_0 be corresponding cooperative expenditures between the blocks. Put

$$N_1 = A - A_0, \qquad N_2 = B - B_0,$$

and assume for simplicity that $k = l$ and $a = b$. If we substitute these quantities in Richardson's equations and add we obtain

$$\frac{d(A + B)}{dt} = (k - a)\left[A + B - \left(A_0 + B_0 - \frac{g - h}{k - a}\right)\right],$$

which says that the rate of change of the combined armament expenditures of both blocks is proportional to the level of the combined amount of expenditures, that is, we have a linear relation between them.

Richardson collected data for this period and made a plot (see Figure 13). He then drew the straight line of the combined equation and

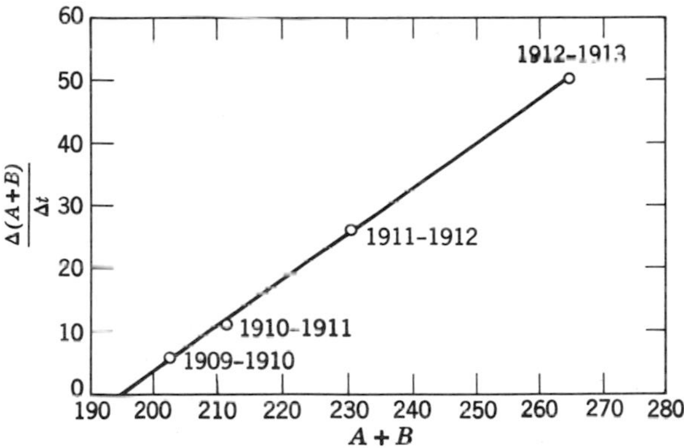

Figure 13

obtained the indicated good fit of the model to the data giving the trend along the line with time. The graph indicates a positive proportionality factor or slope $k - a$. Thus $k - a > 0$ or $k > a$, indicating instability and a runaway race.

In general it is not easy to obtain an accurate statistical measure for warlike preparations that is crucial for the credibility of the model. There are other studies [10a] that have collected data for the purpose of analyzing the stability of the arms race between the United States and the U.S.S.R. in recent years.

The foregoing model is more plausible if instead of armament one speaks of threat since people react to the absolute level of hostility in others and have anxiety proportional to the level of hostility they themselves bear. A noteworthy aspect of this model is the explicit expression of dependence of the level of arms of one side on that of the other. This enables each side to gauge its levels upon its opponents response to its own previous levels. The model does not prescribe a sequence of choices in an arms race, however.

Richardson places no upper bound on expenditures, but actually the wealth of a society minus a minimum amount for the subsistence of its members is an absolute constraint on armament. In general it is more expensive to procure a new weapon than to maintain an old one, and hence the economics of armament are not simply proportional to their level. Long before this economic maximum feasible level is realized the system is likely to explode by increases in international tensions, although these variables are not explicitly included in the model.

There have been attempts to bring Richardson's model closer to reality by introducing additional variables.

In an unpublished paper W. R. Caspary has considered the economic constraint. If M is the cost per unit of maintaining the existing forces and if C is the total resources available for armament, then $C - MN_1$ is the expenditure on new arms. If we put

$$D = a\left(\frac{kN_2}{a} - N_1 + \frac{g}{a}\right),$$

then k/a and g/a are the desired ratio and the minimum levels respectively in case of disarmament by the opposite power. The constant a has the dimension of (1/time) and $1/a$ is the time a nation allows itself to reach the desired level. Expenditures will increase linearly with D for small values of D but the new procurement will approach asymptotically the ceiling value.

The initial slope, when the function is linear in D, and the rapidity of the limiting behavior will differ from one nation to another and hence a parameter p is used to indicate preference for military spending.

Our model now assumes the form

$$\frac{dN_1}{dt} = (C - MN_1)(1 - e^{-pd}),$$

$$\frac{dN_2}{dt} = (C' - M'N_2)(1 - e^{-p'd'}),$$

where the exponential expresses both facts known to hold for small and for very large values of D. One recovers Richardson's model by expanding e^{-pd} in series to first-order terms and letting $MN_1 \ll C$ so that $dN_1/dt \approx CpD$, etc.

For stability we must have $C - MN_1 = 0$ or $1 - e^{-pd} = 0$. The latter leads to $D = 0$ and to Richardson's analysis of stability.

Very interesting conclusions can be obtained by assigning specific values to this model. Put $p = a = p' = a' = 1$; $g = g' = 0$; $k/a = k'/a' = 2$; $C = C'$; $M = M' = \frac{1}{2}$; and $N_1(0) = N_2(0) = .01C$. If a graph of the expenditure as a function of the time in years is drawn it would show that for the first five years the arms race proceeds geometrically, then the slope begins to decrease after the eighth year reaching a level of 95% of the maximum after the thirteenth year and attaining stability. Thus this model has several interesting and realistic features which are improvements on Richardson's equations.

A differential game or control theory variation on Richardson's model is to minimize a cost function of armament given by an integral

$$\int_0^1 (a_1N_1^2 + aN_2^2 + b_1u_1^2 + b_2u_2^2)\, dt$$

where a_1, a_2, b_1, and b_2 are given weights, subject to Richardson's equations as constraints but with the modification that a control function $u_1(t)$ denoting armament policies of the first country is added to the right side of the first equation and a corresponding function $u_2(t)$ for the second country is added to the right side of the second equation.

Later on, we shall give an example of an armament and conflict model demonstrating the use of the theory of optimum control applied to an objective function subject to differential equations as constraints.

In 1965 a Norwegian statistican used a computer to account for 14,531 wars in 5560 years of recorded history, at an average of 2.6135 wars per year. There are high-intensity wars such as the two world wars of this century, mid-intensity wars in which no total offensive or total victory are envisioned such as the Vietnam War, and low-intensity wars which are illustrated by the Dominican crisis and the Congolese rebellions. Forty wars have been counted since 1945, which puts the average for this period somewhat under that previously mentioned.

Richardson's model says nothing about whether arms races lead to war. It may be inferred, however, that such a relationship is sometimes brought about through increased tensions and the incidence of quarrels related to the increase in armament itself. One can even envisage the deliberate provoking of a conflict at what is considered an opportune time rather than continuing armament at a high cost to the general economy or in a situation where the potential enemy threatens to overtake in an arms race.

A generalization of the model to n countries was used by Richardson to study the arms races of 1932–1939. He found that it gave a reasonably good prediction for the outcome. He noted an increasing tendency toward instability for an increasing value of n.

The good fits of Richardson's models show the exponential trends in arms expenditures for both periods. Clearly there are many alternative models that would yield such exponential trends. The coefficients in the model take on different values for different arms races and hence larger historical samples are needed to discover the law governing the values of these variables so that the models may be used to make future predictions.

A more general theory is needed that would be less mechanical and would consider rational behavior accounting for the relationships between arms buildup and the occurrence of conflicts. However, Richardson's model may be used as an indicator to warn nations when their arms buildup has gone beyond the bounds of a certain predetermined threshold which points to danger if the race is continued.

Some have argued that man needs the stimulus of wars to unite him and to integrate his drives for making progress. This idea is usually backed by historical data. There is no denying that man has residual barbarism in his nature. The picture as it now presents itself, however, is influenced by our past, and war is not the only source of inspiration for energy and creativeness. The alternative is to establish peace and security in a world in which we can develop a deeper meaning for our activities and where we can derive a stimulus for progress from security and cooperation rather than from fighting and dissidence.

It may be worth mentioning that Richardson's model is not very different in substance from two well-known models that preceded it in this century. The first was developed by Vito Volterra. It arises in a study of the struggle for existence, in a closed environment, between two species of animals, one of which preys exclusively on the other. Let $N_1(t)$ be the population of the prey, and $N_2(t)$ of the predator, at time t. If N_2 is small, N_1 increases, entailing an increase in N_2. This increase in N_2 is followed by a decrease in N_1, which causes starvation and hence a decrease in N_2. The number of encounters of the two species is proportional to N_1N_2. In an encounter one species decreases while the other increases [77]. Thus

$$\frac{dN_1}{dt} = aN_1 - bN_1N_2$$

and

$$\frac{dN_2}{dt} = -cN_2 + dN_1N_2$$

where a, b, c, d are all positive. Dividing the first equation by the second, integrating and substituting

$$N_1 = x + \frac{c}{d} \equiv x + p,$$

$$N_2 = y + \frac{a}{b} \equiv y + q$$

yield

$$c \log (x + p) + a \log y + q - dx - by = c$$

where c is the integration constant. After expanding in series about the origin and neglecting terms of higher order, we obtain ellipses that describe periodic variations in the prey population (e.g., a host population) and in the predators (e.g., parasites). These ellipses are given by

$$\frac{cx^2}{p^2} + \frac{ay^2}{q^2} = D$$

where D is a constant. The period of oscillation near the origin is given by $2\pi/(ac)^{1/2}$. Volterra also studied the behavior of a two prey and one predator system.

Another differential equation model was developed by Lanchester [11, 38]. It is concerned with the following problem: Suppose that N_1 units of one force A, each of hitting power α, are engaged with N_2 units of an enemy B, each of hitting power β. Suppose further that the engagement is such that the fire power of force A is directed equally against all units of B, and vice versa. The rate of loss of the two forces is given by

$$\frac{dN_1}{dt} = -k\beta N_2 \qquad \text{and} \qquad \frac{dN_2}{dt} = -k\alpha N_1$$

where k is a positive constant.

The strength of the two forces is defined as equal when their fractional losses are equal, that is, when

$$\frac{1}{N_2}\frac{dN_1}{dt} = \frac{1}{N_1}\frac{dN_2}{dt}$$

On dividing the first equation by the second and integrating, we obtain two hyperbolas defined by

$$\alpha N_1{}^2 - \beta N_2{}^2 = C.$$

Taking $C = 0$ gives Lanchester's N^2-law which states that the strength of a force is proportional to the fire power of a unit multiplied by the square of the number of units.

The notion of stability is often troublesome when one speaks of military power and armaments. Care must be exercised in defining the problem and the sense in which stability is to be used. Consider, for example, the differential equation system

$$\frac{dX}{dt} = AX$$

where

$$X(t) = \begin{pmatrix} x \\ y \end{pmatrix}, \quad A = \begin{pmatrix} a & b \\ c & d \end{pmatrix}.$$

We form the characteristic equation

$$|A - \lambda I| = 0$$

and suppose that its roots are λ_1 and λ_2. We note that Richardson's system may be reduced to this form by means of an affine transformation.

An affine transformation has the form

$$x' = a_1x + b_1y + c_1, \qquad y' = a_2x + b_2y + c_2$$

with a nonsingular coefficient matrix. Such a transformation can always be factored into a product of translation, rotation, stretching and contracting, reflections, and simple elongation and compression.

There is a unique solution $x(t)$ of the foregoing system that satisfies the initial conditions $x(t_0) = x_0$, $y(t_0) = y_0$. This solution defines a curve called a characteristic curve with a continuously turning tangent. Note that $x(t - \bar{t})$, $y(t - \bar{t})$ is also a solution for any t but represents the same characteristic; hence a characteristic may belong to more than one solution.

The study of stability involves investigating conditions under which characteristics stay near equilibrium points or tend to an equilibrium point such as $t \to \infty$. At most one characteristic passes through any point of the domain of definition of the system. If a single point is a solution of the system, then clearly no characteristic passes through it, and it is said to be a singularity of the system. Singularities represent points of equilibrium of the system, whereas at any regular point nonzero components of both derivatives (indicating velocity and hence motion) exist, and they are therefore points of disequilibrium. Thus the characteristics represent the trajectories of motion. A point at which both expressions on the right of the equations of the system vanish is called an equilibrium or a critical point. Such a point is called a singular point of the expression obtained by dividing the two equations of the system. Critical points are assumed to be isolated, that is, there is a neighborhood about each of them in which there are no other critical points. We have seen that there is a unique solution to the system for any point chosen as initial point.

Solutions corresponding to all initial points reveal characteristic behavior with regard to the critical points, which from their definition can be obtained by solving $ax + by = 0$, $cx + dy = 0$ simultaneously. Since, by a translation of variables, a singular point can be brought to the origin, it suffices to examine systems having the latter as a critical point [57].

In general, if the roots of the characteristic equation λ_1 and λ_2 are complex numbers with

$$\lambda_1 = \alpha + i\beta \qquad \lambda_2 = \alpha - i\beta,$$

then by means of a real affine transformation the original system may be transformed to

$$\dot{x} = \alpha x - \beta y \qquad \dot{y} = \beta x + \alpha y$$

where

$$\dot{x} = \frac{dx}{dt} \qquad \dot{y} = \frac{dy}{dt}$$

which has a solution of the form

$$x = e^{\alpha t} \cos \beta \qquad y = e^{\alpha t} \sin \beta t.$$

It is easily verified by varying the coefficients that a family of trajectories is obtained, and, depending on the nature of the roots λ_1 and λ_2, we have the following description of the trajectories near the origin (see Figure 14) as t ranges from $-\infty$ to $+\infty$:

1. If λ_1 and λ_2 are real, and if

   (*a*) $\lambda_1 < \lambda_2 < 0$, then all trajectories move towards the origin, forming a stable node there.

   (*b*) $0 < \lambda_1 < \lambda_2$, the origin is an unstable nodal point, since the trajectories move away from it.

   (*c*) $\lambda_1 < 0 < \lambda_2$, the trajectories tend asymptotically to the x_1 and x_2 axes: the origin forms a saddle point. Each axis in this case is called a *separatrix*, since it separates the plane into regions of trajectories.

2. If $\lambda_1 = i\beta$, $\lambda_2 = -i\beta$, that is, they are purely imaginary, then $\alpha = 0$ and $x = \cos \beta$, $y = \sin \beta$, and the trajectories form circles (ellipses before the affine transformation) with center at the origin. The origin is called a *vortex* point and (by definition) is a stable singularity.

3. If $\lambda = \alpha + i\beta$, $\lambda = \alpha - i\beta$, for α, $\beta \neq 0$, and if $\alpha < 0$, the trajectories are spirals that wind around and move toward the origin, which is stable and is called a *focal* point. If $\alpha > 0$, the spirals unwind and move away from the origin, which is an unstable focal point (*focus* or *spiral* point).

Thus we have stability only when the real parts of the roots are zero or negative.

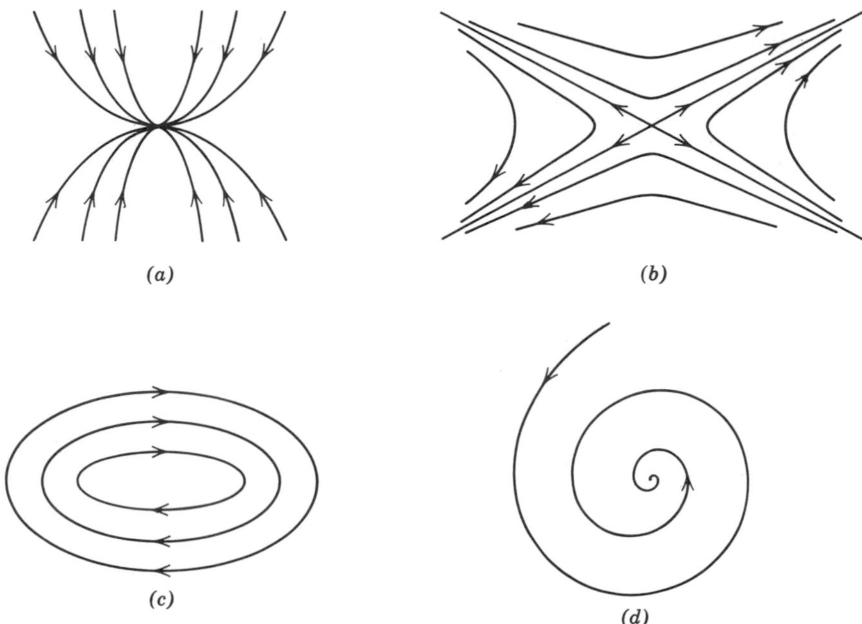

Figure 14. (*a*) Stable nodal point (reverse arrows for instability), (*b*) saddle point, unstable equilibrium; (*c*) center or vortex point, a stable singularity; (*d*) stable spiral or focal point (reverse arrows for instability).

2.7. A DYNAMIC MODEL OF MISSILE WAR

The definition of arms control previously given referred to reducing damage if war breaks out. To reduce damage in a nuclear age requires an understanding of the possible conduct of war and of the optimum strategies for each side. Neither side may wish to annihilate the other. If a nuclear war has started, can it be terminated early with a minimum of destruction? This section develops tools to analyze this question.

M. Intriligator [29a] has studied, through the use of the tools of the mathematical theory of optimum control (see Chapter 5, reference 57), the problem of strategy in a missile war from the viewpoint of an economist. He does this as a problem in allocating scarce resources of missiles, considering both alternative targets and alternative rates of fire. From this viewpoint the paper analyzes the following questions of missile strategy:

1. What is the optimal targeting strategy; that is, should missiles be targeted at enemy missiles (a counterforce strategy) or at enemy cities (a countervalue strategy)? How should these targets vary over time?

2. What is the optimal rate-of-fire strategy; that is, should missiles be fired rapidly, perhaps even all at once (a massive retaliation strategy), or slowly, holding some missiles in reserve (a controlled response strategy)?
3. How can variations in missile strategy affect the opponent's optimal targeting and rate strategies?
4. How can missile defense, including both passive defense (hardening) and active defense (antiballistic missile defense for missile sites), affect the opponent's optimal targeting and rate strategies?
5. How can civil defense, including both passive defense (shelters) and active defense (antiballistic missile defense for cities), affect the opponent's optimal targeting and rate strategies?
6. How would a missile war terminate, and what would be the optimal targeting and rate strategies at war termination?

There has been an ongoing debate over many of these questions of strategy, especially the optimal targeting and rate strategies and the influence of an antiballistic missile system on the opponent's strategy. A major criticism of this debate is that it generally tends to ignore a critically important dimension of a missile war—time. The analysis of the foregoing questions of missile strategy has been made within the context of a dynamic model of a missile war, one in which targets and rates of fire can vary over time during the course of the war.

This work has so far been concerned with various conditions on the terminal manifold of war. Its continuation will be concerned with the initial manifold and how to control the arms and conditions under which war breaks out. The model itself is a pioneering contribution to the analytical tools available so far for studying such problems. We now briefly give some of the underlying concepts and formulations.

A, B; countries at war.

t = time, $0 \leq t \leq T$, T = length of the war,
t = 0: initial time for the war,
t = T: termination time for the war.
$M_A(t)$ = missiles in A at time t, $M_A(0) = M_{A0}$, given
$C_A(t)$ = casualties in A at time t, $C_A(0) = 0$,
$\alpha(t)$ = rate of fire proportion used by A at time t, $0 \leq \alpha(t) \leq \bar{\alpha} < 1$,
$\alpha'(t)$ = counterforce proportion used by A at time t, $0 \leq \alpha'(t) \leq 1$,
$f_A(t)$ = effectiveness ratio for A counterforce missiles,
= B missiles destroyed per A counterforce missile at time t,
$V_A(t)$ = effectiveness ratio for A countervalue missiles,
= B casualties inflicted per A countervalue missile at time t.

$$
\begin{aligned}
M_B(t) &= \text{missiles in } B \text{ at time } t,\ M_B(0) = M_{B0}, \text{ given} \\
C_B(t) &= \text{casualties in } B \text{ at time } t,\ C_B(0) = 0, \\
\beta(t) &= \text{rate of fire proportion used by } B \text{ at time } t, \\
\beta'(t) &= \text{counterforce proportion used by } B \text{ at time } t. \\
f_B(t) &= \text{effectiveness ratio for } B \text{ counterforce missiles,} \\
&= A \text{ missiles destroyed per } B \text{ counterforce missile at time } t, \\
V_B(t) &= \text{effectiveness ratio for } B \text{ countervalue missiles,} \\
&= A \text{ casualties inflicted per } B \text{ countervalue missile at time } t.
\end{aligned}
$$

We have the following differential equations:

$$
\begin{aligned}
\dot{M}_A &= -\alpha M_A - \beta'\beta M_B f_B, & M_A(0) &= M_{A0} \\
\dot{M}_B &= -\beta M_B - \alpha'\alpha M_A f_A, & M_B(0) &= M_{B0} \\
\dot{C}_A &= (1 - \beta')\beta M_B V_B, & C_A(0) &= 0 \\
\dot{C}_B &= (1 - \alpha')\alpha M_A V_A, & C_B(0) &= 0.
\end{aligned}
$$

The dot indicates the derivative with respect to time.

The objective of country A is summarized by a payoff function, P_A, which A seeks to maximize. The payoff function is assumed to depend on the outcome of the war; that is, on the terminal numbers of missiles and casualties in both countries, and is assumed linear:

$$P_A = P_{A1}M_A(T) + P_{A2}M_B(T) + P_{A3}C_A(T) + P_{A4}C_B(T)$$

The constants P_{Ai} ($i = 1, 2, 3, 4$) represent marginal payoffs to A and summarize the viewpoint of country A. Since added terminal missiles can be used to attain political objectives, to threaten the opponent, and to terminate the war, P_A presumably increases with greater A missiles and fewer B missiles:

$$P_{A1} \geq 0,$$

$$P_{A2} \leq 0.$$

Since "damage limitation" is an important objective, P_A presumably increases with fewer A casualties:

$$P_{A3} < 0.$$

Although "assured destruction" would imply that P_A increases with more B casualties, two cases are considered: where added B casualties increase or decrease the A payoff function, referred to as a "vindictive war" or a "nonvindictive war" respectively:

$$P_{A4} \begin{Bmatrix} > \\ < \end{Bmatrix} 0 \quad \text{if} \quad \begin{Bmatrix} \text{vindictive} \\ \text{nonvindictive} \end{Bmatrix}.$$

This payoff function generalizes on previous work by allowing for the influence of terminal missile stocks on the payoff function.

The optimal missile strategy for A where the strategy of B is known consists of the time paths for the counterforce proportion, $\alpha'(t)$, and rate of fire proportion, $\alpha(t)$, which maximize the payoff to A, P_A. This optimal strategy can be obtained by the method of optimal control. According to this method the solutions for $\alpha(t)$ and $\alpha'(t)$ are obtained by introducing supplementary variables $a_1(t)$, $a_2(t)$, $a_3(t)$, and $a_4(t)$ and maximizing the Hamiltonian function H, where:

$$H = \alpha M_A[-a_1 + \alpha'(a_2 f_A - a_4 V_A) + a_4 V_A] \\ + \beta M_B[a_2 - \beta'(a_1 f_B - a_3 V_B) - a_3 V_B].$$

A number of useful conclusions can be drawn from the results of the analysis as it proceeds toward determining the optimal strategies. We shall derive only one conclusion from the foregoing expression for H without proceeding further. If αM_A is positive, that is, country A is firing some missiles, then the choice of targets (summarized by α') is independent of the rate of fire and depends only on the expression $a_2 f_A - a_4 V_A$. If this expression is positive then α' should be maximized (in order to maximize H), but the maximum value of α' is unity in which case A is using counter-force targeting. If $a_2 f_A - a_4 V_A$ is negative, α' must be minimized. The minimum value is zero, which means counter-value targeting by A.

The analysis provides some conclusions about how wars begin, how they are fought and how they end. For example the model suggests regions of stability against war-outbreak [29b], that is, it indicates combinations of missiles which would probably not lead to war. During the war, there are typically 3 phases. The initial phase is an all-out attack against enemy missiles. The final phase is a controlled retaliation against his cities. The intermediate phase is the critical one. Depending on conditions in the model, it can either be an all-out attack against enemy cities or a controlled attack against his missiles.

The termination of a war developed in the model is based on relative missile strengths and casualties. One conclusion for the termination of war is that a country which is nonvindictive can still optimally target enemy cities at the end of war in order to shorten the length of the war and thereby reduce its own casualties. It is precisely on this ground that the allies in World War II bombed Dresden, Tokyo and Hamburg.

OPTIMUM STRATEGIES FOR COORDINATING POLICIES

The problem of coordinating policies within a country involves cooperative bargaining with officials of the same government for agreement on these policies. Here the officials may threaten not to concur with a drawn policy unless certain changes are made. Formally, this situation may be regarded in the context of game theory as a problem of fixed threats.

Important aspects of negotiations with other countries encountered in arms control and disarmament may also be examined from the viewpoint of game theory. Noncooperative games provide one framework. Games with incomplete information studied in Chapter 4 give another framework for a different set of negotiation problems. Chapter 3 is essential for developing background material to examine such ideas. The object is to increase understanding of such problems rather than to carry out computations.

Chapter 3

CONFLICTS AND THE THEORY OF GAMES

3.1. INTRODUCTION

In the next two chapters we shall approach game theory as a significant analytical tool without a comparable rival as a theory for conflict problems with the hope that it will in time provide the necessary models for the analysis of problems of escalation, negotiations, arms races, and arms control and reduction. Its present contributions must be regarded primarily in terms of the conceptualization and structuring it provides to the possible treatment of such problems. At this point of its development this process of conceptualization is an important adjunct and will probably continue to occupy a central place for the next few years. In certain parts of the presentation we shall also see how close this process has come to representing various types of political problems. At present it is easy to point to several areas into which game theory needs to expand in order that it be more suitable for applications. We must give a summary of some of the basic ideas of game theory before we can discuss areas of expansion and some possible applications for which Section 3.7 has been reserved.

We must emphasize that powerful applications of game theory can be made and have been made. Such applications may be used in the decision-making process. Examples illustrating a general method of application are given in Section 3.7. The entire procedure of sanctions discussed under meta-games seems to play a role equivalent to the idea of threats and can be used in a real sense to analyze policies for stability. In many applications, the fact that only ordinal utilities are needed reduces the burden of justifying the magnitude of numbers and makes it clear that numbers primarily serve as a tool to facilitate the expression of preferences in decision making and have no particular deep meaning of their own. This meta-game approach can also be used in a dynamic sense, that is, by altering the preference rankings and repeating the analysis for anticipated changes on the international scene.

Most of the examples given in Chapter 2 analyze the stability of given policies used in a conflict situation. This is done separately for each of the parties, often assuming symmetry for their separate objectives. Game theory goes the last step and attempts to find the "best" strategies or policies which lead to stability, for the parties *taken together*. At least this is its goal although in difficult problems it is not easily achieved. The framework of this chapter and that of the next two is, in the language of Chapter 1, normative rather than descriptive with optimization as the objective. Meta-game theory is the exception: it is descriptive.

In this section, we shall first relate political conflicts and game theory. Then we show that in a classification scheme, game theory is a branch of optimization. Finally, a basic concept of optimization, and hence also of game theory, is discussed—utility theory. A brief presentation of game theory is needed because it is a relatively new subject and will be used for constructing models of arms control.

Because of the complexity of international politics, no mathematical treatment can do full justice to all the essential elements that go into making a political decision. Usually only a few factors are incorporated in a simple model which is used for insight, or occasionally for making specific recommendations. An insight gained from a simple model may direct attention to a new procedure not previously recognized or utilized. Ordinarily, a model is gradually adapted to the real situation, becoming more and more elaborate in the process. Sometimes the reverse happens and an initially complicated model becomes simpler and clearer. Greater sophistication in model building is grounded in the analysis of simpler models.

Among political scientists and diplomats the idea of seeking equilibrium positions in the resolution of conflict problems is a familiar and intuitively acknowledged concept. Politicians instinctively select the best of the worst outcomes as the first step before proceeding to chart a cooperative position. This practice is formalized by the minmax principle of the theory of games and by bargaining procedures of cooperative games. In politics cooperative solutions are constructed through a mixture of imagination and experience.

Whereas game theory is still seeking to define a widely usable notion of a solution for nonzero-sum N-person games, the diplomat politician already has pragmatic knowledge and a working procedure from precedents and examples. No matter how adequate such experience may be to cope with crises, an integrated view based on a sound theory would be preferred. There is no such theory today, but there is one in the making and its progress in the past few years has been remarkable.

Negotiations and bargaining help achieve a compromise which may be the desired solution of the conflict problem. In this process various basic strategies, for example, alliances and threats, are available to the parties involved.

By forming alliances, power blocks can improve their bargaining positions and invite greater cooperation. Subtle uses of threats, sanctions, and even military force are possible devices employed by nations to induce the cooperation of other nations. A threat not to cooperate may result in smaller advantage to both sides. A small nation may persuade a larger nation to cooperate so that together each will obtain a larger return. It may even force the larger nation to share some of the gain made possible by the smaller nation's cooperation. On the other hand a larger nation may force a smaller nation to cooperate because the smaller nation may be desperate for the gain from cooperation.

In this chapter the reader will learn the basic elements of game theory, which provides a formal framework for the foregoing notions. The recently emerging theory of games with incomplete information, which, as a modeling technique, is applicable to arms control, is given in Chapter 4 which is also concerned with the game theoretic approach to the balance of power concept.

Game Theory as a Branch of Optimization

One of the most powerful and effective mathematical techniques which has found diverse applications, particularly in decision making, is the theory of optimization. This theory is usually concerned with maximizing (or minimizing) a function describing a set of objectives, subject to constraints on these objectives.

Ideally, if several parties could agree on a common utility scale, pool their interests cooperatively, and agree on the constraints, they could obtain the best solution for all concerned. Concepts of utility differ, however, and hence each side may wish to obtain more for himself within his utility scale. Even if the problem of utility differences were resolved the constraints on the objectives of one party may be less restrictive than the constraints on the objectives of another party. Hence a solution subject only to the first party's constraints would yield a larger value for his maximum than would be obtained by having his objectives subjected to the more restrictive constraints of another party.

The real situation between nations is not a case of complete cooperation but of strong competition whereby each party is free to choose a strategy and form alliances which it considers to be more profitable in the competition. Thus the problem is one of opposing interests. When interests are opposed it is a conflict situation. In this context conflict does not necessarily mean war. Even though arms control is presently concerned with weapons and war, war itself may arise from conflicts with varying causes, for example, economic and territorial causes, power politics, or ideological clashes.

Game theory is the branch of optimization concerned with the resolution of multiple-interest conflict problems and does not involve direct maximization or minimization. For better perspective, we give a comprehensive chart (Figure 15) that shows the position of game theory as a special branch of optimization theory.

Utility Theory, the Foundation of Optimization

All methods of optimization are based on the concept of utility preferences. It is usual in decision making to examine the available alternatives and choose one which gives the highest return or has the largest utility. In other words we must first define preferences among the alternatives and then attach a utility to these preferences which indicates how much more one preference is worth than another. The attached utilities define a function from the alternatives to the real numbers which is called the utility function. It must reflect the order of the preferences. If the intensity of preference (in a sense defined more precisely in Section 3.2) is reflected in the utility function on an absolute scale, then we have cardinal utilities. If the utility function only reflects the order of preference, we have an ordinal utility function. A preference relation is not a numerical relation; it is simply an ordering. The quality of an ordering is expressed numerically through a utility function. Having formulated a utility function, a decision maker optimizes this function in search of the best alternative to be chosen, subject to constraints that limit the courses of action to alternatives that are feasible. The optimum is a feasible alternative which is preferred or indifferent to all feasible alternatives.

Classical optimization techniques ranging from linear and nonlinear programming to the calculus and the calculus of variations provide the mathematical techniques for selecting a preference with optimum (maximum or minimum) return. The theory of games, which involves more than a single interest, provides another framework for optimum decision making.

Among the most important practical problems encountered in utility theory is the ordering of preferences. Preferences are generally partially ordered rather than totally ordered. A desperately hungry man, for example, may prefer an apple to a Cadillac. In arms control, utility ordering may depend on its contribution to diminishing the risk of war.

On other occasions the opposite would hold. The next section is given to a discussion of the subject of defining individual utility preferences.

Another problem is that of representing the utility of a group. The problems inherent in this situation are greatly magnified when an individual with a different personal preference ordering tries to represent or mediate for the group.

Many political decisions are based on either a majority vote or on negotiation within the group to obtain a compromise position. If the majority decision does not take into consideration minority positions, the utility function is not representative of the whole group. The compromise approach employed by a family deciding how to spend their evening is more like a social utility function which is an aggregation of individual utility functions. In a hierarchy of decision makers where higher-level members have greater information about the broader aspects of a problem, the first step for obtaining a group decision is to have decision makers of a certain level get together to work out their views. If they agree, the matter is settled and a decision on that level is passed on. If they do not agree, an arbitration is made by the next higher authority. This is the method by which high political circles reach their world-shaking decisions. Group decision making strongly depends on the ability of the individual to bargain so that on occasion he can gain the support of others even when they do not fully agree.

An alternative approach is to assign a group of competent individuals to study the problem and define actions and outcomes. In this manner critical judgments and preferences are brought together into the fine structure of the problem giving the analysis broader scope and greater objectivity. Aggregation in this sense begins with the determination of the preferences themselves; a utility function describing this "collective preference" is then adopted.

3.2. DECISION, UTILITY, PREFERENCE

We now turn to the subject of individual assignment of utilities. In the single-interest case one is frequently concerned with the maximization of utilities. The utility function is defined in such a way that preferred objects are assigned higher utility than less preferred objects and equally preferred objects are associated with equal utilities. The objects with which utility is associated may be scalars, for example, money or bundles of commodities such as "five potatoes, six apples, and three beds." Before we associate a utility number with each bundle of commodities we cannot in general compare the values of different commodity bundles. We can say, for example, that four apples and two pears are preferred to three apples and one pear, but we cannot say whether the first combination would be preferred to three apples and three pears.

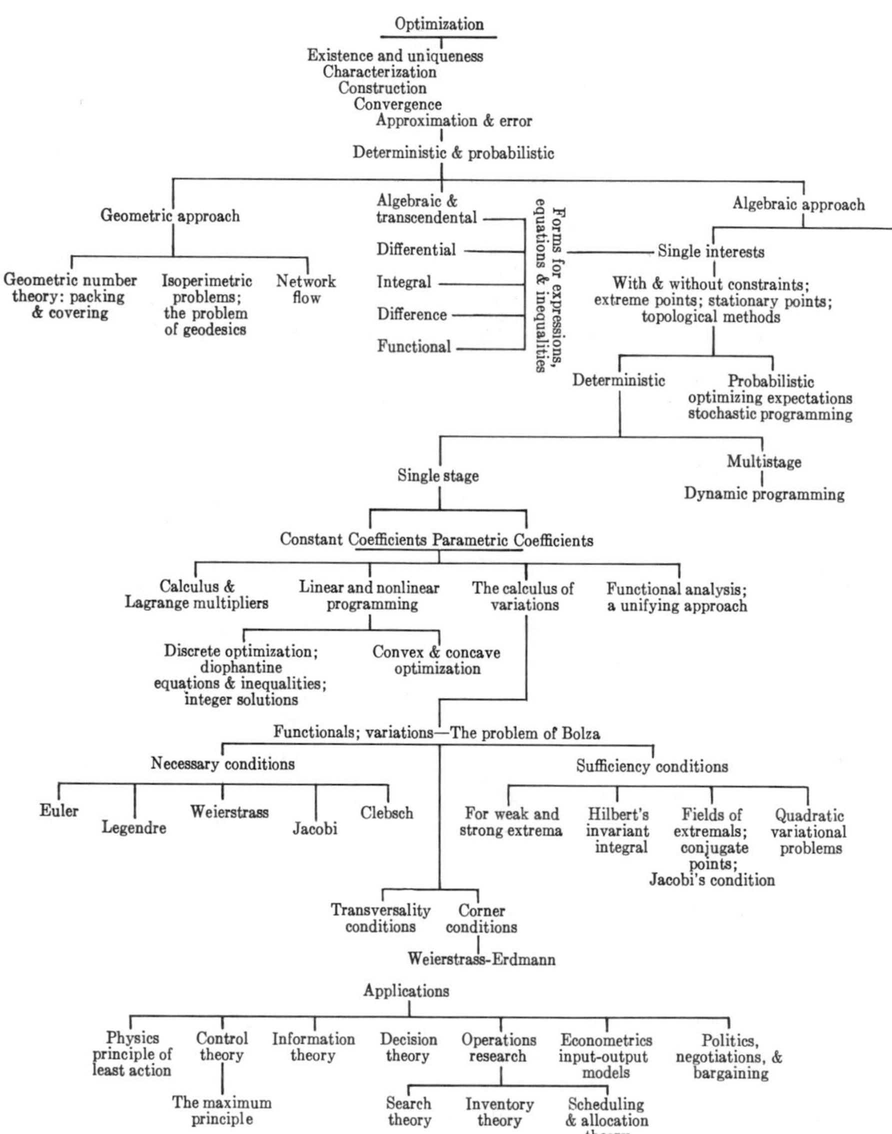

Optimization
Existence and uniqueness
Characterization
Construction
Convergence
Approximation & error
Deterministic & probabilistic
Geometric approach
Algebraic & transcendental
Differential
Integral
Difference
Functional
Forms for expressions, equations & inequalities
Algebraic approach
Single interests
With & without constraints; extreme points; stationary points; topological methods
Geometric number theory: packing & covering
Isoperimetric problems; the problem of geodesics
Network flow
Deterministic
Probabilistic optimizing expectations stochastic programming
Single stage
Multistage
Dynamic programming
Constant Coefficients Parametric Coefficients
Calculus & Lagrange multipliers
Linear and nonlinear programming
The calculus of variations
Functional analysis; a unifying approach
Discrete optimization; diophantine equations & inequalities; integer solutions
Convex & concave optimization
Functionals; variations—The problem of Bolza
Necessary conditions
Sufficiency conditions
Euler
Legendre
Weierstrass
Jacobi
Clebsch
For weak and strong extrema
Hilbert's invariant integral
Fields of extremals; conjugate points; Jacobi's condition
Quadratic variational problems
Transversality conditions
Corner conditions
Weierstrass-Erdmann
Applications
Physics principle of least action
Control theory
Information theory
Decision theory
Operations research
Econometrics input-output models
Politics, negotiations, & bargaining
The maximum principle
Search theory
Inventory theory
Scheduling & allocation theory

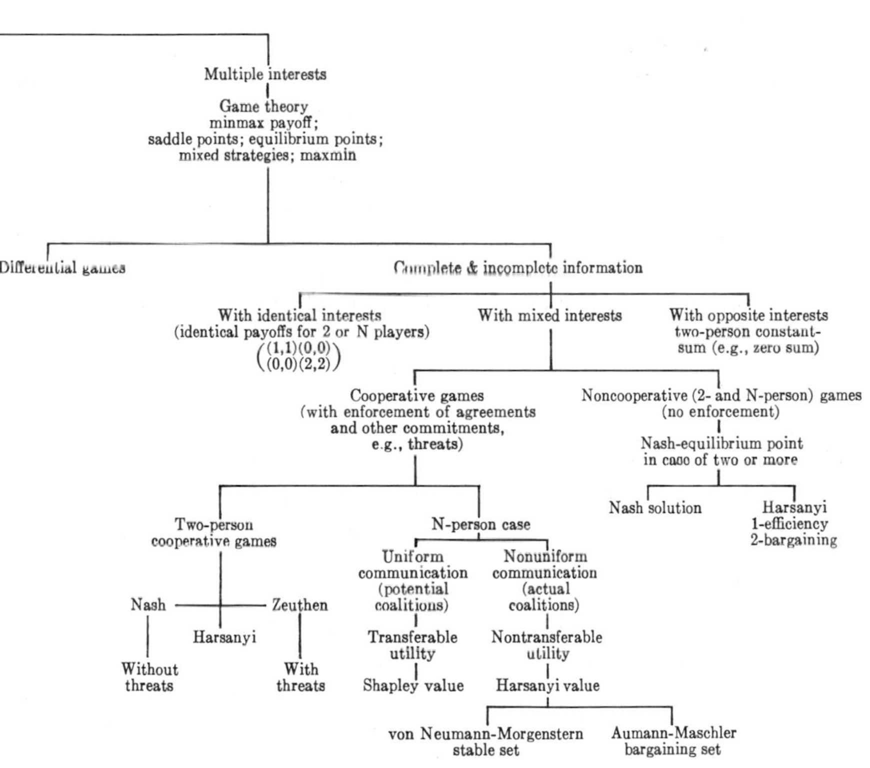

Multiple interests
Game theory
minmax payoff;
saddle points; equilibrium points;
mixed strategies; maxmin
Differential games
Complete & incomplete information
With identical interests
(identical payoffs for 2 or N players)
(1,1)(0,0)
(0,0)(2,2)
With mixed interests
With opposite interests
two-person constant-
sum (e.g., zero sum)
Cooperative games
(with enforcement of agreements
and other commitments,
e.g., threats)
Noncooperative (2- and N-person) games
(no enforcement)
Nash-equilibrium point
in case of two or more
Nash solution
Harsanyi
1-efficiency
2-bargaining
Two-person
cooperative games
N-person case
Uniform
communication
(potential
coalitions)
Nonuniform
communication
(actual
coalitions)
Nash
Zeuthen
Harsanyi
Without
threats
With
threats
Transferable
utility
Nontransferable
utility
Shapley value
Harsanyi value
von Neumann-Morgenstern
stable set
Aumann-Maschler
bargaining set

Figure 15

"To decide" is to make a choice among alternatives. In order that the choice be rational, a preference order among the alternatives must be known. The purpose of a utility function is to represent this order of preferences in a mathematically convenient way. The process may be complicated by uncertainty and risks, hence probability theory enters into the problem.

Decision theory concerns itself with the gamut of problems, ranging from individual decision making under certainty and under risk to group decison making, as well as to competitive decision making by strategically interacting individuals, both under complete information and incomplete information. Figure 16 is a rough skeletal chart of some of the important ideas with which decision theory is concerned.

When the utility function is decided on and the constraints on implementing the preferences (that is, the feasible set or opportunity set) are known, we attempt to use an appropriate optimization technique to select the best alternative from the feasible set. The best alternative is the one that yields a maximum or a minimum, according to the problem, or which gives a minmax solution or satisfies some other kind of decision rule.

When considering decision making under certainty where no probabilities are involved we need only an ordinal utility function, that is, we are interested only in the questions: Which alternatives have higher utilities and which alternatives have equal utilities? When there are no probabilities we are only interested in comparing utilities, not in comparing utility differences. Thus if x is preferred to y and y is preferred to z then we may assign utility 3 to x, 2 to y, and 1 to z, making the utility distance between x and y equal to the utility distance between y and z. But with equal justification we could assign the utility 100 to x, 2 to y, and 1 to z, making the utility distance between x and y much larger than that between y and z. Both utility assignments will represent our preferences equally well. When interested only in the ordering of utilities but not in comparing utility distances we speak of *ordinal utilities.* If also interested in comparing utility differences, we speak of *cardinal utilities.* In analyzing choices under risk or under uncertainty (that is, choices involving probabilities) ordinal utilities are insufficient and cardinal utilities are required.

The notion of utility may be introduced in a variety of ways. In heuristic language the criteria for utility which indicate "rational behavior" of an individual are

1. The axiom of comparability: Given any two alternatives x and y, one can always express clear preference or clear indifference between them. Thus either $x \succ y$ or $x \prec y$. Otherwise $x \sim y$ indicates indifference. Here $x \succ y$ says that x is preferred to y and $x \sim y$ says they are

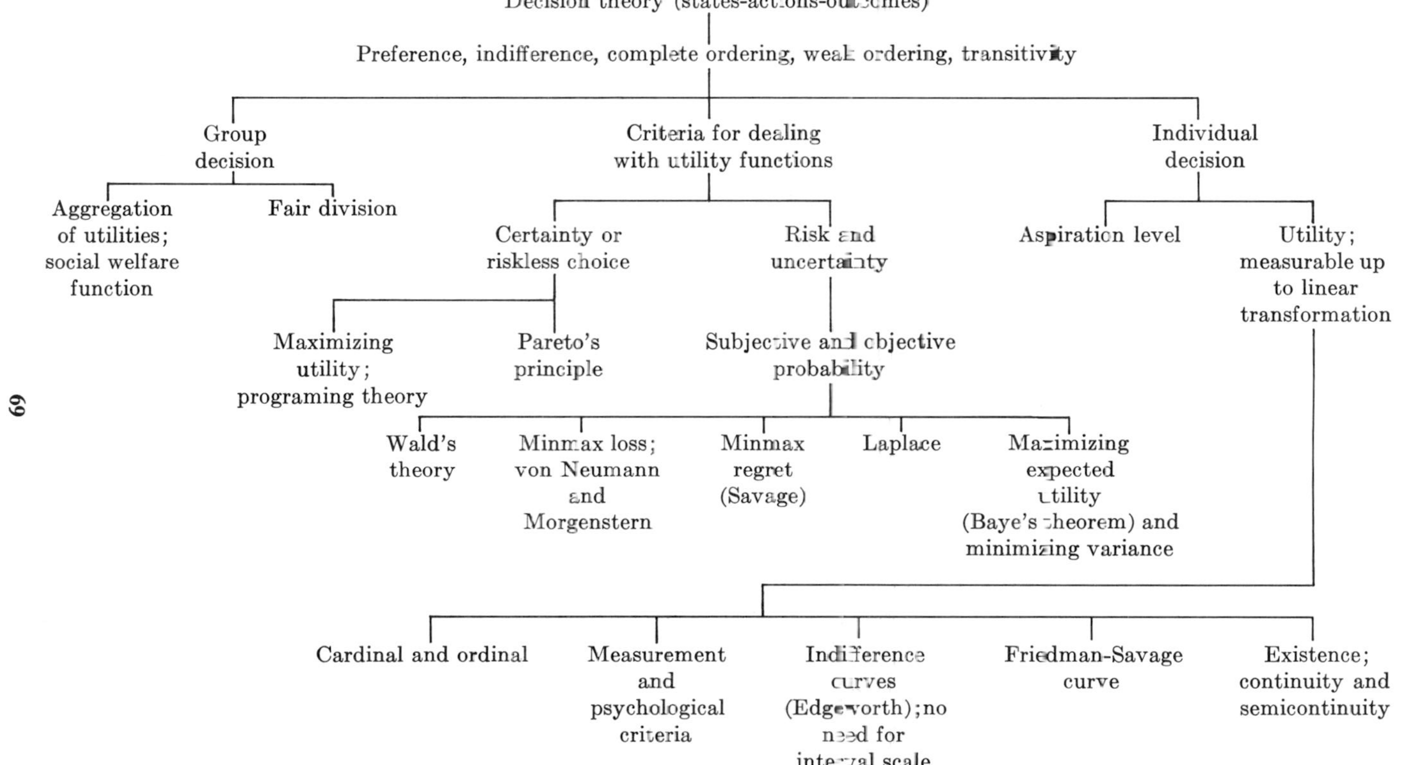
Decision theory (states-actions-outcomes)
Preference, indifference, complete ordering, weak ordering, transitivity
Group decision
Criteria for dealing with utility functions
Individual decision
Aggregation of utilities; social welfare function
Fair division
Certainty or riskless choice
Risk and uncertainty
Aspiration level
Utility; measurable up to linear transformation
Maximizing utility; programing theory
Pareto's principle
Subjective and objective probability
Wald's theory
Minmax loss; von Neumann and Morgenstern
Minmax regret (Savage)
Laplace
Maximizing expected utility (Baye's theorem) and minimizing variance
Cardinal and ordinal
Measurement and psychological criteria
Indifference curves (Edgeworth); no need for interval scale
Friedman-Savage curve
Existence; continuity and semicontinuity

Figure 16

equally preferred or indifferent. When y is not preferred to x we may write $x \gtrsim y$.

2. The axiom of transitivity: If $x > y$ and $y > z$ then $x > z$; and if $x \sim y$, $y \sim z$ then $x \sim z$.

3. Noncomplementarity of options; that is, if $x > y$ and if α is the probability x will occur and $(1 - \alpha)$ that of the occurrence of alternative y then $x > \alpha x + (1 - \alpha)y$. Note that $>$ here does not mean larger than but means preferred to.

4. The continuity of preference: If $x > z > y$ then there is a probability α that x will occur and a probability $(1 - \alpha)$ that y will occur such that $\alpha x + (1 - \alpha)y \sim z$.

5. Probability one means certainty: $1 \cdot \alpha + 0 \cdot \beta \sim \alpha$.

6. Commutativity: $\alpha x + (1 - \alpha)y \sim (1 - \alpha)y + \alpha x$.

7. Rule of composition:

$$\alpha[\beta x + (1 - \beta)y] + (1 - \alpha)y \sim \alpha\beta x + (1 - \alpha\beta)y.$$

The reader may wish to interpret these rules when the alternatives refer to probabilities of escalating and not escalating conflict.

Besides these axioms, utility functions may also have additional properties such as monotonicity. The greater a gain the higher its utility and the greater a loss the lower its utility (that is, the higher its disutility).

To show how the ordinal concept of utility is applied, suppose that a military expert is asked to assign relative numerical values indicating preference among several weapon systems from the standpoint of strategic power and flexibility in performing various types of missions. Let us denote these systems by A, B, C, D, and E. He can then assign them preference ranks, or ordinal utilities. If better knowledge based on the characteristics of the weapons is available, they may be assigned relative values (see the following for relation to ranks). These numerical values need not have any absolute significance, they only indicate the order of relative preference. A different set of numbers may be used indicating their relative values. Thus we may have

System	Rank	Value Assigned	Difference
E	5	2	
			+5
B	4	7	
			+12
C	3	19	
			+2
A	2	21	
			+79
D	1	100	

Here D has the highest rank and E has the lowest. Thus we may write $E \prec B \prec C \prec A \prec D$.

The fourth column shows the differences among consecutive assigned values. These differences have no direct meaning. Any other scale that preserves the same order of utility numbers may be used. Such a scale is known as a monotonic transformation of the first scale.

An ordinal utility function is unique up to a monotone transformation of it. Thus if we use a utility function $u(x)$ we can equally well use a monotone transformation $g(x) = t[u(x)]$ and, in particular, maximization of $u(x)$ will be equivalent to the maximization of $g(x)$. The point that minimizes $\exp\left(\sum_{i=1}^{n} x_i\right)$, for example, is the same as that which minimizes $\sum_{i=1}^{n} x_i$ since the exponential function is monotone and hence preserves the relative order of preference.

If $u(x)$ denotes cardinal utility then we can no longer replace $u(x)$ by arbitrary monotone transforms of $u(x)$ but only with monotone linear transforms of $u(x)$ which have the form $v(x) = au(x) + b$, $a > 0$. Consequently, a cardinal utility is unique up to order preserving linear transformations. The difference of magnitudes of preferences can be compared but not ratios of the magnitudes themselves. Such a measurement scale is called an interval scale. If the ratios of the magnitudes are also known the magnitudes are said to be given on a ratio scale. Such a scale is unique up to a similarity transformation (i.e., put b = 0). Clearly, if the zero point and the unit of measurement are given the cardinal utility function is fully determined.

An illustration of a linear transformation is the scale giving the change in temperature measurement from centigrade to Fahrenheit:

$$\text{Fahrenheit} = (\text{centigrade})\,\tfrac{9}{5} + 32.$$

If an individual's choices under risk satisfy the foregoing axioms then the utility he will attach to risky alternatives (e.g., lottery ticket) can be computed by taking the expected value of his utility. For instance suppose that an individual has probability p of obtaining a given prize x and a probability $1 - p$ of obtaining another prize y and suppose that the cardinal utility of the first is u_1 and that of the second is u_2, then the cardinal utility he will attach to this situation will be

$$u^* = pu_1 + (1 - p)u_2.$$

In general we obtain a person's expected utility by taking the product of the utility associated with each possible alternative and of the probability of obtaining that alternative and then adding the numbers obtained.

In the case of uncertainty where some or all of the relevant probabilities are not known, essentially the same procedure can be used as in the case of risk except that the unknown objective probabilities are replaced by our subjective estimates called subjective probabilities.

In discussing game theory, we assume that individuals are capable of making rational choices and assigning numerical values indicating their preferences among alternative courses of action. At the beginning of our study where the notion of a chance move or a mixed strategy involving probabilities is used, cardinal utilities are needed. In sections 3.6-3.7 on meta-games, ordinal utilities suffice. In neither case is the manner of how the utilities are arrived at always considered. However, this problem is not ignored and a few examples of the determination of utilities are given.

3.3. ZERO-SUM, TWO-PERSON GAMES

A game is a set of rules which describe the formal structure of a competitive situation by specifying:

1. The alternatives or strategies among which a choice is to be made by the players, where a strategy is a set of directions that a player follows in playing the game from start to finish. Each play in a strategy is called a move.
2. The information available to a player when he makes the choice.
3. The payoff to each player at the end of the play.

A payoff is associated with each selection of strategies by the opposing sides; that is, a payoff is associated with every conceivable play of the game from start to finish.

Consider the following example of a game involving two players I and II. Let the ith column $i = 1, 2, 3$ of the following matrix be the payoff II makes to I for playing his strategy B_i, $i = 1, 2, 3$ against each of I's strategies A_1, A_2, A_3.

		Player II's strategies		
		B_1	B_2	B_3
Player I's strategies	A_1	0	-2	1
	A_2	2	0	-2
	A_3	-1	2	0

Each time the game is played one strategy is used by each player. This matrix represents the payoff to player I from player II (to obtain the payoff to player II multiply the entries by -1). Each play of this game consists of a choice of one of the numbers 1, 2, 3 to be made by each player.

The player with the smaller number wins one point unless his number is less than his opponent's by one unit in which case he loses two points. The score is zero when the numbers are equal. This game is symmetric with respect to the players; that is, the payoff to each player is the same for corresponding choices of strategies. Here A_1, A_2, A_3 correspond to I's choices of the numbers 1, 2, 3 respectively. Similarly, B_1, B_2, B_3 correspond to II's respective choices of the numbers 1, 2, 3.

One problem is how to advise the players to choose their strategies so that each one when playing rationally does the best for himself. The foregoing example illustrates a zero-sum game because what one player loses the other gains and no payoff enters the play from an outside source. But in general this may not be the case and each entry of the payoff matrix must give two payoffs, one to each player.

If the payoffs are sums of money we can use these monetary payoffs as ordinal utilities, but they may not represent the two parties' cardinal utilities. This will be true only if both players have utility functions linear in money (which implies constant marginal utility for money). But in the real world it is unlikely that people should have constant marginal utility for money. If a rich man and a poor man were offered the opportunity to place a bet of $100 with the odds 5 to 1 in favor of their winning $200, for example, the poor man might refuse to gamble because the $100 has more utility for him than for the rich man. If these two men play a zero-sum game in mixed strategies, however, this comparison of worth must be ignored. (In order for utilities to be consistent they must be invariant under linear transformations of the form $y = ax + b$, $a > 0$, and hence a strategy solution of a game problem must remain the same before and after the transformation is made.)

Examples of Utility Computation

In some games the utilities are easily decided on. In a coin matching game in which each player shows one side of his coin, player I winning one unit if they are alike and losing a unit if they are not, the essential point for utility selection is the symmetry of the game.

The payoff matrix may be represented by

		Player II	
		Heads	Tails
Player I	Heads	1	−1
	Tails	−1	1

Here is another example: two airplanes belonging to player I wish to destroy a target of player II to which there are three routes, but the adversary has three guns that he can place on any of the routes. If an airplane travels over a route on which there is a gun it is put out of action. If two airplanes go over one gun, only one is destroyed. Player I wishes to destroy the target and player II to defend it.

Player I has two strategies whereby he may send each airplane by a different route or send both on the same route. Player II may assign each gun to a different route, two guns to one and one gun to another, or all three on the same route. If the payoff for destroying the target is unity, it is easy to show that $a_{11} = 0$, $a_{21} = 1$, $a_{12} = \frac{2}{3}$ (the pattern of gun allocation to the routes is 0, 1, 2. The planes may be assigned to these patterns as follows: 0, 1, 1; 1, 0, 1; and 1, 1, 0. Two of these use an undefended route. Thus the probability of getting through is $\frac{2}{3}$), $a_{22} = \frac{2}{3}$, (the probability that at least one plane gets through is equal to that of choosing a route not defended by two guns), $a_{13} = 1$, $a_{23} = \frac{2}{3}$. Here a_{ij}, $i = 1, 2$; $j = 1, 2, 3$, denotes the payoff which II playing the strategy of the *jth* column, pays I for playing his *ith* row strategy. This gives the payoff matrix:

		II		
		A gun on each route	A gun on one route and two on another	Three guns on one route
I	Planes on different routes	0	$\frac{2}{3}$	1
	Planes on same route	1	$\frac{2}{3}$	$\frac{2}{3}$

In general, it is not easy to write down a cardinal payoff matrix. Frequently, it is even difficult to compute ordinal payoffs. For comparison of weapon systems designed for different missions, the payoff may be computed by means of simulation in which a weapon system is theoretically tested against the different missions for various effectiveness measures of destruction, deterrence, reliability, cost, etc. The reader can imagine the added difficulty when the utility scales of the players are different as may be true in nonzero-sum games.

Games may be classified according to

1. The number of strategies available: whether finite or infinite.
2. The number of individuals involved:

a. One person who plays against nature (such games involve notions of certainty, risk, and uncertainty).

b. Two persons who play a zero-sum game or a nonzero-sum game. In the former, the gains of one player are the losses of the other (here the von Neumann and Morgenstern theory has made its most effective contribution, that is, every finite zero-sum game is known to have a solution). In the latter, pure competition may be possible but usually not the most profitable, and cooperation may be a better policy for both parties (each player may be able to improve on the returns of purely competitive behavior).

c. N-person games ($N > 2$) which may or may not be zero-sum, in either case permitting the formation of coalitions and opening the possibility for cooperation. A person or player may consist of several people who have identified their interests and pursue them as one person.

3. Whether they are in extensive or normalized form. The former involves a representation by means of a tree diagram in which each alternative move in each strategy for each player is indicated. The moves may be dictated by a chance device with given probabilities or they may be behavioral choice of the player as in chess or checkers, or a mixture whereby some moves are done probabilistically and some by an act of choice.

The normal form of a game utilizes a payoff matrix as given in the foregoing examples. It is analyzed without reference to moves but only to the payoffs corresponding to strategies. The extensive form can always be reduced to normal form. In the extensive case a player is said to have *perfect information* or perfect recall if he knows all previous moves made in the game and they are all behavioral and not chance moves. A player in a game given in extensive or normal form has "complete" information if he knows the rules, for example, the payoff matrix and the strategies, both his and those of the opponents. Conflict problems, for example, often involve incomplete information on the payoff matrix. It is known that every zero-sum, two-person game with perfect information has a solution in pure strategies, that is, the game can either always be won by one player or can always be tied. In either case each player has the same best strategy to follow in any play of the game. The proof is intuitively clear if we consider all possible paths from start to finish in the extensive form of the game.

The following is a proof of this fact in a case where no draw is allowed: consider a crisis situation between two nations A and B and suppose that it is desired to resolve the crisis by negotiations. Let us also suppose that this particular situation does not permit a draw (standoff or stalemate), that offers or moves are made alternately, and that the number of rounds n is finite (that is, the bargaining terminates). By a strategy for a nation we mean a sequence of moves from beginning to end, each of which may depend on the moves of the other nation. A winning strategy for a nation is a strategy which eventually leads to a win no matter what strategy the other nation follows. We prove [80]:

Theorem. There is a strategy ensuring a win for nation A or there is a strategy ensuring a win for nation B.

Proof. The fact that there is a finite sequence of moves makes it easy to see that one of the negotiators must have a winning strategy determined at the very first move he makes. The first move is made from a winning position which has the property that with proper subsequent play he can win no matter what the other player does. First note that no draw means that one nation must win (regardless of who moves first). If one of them is to win, somewhere toward the end he is in a winning strategy position. Consider the very first time that one of them, for example, A, has a winning strategy; the move which B makes just before putting A in that position must be a mistake, otherwise A's winning strategy position would have started a move earlier. Thus if A wins, B must make a mistake. On the other hand if B does not make a mistake, A cannot win. Alternatively, unless A makes a mistake, B cannot win. So neither of them would win if neither of them makes a mistake. This is a contradiction because the game must terminate without a draw in a finite number of moves. Thus one of them must have a winning strategy from the start. This completes the proof.

Among all games those dealing with zero-sum, two-person problems are the best understood. Recall that a zero-sum, two-person game between players I and II with a finite number of strategies $A_1, \ldots, A_n$ for I, and $B_1, \ldots, B_m$ for II may be represented in normal form by means of a payoff matrix. Since the game is zero-sum the payoff entries a_{ij} of the matrix will be understood to be the amount II pays I if he chooses strategy A_i and II chooses strategy B_j. To obtain the payoff to II it suffices to multiply the entries by -1. Otherwise the entries of the matrix may be given as a vector whose general form would be $(a_{ij}, -a_{ij})$ and the sum of whose two components is zero. The payoff matrix of a zero-sum, N-person game has entries that are vectors whose ith component is the payoff to the ith player and the sum of the components is zero.

For a zero-sum, two-person game, game theory counsels player I to assess his choice by the payoff gain independently of the actions taken by II. Thus I assumes that II knows what his choice will be and that II will try to yield him the minimum return. Thus I runs through each of his strategies and notes the minimum payoff in the row of that strategy. Naturally, he will choose that strategy which has the maximum payoff among these minima. On the other hand II will attempt to minimize the maximum loss which he may have. Thus he notes the maximum payoff in each column and chooses that strategy which yields the minimum among these maxima. Since I cannot gain more than II can lose we have

$$\max_j \min_i a_{ij} \leq \min_i \max_j a_{ij}.$$

An entry that yields equality is known as a saddle point and the corresponding strategies are the two pure strategies always to be used by I and II in playing the game. In the following example we have a saddle point at A_1, B_1 and 5 is the value there.

		Player II			
		B_1	B_2	B_3	Row minima
Player I	A_1	5	7	20	(5)
	A_2	4	-1	10	-1
	Column maxima	(5)	7	20	

An example of a game with no saddle point is the coin matching game described previously. If a game has no saddle point, it is essential that the strategies be chosen by a chance device to hide a player's choice. In that case the player would be concerned with maximizing the expected payoff. Here we speak of a mixed strategy which is a vector whose components are probabilities for playing the corresponding strategies. The sum of the components must be unity since a choice of strategy is always made. If I uses strategy x and II uses y then the expected payoff to I, for example, in repeated plays of the game, is xAy when A is the payoff matrix. This is a simple expression for a sum whose terms are products of a payoff and the two probabilities that each player will choose the strategy leading to this payoff.

The ideas of expected payoff and mixed strategy are also the best policy if a game is played only once, for then we may regard the game as a situation presenting itself in various possibilities (mixed strategy) among which we must make one good choice.

Von Neumann has proved that in a zero-sum, two-person game in normal form, an assignment of probabilities to the choice of strategies for each player exists and yields the equality

$$\max_x \min_y xAy = \min_y \max_x xAy \equiv v$$

for the value v of the game, which is a generalization of the previous idea involving saddle points. If we consider a simplex whose vertices correspond to the pure strategies of player I, then a mixed strategy for I is any point of the simplex, since it is a convex combination (with coefficients ≥ 0 whose sum is unity) of the pure strategies. A simplex is a generalized tetrahedron in n-dimensional space. Each of its $n + 1$ vertices is joined by an edge to every other vertex.

To solve a two-person, zero-sum game we first look for a saddle point; if none exists we eliminate every row that is dominated (since player I would not use the strategy corresponding to that row, for example, the second row in the saddle point matrix just given). Dominance means that every element of that row is not more than the corresponding element of another row or of a convex combination of other rows. By analogy every column that dominates is eliminated. We then proceed to find a mixed strategy solution. The coin matching game has no saddle point, and hence has no solution in pure strategies. The optimal strategies are so determined that player I would get the same amount for each column corresponding to a pure strategy of player II which has a nonzero probability component in II's solution vector. In the coin matching game both strategies are active and hence to insure that the payoff is the same for each column, if we suppose that heads will be used by player I with probability x and hence tails are used with probability $1 - x$ so that $x + (1 - x) = 1$, we have on equating the expected payoffs from both columns: $x - (1 - x) = -x + (1 - x)$. From this we obtain $x = \frac{1}{2}$, $1 - x = \frac{1}{2}$. Similarly, II may equalize the expected return on both rows, since both strategies are active for I and obtain $y = \frac{1}{2}$, $1 - y = \frac{1}{2}$. The value, or expected value, of the game is zero to both players, thus, for example, $x - (1 - x) = \frac{1}{2} - \frac{1}{2} = 0$.

The matrix game

		Player II	
		B_1	B_2
Player I	A_1	1	2
	A_2	3	0

has no saddle point. Suppose that x and $1 - x$ are the relative frequencies with which player I chooses his A_1 and A_2 strategies respectively and y and $1 - y$ those with which player II chooses his B_1 and B_2 strategies respectively; then

$$1x + 3(1 - x) = v \text{ if II selects } B_1,$$

$$2x + 0(1 - x) = v \text{ if II selects } B_2.$$

We can now solve for x, $(1 - x)$, and v. An analysis of the game from II's point of view leads to a similar set of equations. Without difficulty we can write these equations and compute y and $1 - y$. We obtain $x = \frac{3}{4}$, $y = \frac{1}{2}$, $v = \frac{3}{2}$. Thus $(\frac{3}{4}, \frac{1}{4})$ is player I's mixed strategy and $(\frac{1}{2}, \frac{1}{2})$ is player II's mixed strategy and $v = \frac{3}{2}$ is the value of the game. Note that utility or payoff expectation, rather than the precise saddle point payoff assured a player on each play, is an important basis in the analysis since on no single play of the game can I win precisely $\frac{3}{2}$ units of utility.

The optimum mixed strategy of player I in the number matching example may be obtained by subtracting the last column from each of the other two and taking the 3 by 2 matrix C of the resulting two columns. Let x_1, x_2, x_3, be the probabilities for playing A_1, A_2, A_3 in the optimum mixed strategy of player I. To compute x_1 the probability of playing A_1, we compute the determinant of the 2 by 2 submatrix whose rows correspond to A_2 and A_3 and take the absolute value of this determinant. We proceed analogously for x_2 and x_3, that is, in C we take the absolute value of the determinants whose submatrices are the rows of A_1 and A_3 for x_2 and of A_1 and A_2 for x_3. We then divide each of these values by their sum, obtaining $x_1 = \frac{2}{5}$, $x_2 = \frac{1}{5}$, $x_3 = \frac{2}{5}$. Thus we have $(\frac{2}{5}, \frac{1}{5}, \frac{2}{5})$ for the optimum mixed strategy of player I. A similar procedure gives $(\frac{2}{5}, \frac{1}{5}, \frac{2}{5})$ for player II because of symmetry.

A zero-sum, two-person game may be reduced to a linear programming problem and solved. Thus a minmax problem is reduced to a pure maximization problem. This is done for player I by multiplying his probability vector $(x_1, x_2, \ldots, x_n)$ by each column and requiring that each of these satisfy the condition $\geq v$ where v is the minimum expected value of any column. Note that every entry of the payoff matrix can be made positive by adding a suitable constant to all the a_{ij}. Thus $v > 0$ may be assumed. This does not alter the solution and the original value may be recovered by subtracting the constant. The sum of the x_i must be equal to unity and all $x_i \geq 0$. If the inequalities are reduced to equations by using nonnegative slack variables and one of them is subtracted from those involving v, only this one will have v appearing in it and it will be the expression to be maximized (to obtain the largest payoff) subject to the others as constraints. The well known simplex process can then be used to solve the problem. The solution of the dual problem gives II's optimal strategy.

3.4. NONZERO-SUM GAMES

We now illustrate a nonzero-sum, two-person game. For such a game each entry must consist of a_{ij} and b_{ij}, the payoffs to players I and II respectively, corresponding to strategies A_i and B_j.

Examples of nonzero-sum games are the Prisoner's Dilemma game and the game of Chicken shown in normal form:

		Player II	
		N	E
Player I	N	3, 3	1, 4
	E	4, 1	2, 2

Prisoner's Dilemma

		Player II	
		N	C
Player I	N	3, 3	2, 4
	C	4, 2	1, 1

Chicken

In the first game two prisoners are urged by the police to confess or give evidence (E) to a crime they are strongly suspected to have committed together. They are guilty, and everyone knows it, but it cannot be proven. If they both confess and hence do not cooperate with each other, their respective payoffs are worse than if neither does (N), that is, if they cooperate, whereas if one does and the other does not confess the gain to the confessor is greater, and the loss to the nonconfessor is also greater. The dilemma is that no matter what his colleague does, a suspect prefers the outcome which results by not cooperating, but if both confess, the outcome is less preferred than if neither does. How should they behave if they are not bound by any rules? The resolution of this problem is a subject of particular interest to meta-game theory discussed later.

In the game of Chicken two teenage car riders drive in a head-on collision course. The one who swerves, that is, does not head toward collision (we denote this strategy by N) loses in prestige by being called "chicken" whereas the other wins if he continues on a collision course (we denote this strategy by C). If they both swerve they are both far better off than if neither does (collision course), because if they collide their payoff is a substantial loss, perhaps of their lives. How should they behave?

To develop the concept of a solution for an N-person game (zero-sum or otherwise) we use a function $U_i(\mathbf{s}_1, \ldots, \mathbf{s}_N) \equiv U_i(\mathbf{s}), i = 1, \ldots, N$ to denote the payoff to player i as a function of the strategy vector $\mathbf{s} = (\mathbf{s}_1, \ldots, \mathbf{s}_N)$. This payoff is linear in the mixed strategy $\mathbf{s}_i$ of each player. Let $(\mathbf{s}, t_i)$ stand for $(\mathbf{s}_1, \mathbf{s}_2, \ldots, \mathbf{s}_{i-1}, t_i, \mathbf{s}_{i+1}, \ldots, \mathbf{s}_N)$. A strategy $\mathbf{s}$ is an equilibrium point if and only if

$$U_i(\mathbf{s}) = \max_{\text{all } t_i} U_i(\mathbf{s}, t_i) \qquad i = 1, \ldots, N.$$

Thus at an equilibrium point a player's mixed strategy maximizes his payoff for each choice of the other player's strategies. Nash [49] has shown that every finite N-person game has an equilibrium point.

Although some of our remarks are valid in general, we shall confine our attention to two-person, nonzero-sum games.

The underlying notion behind the choice of an equilibrium strategy for player I is for player I to choose his strategy so that no matter what player II does, player II gets the same expected payoff. It is useful to remember that an equilibrium strategy is a strategy which, if either player deviates from using it while the other does not, the deviating player's return would not be increased. If the other player also abandons his equilibrium strategy, the payoff to each may be the same or more or less. If both players are required to announce their strategies, neither of them alone will make more by deviating. Whereas the maxmin strategy is a conservative one assuring each player a modest but sure return, an equilibrium strategy is more daring and involves risk.

In the ordinary mixed-strategy game, rational players will of necessity mistrust each other and play a noncooperative game unless agreements between the players can be made binding, in which case they may cooperate. Bargaining is made easier if their cardinal utilities are computed on the same scale. Cooperative games may be reduced to noncooperative ones if promises and credible threats are included in the strategies, and penalties for breaking promises appear in the payoff matrix.

Rationality requirements in game theory (to be discussed later) demand that the same choice of strategy be used whether the stakes (payoffs) are small or large as long as they are related by the same linear transformation. In simple terms, a player is rational if he takes more when offered more.

While ethics deal with a rational pursuit of long-range interests of society, game theory is occupied with optimization of individual utility against other individuals who rationally pursue their own utility [25].

Rationality requires the prescription of rules for one's own behavior. Such rules require: (a) following the maxmin strategy in an unprofitable game; (b) using an equilibrium solution for a profitable noncooperative game (an equilibrium strategy is called profitable if its payoff exceeds the maxmin payoff; otherwise it is called unprofitable); (c) using a bargaining strategy as a best reply to the bargaining strategies expected from others (if a player is willing to settle for less and can get more if others get more then he must accept more if offered, etc.); (d) prescribing what behavior may be expected from others such as not expecting others to make concessions that one would not make; (e) that others would also follow their rationality postulates; (f) that variables that are not relevant cannot be expected to affect a rational opponent's strategy choice, and so forth.

Let $\mathbf{s}_1$ be the equilibrium point strategy for player I.

Let $\mathbf{s}_2$ be the equilibrium point strategy for player II.

Let σ_1 be the maxmin strategy for player I.

Let σ_2 be the maxmin strategy for player II.

Let $(w_1, w_2) \equiv [U_1(\mathbf{s}_1, \mathbf{s}_2), U_2(\mathbf{s}_1, \mathbf{s}_2)] \equiv U(\mathbf{s}_1, \mathbf{s}_2)$ be the equilibrium point value.

Let $(v_1, v_2) = [\underset{\xi_1}{\text{Max}}\ \underset{\xi_2}{\text{Min}}\ U_1(\xi_1, \xi_2), \underset{\xi_2}{\text{Max}}\ \underset{\xi_1}{\text{Min}}\ U_2(\xi_1, \xi_2)]$ be the maxmin value.

Theorem. $w_1 \geq v_1$, $w_2 \geq v_2$.

Proof. Suppose $w_1 < v_1$ and let player I use σ_1 instead of $\mathbf{s}_1$, while II uses $\mathbf{s}_2$. Since I uses his maxmin strategy, we have

$$U_1(\sigma_1, \mathbf{s}_2) \geq v_1 > w_1.$$

This implies that $(\mathbf{s}_1, \mathbf{s}_2)$ is not an equilibrium strategy since (repeating what was said before) for such a strategy if one player switches from using it he cannot increase his return if the other player adheres to his equilibrium strategy; this is a contradiction. Thus $w_1 \geq v_1$. Similarly, it can be shown that $w_2 \geq v_2$.

It is obvious that if $w_1 = v_1$ and $w_2 = v_2$ and $(\mathbf{s}_1, \mathbf{s}_2)$ is unique $\mathbf{s}_1 \neq \sigma_1$, $\mathbf{s}_2 \neq \sigma_2$ and the opponent cannot be depended on to play $\mathbf{s}_2$, it is better for I to play his maxmin strategy and assure himself the equilibrium value which is also the maxmin value. If the equilibrium strategy is not unique (as in Chicken), it is difficult to decide how the players should play in a game where there is no cooperation, since each player may aim at one equilibrium point while the other aims at another and the strategies may have a payoff which is worse for both players.

In the introduction to this chapter it was stated that game theory is normative. An open question is: In what sense are the Nash equilibrium payoff and its corresponding strategies best? Here we are speaking of optimization for an entire group and not for any single player. This criterion may be the first rigorous definition the reader has encountered that satisfies the intuitive requirement that the players assure themselves at least the maxmin payoff and perhaps more by playing the equilibrium strategies. In fact this is a stepping stone to further refinements involving cooperation and bargaining.

In general an algorithm may be developed for finding equilibrium points based on inequalities which are, for example, in the 2 by 2 case:

$$U_1(\xi_1, \mathbf{s}_2) \leq U_1(\mathbf{s}_1, \mathbf{s}_2),$$

$$U_2(\mathbf{s}_1, \xi_2) \leq U_2(\mathbf{s}_1, \mathbf{s}_2).$$

The object is to find $(\mathbf{s}_1, \mathbf{s}_2)$ which satisfy these inequalities for all ξ_1 and ξ_2.

To see how an equilibrium point is computed, consider a nonzero-sum, two-person game with the following payoff matrix; the first number in parentheses represents I's payoff and the second II's payoff.

		Player II		
		B_1		B_2
	A_1	(2, 6)	←	(3, 4)
Player I		↓		↓
	A_2	(5, 3)	←	(7, 1)

Vertical arrows indicate I's preference of the strategy to which the arrow points because of a larger payoff. Similarly, horizontal arrows indicate II's preference. An equilibrium point is such that both arrows are directed toward it. (The first number is largest in its column and the second number is largest in its row.) Thus the strategy (A_2, B_1) yields an equilibrium point with payoff 5 to I and 3 to II.

The security level or maxmin strategies are obtained in ignorance of what the other player would do by playing a zero-sum game. For player I we consider his payoff matrix

A_1	2	3
A_2	5	7

Thus I should play the pure strategy A_2 since 5 is a saddle point because it is both the minimum coefficient in its row and the maximum coefficient in its column. For II we find from his payoff matrix

B_1	B_2
6	4
3	1

(by examining the columns) that there is a saddle point with payoff 3. Thus he should play pure strategy B_1. In this case both maxmin and equilibrium strategies are the same.

In the absence of an equilibrium point in pure strategies we seek such a point in mixed strategies from which the payoff is obtained as an expected value. Ordinarily, we must test for a pure strategy equilibrium point and also apply dominance rules to the payoff matrix. For a 2 by 2 game the calculations are straightforward. Consider the payoff matrix:

$$
\begin{array}{cc|cc}
 & & \multicolumn{2}{c}{\text{Player II}} \\
 & & B_1 & B_2 \\
\hline
 & A_1 & (5, -3) \rightarrow & (-4, 4) \\
\text{Player I} & & \uparrow & \downarrow \\
 & A_2 & (-5, 5) \leftarrow & (3, -4)
\end{array}
$$

The arrows show that there is no equilibrium point in pure strategies. To assure that I obtains the same payoff no matter what he does, II concentrates on I's payoff and computes his mixed strategy. Hence if II plays B_1 with probability q and B_2 with probability $1 - q$ the expected values of the two rows in I's payoff matrix must be equal, that is, $5q - 4(1 - q) = -5q + 3(1 - q)$ and $q = \frac{7}{17}$, $(1 - q) = \frac{10}{17}$. Thus II should play B_1 with probability $\frac{7}{17}$ and B_2 with probability $\frac{10}{17}$. This yields I the expected payoff $v_1 = -\frac{5}{17}$. Note that whatever mixture $(p, 1 - p)$ I uses for his strategies A_1 and A_2, his expected payoff is

$$5p\,\tfrac{7}{17} - 4p\,\tfrac{10}{17} - 5(1 - p)\,\tfrac{7}{17} + 3(1 - p)\,\tfrac{10}{17} = -\tfrac{5}{17}.$$

Similarly, to ensure that II obtains the same expected payoff no matter what strategy mixture he chooses, I uses II's payoff matrix and writes $-3p + 5(1 - p) = 4p - 4(1 - p)$ from which $p = \frac{9}{16}$ and $1 - p = \frac{7}{16}$. Thus the equilibrium strategy is

$$(\mathbf{s}_1, \mathbf{s}_2) = (\tfrac{9}{16}A_1 + \tfrac{7}{16}A_2, \tfrac{7}{17}B_1 + \tfrac{10}{17}B_2)$$

and the equilibrium payoff is

$$(w_1, w_2) = (-\tfrac{5}{17}, \tfrac{1}{2}).$$

The maxmin strategies for each player are obtained from their respective payoff matrices:

$$(\sigma_1, \sigma_2) = (\tfrac{8}{17}A_1 + \tfrac{9}{17}A_2, \tfrac{1}{2}B_1 + \tfrac{1}{2}B_2),$$

$$(v_1, v_2) = (-\tfrac{5}{17}, \tfrac{1}{2}).$$

In this case again $(v_1, v_2) = (w_1, w_2)$. In order that the reader not get the idea that $(v_1, v_2) = (w_1, w_2)$ always, the following game:

	B_1	B_2
A_1	(6, 2)	(5, 6)
A_2	(1, 0)	(9, 4)

has

$$(\mathbf{s}_1, \mathbf{s}_2) = (A_2, B_2),$$

$$(w_1, w_2) = (9, 4)$$

and

$$(\sigma_1, \sigma_2) = (\tfrac{8}{9}A_1 + \tfrac{1}{9}A_2, B_2)$$

$$(v_1, v_2) = (\tfrac{49}{9}, 4).$$

The following is an example of a three-person, nonzero-sum game with coalitions. Player I plays his first strategy with probability p and his second strategy with probability $1 - p$. Player II uses q and $1 - q$ and player III uses r and $1 - r$ [31]. Then the payoffs are represented as in Figure 17. The expected payoff to player I is obtained by multiplying

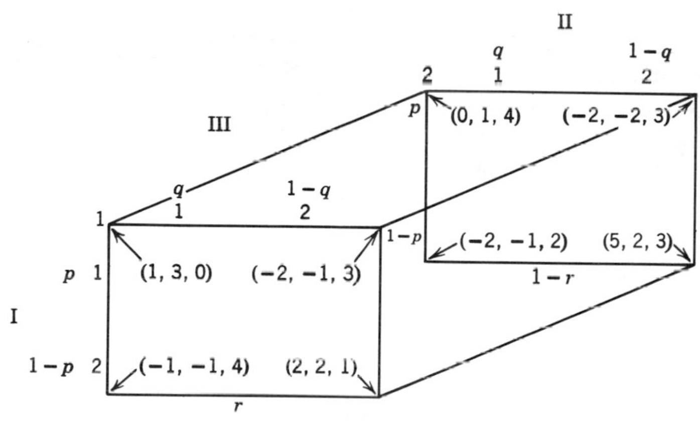

Figure 17

the probabilities with which a strategy is played by the corresponding payoff to player I. We have

$$\begin{aligned} v_1 = pqr &- 2p(1-q)r - (1-p)qr + 2(1-p)(1-q)r \\ &- 2p(1-q)(1-r) - 2(1-p)q(1-r) + 5(1-p)(1-q)(1-r) \\ &= p(-3qr + 9q + r - 7) + 6qr - 7q - 3r + 5. \end{aligned}$$

Similarly, the payoffs v_2 and v_3 to players II and III respectively are

$$v_2 = q(pr - 6p - 3) + pr - 4p + 2,$$

$$v_3 = r(-8pr + 6p - 2) + 2pq - p + 3.$$

Note that player I cannot lose more than 2, that is, his minimum payoff is -2. Players II and III are each guaranteed a minimum payoff of -1 and 2 respectively. These are the players' security levels. Notice that each strategy has four possible payoffs for each player. Player I's first strategy has the payoffs 1, -2, 0, -2 and his second strategy has payoffs -1, 2, -2, 5, for example. The first is obtained from the face at the top of the box and the second from the face at the bottom. For player II the two side-faces are used.

To improve his minimum payoff player I, who cannot control q and r, considers a coalition with another player. He says, "Suppose that I play my first pure strategy, then $p = 1$ and $v_1 = r(3q - 2) + 2q - r$, and suppose that player II agrees to play his first pure strategy, giving $q = 1$. Since $v_1 = r$ and $0 \leq r \leq 1$, it follows that $0 \leq v_1 \leq 1$, which is an improvement on the previous payoff of -2." By looking at v_2, player II finds that such a coalition would yield him $1 \leq v_2 \leq 3$, which is an improvement over -1. This coalition and agreement may still not be the best. In Reference 31 after having considered all possible coalitions of players and all possible strategies for such coalitions, it was found that players I and II can form a coalition in which they can each obtain the maximum of the minimum guaranteed payoff by playing their second pure strategies. Then $2 \leq v_1 \leq 5$ and $v_2 = 2$. The problem of 10 players with 10 strategies each has 10^{10} possible outcomes and 637 possible coalitions.

3.5. TWO-PERSON COOPERATIVE GAMES

Fixed-Threats Case

Nash [50] also studied cooperative games. He first examined the simpler case in which the payoffs the players would obtain if no agreement was reached, called the conflict payoffs, are determined by the rules of the game and do not depend on the players' own actions. The vector consisting of the two players' payoffs is known as the conflict point. In many game situations the conflict point will be simply the status quo point that the players occupied before playing the game. Games satisfying these conditions are called two-person bargaining games or two-person cooperative games with fixed threats.

For example, suppose that the players I and II are free to choose any payoff vector $\mathbf{u} = (u_1, u_2)$ from the feasible set F represented by the convex region shown in Figure 18.

Then the feasible (or negotiation) set is convex because the players are assumed to be free to use joint randomized mixed strategies, that is, for any two points it contains the line segment joining them. The point $\bar{\mathbf{u}}$

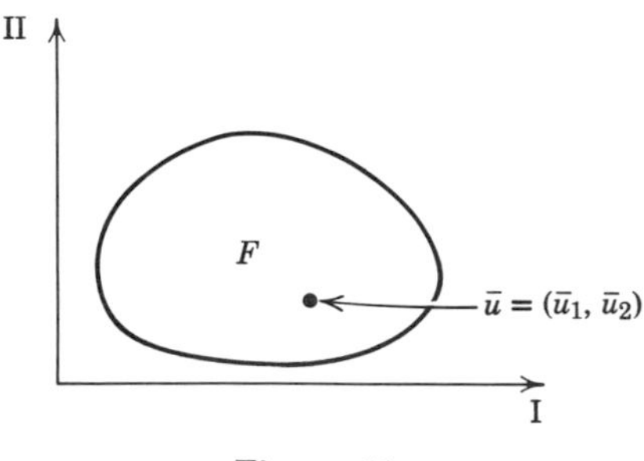

Figure 18

shown in the diagram represents the conflict point. For any feasible point both players have a common interest in moving to points that lie higher and further to the right. This means that the players have common interest in moving to the upper right boundary, also called efficient boundary, of the feasible set, but they have opposite interests as far as choosing among different points of this boundary. Player I would like to move to the right and Player II would like to move up as much as possible.

Nash proposes certain rationality postulates to choose the solution for this game and obtains the result that if the players satisfy these postulates, a unique solution they will accept is the payoff vector $\mathbf{u} = (u_1, u_2)$ which maximizes the Nash product

$$(u_1 - \bar{u}_1)(u_2 - \bar{u}_2)$$

(in which $u_i - \bar{u}_i$, $i = 1, 2$ is the benefit to player i as the difference between playing cooperatively and carrying out his threat) subject to the constraints

$$u_1 \geq \bar{u}_1, \; u_2 \geq \bar{u}_2, \; \mathbf{u} = (u_1, u_2) \epsilon F.$$

These Nash postulates state that (a) the solution should not depend on the manner in which the players are labeled (symmetry), (b) it should be in the negotiation set (efficiency), (c) the payoff corresponding to the solution not be affected by a linear transformation (independent of utility scale), and (d) if the payoff matrix is reduced in size by eliminating strategies, for either or both players, and if the original solution is still feasible in the new game, then the solution of the old game will also be a solution of the new game (independent of irrelevant variables).

The strategies leading to this unique solution may not be unique. Note that the product given above represents a family of hyperbolas if we equate it to a constant that is then assigned different values. In this

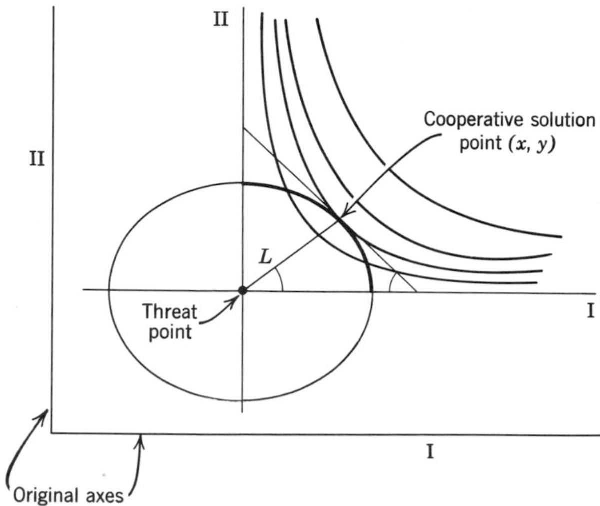

Figure 19

family there is a curve that is tangent to the boundary of the convex payoff region at a point that is the unique solution. At this point the slope of the tangent hyperbola is the same as that of the boundary curve of the convex region [44] (see Figure 19).

The threat point must lie on a line L passing through the point of tangency having numerically the same slope as the tangent but with negative sign. Since the object is to determine the coordinates of (x, y) (which is then translated to the threat point which is treated as an origin), we examine all possible points of the boundary with negative slope, called the "efficient boundary," as possible points of tangency (see bold part of figure). Noting that the threat point is on some line L lying in the convex region, we examine all such combinations relevant to the efficient boundary. Players I and II each respectively wants his threat point to be as far to the "right and down," to the "left and up" as possible. By a modification of the minmax theorem we can show that there is always a unique threat point lying on L. This, of course, assumes that the threat must be enforceable so that the players would accept the cooperative solution and that they can communicate to draw up their convex region of mixed strategies. The part of the efficient boundary which is not worse than the security (maxmin) level for either player is known as the Edgeworth Curve.

Variable Threats Case

Nash has also investigated the more general case in which the conflict point is not determined by the rules of the game as such but rather by the retaliatory strategies the players would use against each other in a conflict situation, that is, if no agreement is reached. He assumes that a player must announce his retaliatory strategy at the beginning of the game and, for this reason, they are also called threat strategies. Once these strategies are announced, the players are compelled to implement them if a conflict situation arises. As an example, the game [42, 53]:

		Player II		
		B_1		B_2
	A_1	$(1, 0)$	$\leftarrow$	$(-a, -b)$
Player I		$\uparrow$		$\downarrow$
	A_2	$(-c, -d)$	$\rightarrow$	$(0, 1)$

with a, b, c, d positive has two equilibrium points, one at $(1, 0)$ and one at $(0, 1)$. The expected payoff to both players from mixed strategies lies in a convex polygon. It is the smallest convex set containing the payoff points and is known as their convex hull. Clearly, any payoff lies in this set and neither of its components can exceed those of corresponding points on the boundary. We may assume convexity if the players cooperate after the threats and take into consideration all mixed strategies. The origin is taken as the threat point (see the following regarding how this point is determined). Thus for the foregoing game we have the diagram in Figure 20.

Unless the players agree on the strategies leading to an equilibrium

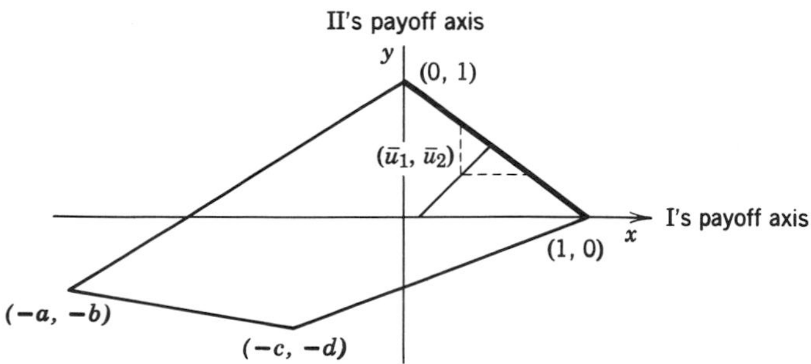

Figure 20

point they can proceed independently and both lose. They can also threaten each other with loss, however, by playing a strategy unfavorable to one another. For example, II can threaten to play B_2 if I plays A_1, causing a loss to both. The threat is more credible whenever the opponent stands to lose more than the forcing player himself (except if we assume that the players are free to implement any threat they may make, as Nash does).

To compute the cooperative solution $\mathbf{u}$, which lies on the boundary, note that the efficient boundary is given by the straight line $u_1 + u_2 = 1$. The line L on which the threat point $\bar{\mathbf{u}}$ lies is perpendicular to it and is given by $u_1 - \bar{u}_1 = u_2 - \bar{u}_2$. Eliminating u_2 we have $u_1 = (1 + \bar{u}_2 - \bar{u}_2)/2$, $u_2 = (1 + u_2 - u_1)/2$.

Who Should Make the Next Offer? In a bargaining situation suppose that player I suggests a payoff vector $\mathbf{u}^1 = (u_2^1, u_2^1)$, whereas player II suggests $\mathbf{u}^2 = (u_1^2, u_1^2)$ with $u_1^1 > u_1^2 > v_1$, $u_2^2 > u_2^1 > v_2$, where v_1, v_2 refer to the maxmin payoffs. Then player I's behavior, for example, will depend on whether he thinks that player II, with probability p_{21}, will not make a concession beyond the last offer $\mathbf{u}^2$. Thus player I will refuse any concession if

$$p_{21}v_1 + (1 - p_{21})u_1^1 \geq u_1^2,$$

that is, if

$$p_{21} \leq \frac{u_1^1 - u_1^2}{u_1^1 - v_1} \tag{1}$$

Similarly, player II will refuse further concessions if his subjective probability that player I will make no concessions beyond u_1^1 is

$$p_{12} \leq \frac{u_2^2 - u_2^1}{u_2^2 - v_2} \tag{2}$$

Zeuthen's principle advises that I or II or both make concessions depending on whether the quantity on the right in (1) is less than that in (2) or exceeds it or is equal to it respectively.

How to Estimate a Strategy [31]. Assume that in a two-person, nonzero-sum negotiation problem the strategies available to the opponent are known, but his utilities are not. These utilities can be estimated from the opponent's value system, however, or through the use of previous experience or special information. We want to estimate the opponent's strategy and modify the estimate at the negotiations by "feeling him out" as he is observed to apply his strategy. The negotiations are assumed to occur in stages. For simplicity assume that he has two strategies to play against two for us. Let the payoffs corresponding to his first and second strategies be $\begin{pmatrix} b_{11} \\ b_{21} \end{pmatrix}$ and $\begin{pmatrix} b_{12} \\ b_{22} \end{pmatrix}$ respectively. Assume that his strategy guarantees him a minimum expected payoff v. If he plays his first pure strategy with probability p and the second with probability $1 - p$ we have

$$p = \frac{b_{22} - b_{12}}{b_{11} - b_{12} + b_{22} - b_{21}}, \qquad v = \frac{b_{11}b_{22} - b_{12}b_{21}}{b_{11} - b_{12} + b_{22} - b_{21}}$$

If estimates are available on the b_{ij}, we would have an estimate for p and v. If the same constant is added to all the b_{ij}, the estimates for p and v remain the same. Thus if an estimate with lowest confidence is taken for the b_{ij} and another estimate with highest confidence are used, two values are obtained for p. The average may then be used. We may consider these three values of p as defining a probability distribution. We assign each of the two extreme values a probability β and assign their average the probability $1 - 2\beta$. We can then use the negotiations to improve these estimates using the method of Baye's theorem discussed in Chapter 5. Conceptually, at least, this process has some validity. In practice, small changes in the probability estimates may have no operational significance.

A Problem of Transferring Utilities. Game theory forces one to represent his utilities with numbers, even when, as with satisfaction or happiness, they are difficult to quantify. He does this in order to get a better idea of what to do in a given situation. In negotiations, however, it is not clear how to transfer happiness unless it involves promises of compromise in other situations: for example, the promise that if "You do this for me, I promise to do something specified in advance for you in the future."

Consider the example of the wife and husband, each of whom prefers one of two activities for the evening, with different utilities. The activities are Hockey and Ballet. The husband prefers the first and the wife the second, but they are miserable when they do not go together. If they go together the return to both is higher. The husband obtains what is indicated by the first of the two numbers and the wife the second. What should they do?

		Wife: Hockey		Wife: Ballet
Husband	Hockey	(2, 1)	←	(−1, −1)
		↑		↓
	Ballet	(−1, −1)	→	(1, 2)

How to derive a utility measure of their collective satisfaction remains a problem. The best suggestion is to go together to satisfy one of them, and satisfy the other on another occasion.

Some problems yet to be adequately studied by game theory follow [61, 61a]:

1. The problem that there is a well-defined set of players.
2. Can nations' preferences be aggregated so that each can be regarded as a player in the sense of game theory?
3. There is the possibility of major inaccuracies residing in the development of numerical payoffs.
4. *a*) Can the players obtain a measure for their preferences; *b*) do they at least know their own payoffs; *c*) do players know each other's value systems?
5. Organizing a diplomatic game in extensive form to portray the possible moves is not as effective as it may be in economics, for example, where time does not affect the layout. Here time is of importance and both the extensive and normal forms of a game need to be modified to include dynamics of strategy and payoffs.
6. It is difficult to define moves in the diplomatic area where statements made are sometimes important and sometimes trivial and have no bearing on the problem. Even certain acts of nations that seem to have bearing on a conflict may actually have none.
7. What is the effect of teams and alliances on a conflict; the gains and losses (including economic gains and losses) resulting from such groupings as they ultimately affect a conflict?
8. There is no adequate idea of a solution for general game theoretic problems.
9. There is no code for the language or ideas of diplomacy.
10. Are all agreements enforceable?
11. Are all decisions clear and correct and not subject to errors?
12. Is communication completely understood?

3.6. META-GAMES; POLICIES AND SANCTIONS

In the example of the Prisoner's Dilemma, in which the general type of payoff matrix is applicable to competitive situations, it has been noted that the Nash equilibrium is not the stability point reached by playing the game repeatedly. Rather, it is the other payoff on the diagonal that yields both players a higher return than the Nash equilibrium payoff. It has been tested experimentally [52a] that this higher payoff may be achieved after repeated plays. The game is continued in consistent unchanging play, each player doing what the other player expects him to do. A generalization of the theory has been needed to account for this paradox. One explanation is to be found in the theory of cooperative games in which binding and enforceable agreements would insure that the players play strategies with greater payoff to both than the Nash equilibrium yields.

N. Howard [29] has taken this payoff matrix and augmented its strategies by introducing responses or policies (patterns of reaction) that counter the opponents' strategies and counter policies for the opponents as a response to these policies. In this manner he was able to develop a theory of meta-games to account for the paradox. At this point it may be best to illustrate with an example. The theory uses only ordinal utilities.

Consider a military conflict between two powers, I and II. Each has the simple choice of whether or not to escalate the conflict. If one escalates and the other does not, the one who escalates wins a victory. If both escalate, however, both are worse off than if neither does. This can be represented by a Prisoner's Dilemma type of game as shown in the following matrix. Here E stands for escalation and N for nonescalation:

		II's Alternatives	
		N	E
I's alternatives	N	(3, 3) de-escalation	(1, 4) II's victory
	E	(4, 1) I's victory	(2, 2) escalation

The essential feature of the payoffs is their relative magnitudes. These magnitudes were chosen according to which outcome each side prefers. For example, I prefers victory to de-escalation to escalation to defeat. (It has been shown that there are 78 essentially different such 2 by 2 payoff matrices of which this is one important example.)

In order to appreciate the mathematical nature of the Prisoner's Dilemma we introduce the following ideas:

Individual Rationality. In a two-person game, an outcome is called rational for player I (the row player) if it is the largest value to him in its column (where each column corresponds to the payoffs from a strategy choice by player II for each of I's strategies) and plays the strategy corresponding to this payoff for each choice of player II. A similar definition holds for player II (the column player). For each player we can define similarly a rational outcome in the case of N players.

Group Rationality (or Pareto Optimality). A payoff (a_{ij}, b_{ij}) is rationally better for the two players if there is no other payoff (a_{hk}, b_{hk}) which dominates it, that is, $a_{hk} \geq a_{ij}$, $b_{hk} \geq b_{ij}$. The Prisoner's Dilemma is a dilemma between individual and group rationality because the Nash payoff is a result of individual rationality and violates group rationality since there is a payoff dominating it coefficientwise. Hence a theory is required in which this contradiction is impossible.

The question arises: Which of the four possible outcomes of this game can be stable? According to game theory, the Nash equilibrium point occurs when both sides escalate (*E*-*E*). As already mentioned, experimental work with this game has shown that in repeated play, stable equilibrium is more likely to occur when there is deescalation (*N*-*N*). Meta-game theory shows that both the escalation and deescalation entries are equilibrium points (in an extended sense) and that a stable outcome (achieved by any spoken or unspoken agreement between the two sides) will result from either of them. Note that (*N*-*N*) is the outcome satisfying the concept of group rationality.

To extend the original game for the purpose of determining the equilibrium points, we consider all of the possible ways that II might react to I's choices, all of the possible ways that I might react to II's reactions, and so on, ad infinitum. In this way the theory finds policies by which each side may mutually reinforce the other's choice of no escalation of conflict.

To illustrate: II's possible reactions to I's choices are *AN* ("always not-escalate, regardless of I's choice"), *AE* ("always escalate, regardless of I's choice"), *T* ("tit-for-tat," that is, choose the same as I), and *O* ("tat-for-tit," that is, choose opposite to I). By considering these alternative reactions we obtain the following matrix:

		II's meta-alternatives			
		AN	*AE*	*T*	*O*
I's alternatives	*N*	*N* 3, 3 de-escalation	*E* 1, 4 II's victory	*N* 3, 3 de-escalation	*E* 1, 4 II's victory
	E	*N* 4, 1 I's victory	*E* 2, 2 escalation	*E* 2, 2 escalation	*N* 4, 1 I's victory

The alternatives of player II are called meta-alternatives, or policies. They constitute the set of all functions from I's alternatives to II's choices.

If we look for the Nash equilibrium outcomes in this matrix, we find that only *E*-*AE* (leading to *E*-*E* as before) contains the maximum point-scores in its column (for the first number) and in its row (for the second number). Thus we have no new Nash equilibria.

Next consider player I's possible reactions to II's reactions—the set of all functions from II's meta-alternatives to I's alternatives. There are 16 of these, as indicated in the following matrix.

I's meta-alternatives	II's meta-alternatives *AN*	*NE*	*T*	*O*
NNNN	3, 3	1, 4	3, 3	1, 4
EEEE	4, 1	(2, 2)	2, 2	4, 1
EEEN	4, 1	2, 2	2, 2	1, 4
EENE	4, 1	2, 2	(3, 3)	4, 1 ✓
EENN	4, 1	2, 2	3, 3	1, 4
ENEE	4, 1	1, 4	2, 2	4, 1
ENEN	4, 1	1, 4	2, 2	1, 4
ENNE	4, 1	1, 4	3, 3	4, 1
ENNN	4, 1	1, 4	3, 3	1, 4
NEEE	3, 3	2, 2	2, 2	4, 1
NEEN	3, 3	2, 2	2, 2	1, 4
NENE	3, 3	2, 2	(3, 3)	4, 1
NENN	3, 3	2, 2	3, 3	1, 4
NNEE	3, 3	1, 4	2, 2	4, 1
NNEN	3, 3	1, 4	2, 2	1, 4
NNNE	3, 3	1, 4	3, 3	4, 1

In this matrix there are three equilibria—one leading to *E-E* as before, and two leading to *N-N*. Consider, for example, the row marked with a check. This represents the counter policy for I of escalating in response to any of II's policies except *T* ("tit-for-tat"). This counter policy *EENE* and the policy *T* of tit-for-tat for II are in equilibrium and lead to mutual nonescalation. The other new pair is *NENE* for I and *T* for II.

It can be proved that the equilibria in all further matrices derivable from the 4 by 16 matrix give no additional potentially stable outcomes.

Meta-game theory is an analysis of a conflict situation to find the equilibria and their corresponding policies. By a choice of policies and counter policies the players can induce each other toward equilibrium. It is essential to identify the actual strategies available to the opponents and to recognize that policies can and must be formulated by each player, and that both players will seek an equilibrium outcome.

Let us now consider a meta-game analysis of Chicken.

			Player II	
			Swerve 0	Not swerve 1
Player I	Swerve	0	(3, 3) Compromise	(2, 4) II's victory
	Not swerve	1	(4, 2) I's victory	(1, 1) Collision

Here we assume that both I and II have to decide whether or not to swerve. The various possible outcomes are assumed to be as shown, with the preference orderings indicated. What are the equilibria of this game? Here we have used numbers to designate strategies. This facilitates the identification of policies in further expansion. The two expansions as before lead to the meta-equilibria circled in the following abbreviated table.

		II's policies			
		00	11	01	10
I's counter policies	0000	3, 3	(2, 4)	3, 3	2, 4
	1111	(4, 2)	1, 1	1, 1	(4, 2)
	....	...	...	...	...
	1001	4, 2	(2, 4)	3, 3	4, 2
	....	...	...	...	...
	1101	4, 2	1, 1	(3, 3)	4, 2

The Nash equilibria and hence also meta-equilibria for this game are (2, 4) and (4, 2). However, (3, 3) is also a meta-equilibrium. It can be considered a "good compromise" because it is fairer since it gives each the same amount.

An important theorem of meta-game theory is called the identification theorem. It identifies those outcomes that are meta-rational. This theorem will be given in its generality but its implication will be discussed in the case of two players expanding once for each player. Indications for the general case will also be made. In the two examples previously given we chose to expand in the policies of player II first and then followed this with an expansion in player I's counter policies. Examine the first expansion for a general two-person game. Denote the utility functions of players I and II respectively by $U_i(\mathbf{s}, \mathbf{t})$ $i = 1, 2$ where $\mathbf{s}$ denotes a strategy for player I and $\mathbf{t}$ denotes a strategy for player II. Let S be the set of I's strategies and let T be the set of II's strategies.

What is player I's best response to each of II's policies?

Recall that before we made the expansion, his best choice $\mathbf{s}$ for each of II's strategies $\bar{\mathbf{t}}$ satisfied the condition $U_1(\bar{\mathbf{s}}, \bar{\mathbf{t}}) \geq U_1(\mathbf{s}, \bar{\mathbf{t}})$ for all $\mathbf{s}$. This is a condition on the Cartesian product $S \times T$. It defines a subset $\mathfrak{S}$. Similarly, we can produce a set $\mathfrak{T}$ for player II before expanding. The subsets $\mathfrak{S}$ and $\mathfrak{T}$ are the sets of rational outcomes for I and II respectively in the initial game. The intersection of $\mathfrak{S}$ and $\mathfrak{T}$ are the Nash equilibria (in the original game).

After the first expansion (for instance, for player II) sets are obtained which are denoted by $2\mathfrak{S}$ and $2\mathfrak{T}$. The 2 indicates that we have expanded first by the second player. The intersection of $2\mathfrak{S}$ and $2\mathfrak{T}$ are the Nash equilibria in the game in which II expands first and are meta-equilibria of the original game derived from this particular expansion. (The symbol $12\mathfrak{S}$ would denote the set of rational outcomes for player I in the game which is expanded first by player II and then by player I.)

The identification theorem permits characterization of the sets $\mathfrak{S}$, $\mathfrak{T}$, $2\mathfrak{S}$, $2\mathfrak{T}$, $1\mathfrak{S}$, $1\mathfrak{T}$, $12\mathfrak{S}$, $12\mathfrak{T}$, $21\mathfrak{S}$, and $21\mathfrak{T}$. The characterization for $2\mathfrak{S}$ and $12\mathfrak{S}$, $2\mathfrak{T}$ and $12\mathfrak{T}$ is interesting. We always have $2\mathfrak{T} = \mathfrak{T}$ and $2\mathfrak{S} \supseteq \mathfrak{S}$. The reason for the first equality is that player II makes his best choices by examining rows, and the rows and their elements do not change after he makes his expansion. The reason for the second is that the number of columns and their elements increase for player I. An element $(\bar{\mathbf{s}}, \bar{\mathbf{t}})$ belongs to 2 if and only if it satisfies $U_1(\bar{\mathbf{s}}, \bar{\mathbf{t}}) \geq \max_s \min_t U_1(\mathbf{s}, \mathbf{t})$. Note that the right side is a constant and hence is a critical level associated with the structure of the game. It may be that several outcomes $(\bar{\mathbf{s}}, \bar{\mathbf{t}})$ will satisfy the inequality.

Again we have $12\mathfrak{S} = 1\mathfrak{S}$ and $12\mathfrak{T} \supseteq 2\mathfrak{T}$. The justification for these two relations is analogous to that just given.

Elements of 12 satisfy the following necessary and sufficient condition:

$$U_2(\bar{\mathbf{s}}, \bar{\mathbf{t}}) \geq \min_s \max_t U_2(\mathbf{s}, \mathbf{t})$$

Note that the right side is a constant which is a second critical level associated with the game.

As a consequence of $21\mathfrak{S} \cap 12\mathfrak{T} \supset \mathfrak{S} \cap \mathfrak{T} =$ Nash equilibria, it follows that any Nash equilibrium is above the minmax which we already know is always above the maxmin.

Consider the following diagram:

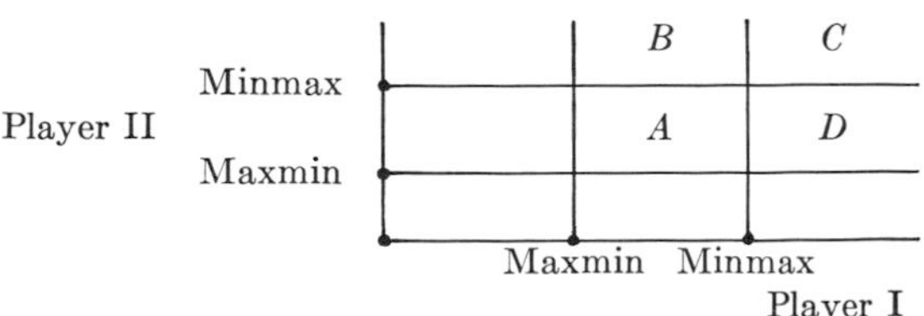

All Nash equilibria are included among points that fall in C. All points that fall in B, C, or D are meta-equilibria in some expansion and therefore they are meta-rational for both players. Points in A are not equilibrium points in any meta-game, but players could stabilize at such an outcome if each perceives different meta-games. All points that fall in C are meta-equilibria in all complete expansions. A complete meta-game is a meta-game in which every player has made at least one expansion. There is a special attractiveness for points in C because each player can see he is in his best expansion.

In the Prisoner's Dilemma and in Chicken the maxmin and minmax for both players are equal to 2.

Remark. It can be proved that we can consider policies as the offering of an outcome together with a sanction which will be applied if the offer is not accepted by the other player. Therefore an outcome is meta-rational for a player if there is a combined choice for the other players so that whatever the given player does, his outcome becomes worse. If departure from an outcome by any player permits an inescapable sanction against the player (an outcome in which he is worse off) it can be shown that this outcome is a meta-game equilibrium. This remark is applied to the examples given in Section 3.7.

Remark. In a two-person game there is no need to go further than the second expansion as far as meta-rational outcomes and equilibrium points are concerned. This generalizes to N-person games; in such games it is not necessary to go beyond Nth expansions for meta-rational outcomes and $2N - 1$ expansions for equilibrium points, provided that each meta-game involves at least one expansion for each player.

In the case of several players, more than two critical levels (in the sense just given) must be introduced in order to characterize the different sets of meta-rational outcomes.

Now consider the payoff matrix M of an N-player, nonzero-sum game and put numbers from 1 to N before it to indicate the order in which the meta-game expansions are to be made. Thus if $N = 3$, $1323M$ indicates that the first expansion is made with regard to player 3's policies followed by an expansion for player 2, and then player 3 expands again, and finally an expansion with regard to player 1's policies is made. No matter how many players there are, the expansion can be continued indefinitely. Each of these expansions, no matter at what level it is stopped, is called a meta-game expansion. An outcome in the policies of a meta-game that is rational is a meta-rational outcome in the original game.

As a simple illustration, suppose that $N = 5$, and consider the expansion 121341M in which 5 is not mentioned. Moving from right to left, leave the first occurrence of a player's identity, but strike out all subsequent ones. This gives 2413M. Consider, for example, player 4 in the foregoing discussion. In this expansion, an outcome $\bar{\mathbf{s}} = (\bar{\mathbf{s}}_1, \bar{\mathbf{s}}_2, \bar{\mathbf{s}}_3, \bar{\mathbf{s}}_4, \bar{\mathbf{s}}_5)$ is meta-rational for player 4 if and only if

$$U_4(\bar{\mathbf{s}}) \geq \min_{s_2} \max_{s_4} \min_{s_1} \min_{s_3} U_4(\mathbf{s}_1, \mathbf{s}_2, \mathbf{s}_3, \mathbf{s}_4, \bar{\mathbf{s}}_5).$$

Note that the maximum is taken only with respect to player 4. In addition it is applied in the second position because that is the position of player 4 in 2413M.

Even though an expansion for player 5 is not included we obtain for him

$$U_5(\mathbf{s}) \geq \max_{s_5} \min_{s_1} \min_{s_2} \min_{s_3} \min_{s_4} M_5(\mathbf{s}_1, \ldots, \mathbf{s}_5).$$

This inequality would hold, of course, if we also have an expansion with respect to 5 appearing after the expansion just given. Thus we now examine the entries in the meta-game and find those where each player gets at least his computed value on the right side of his inequality. These are the meta-equilibrium points. In the case of two players, for example, we compute the minmax value for the player who expands into a meta-game first. We then compute the maxmin value for the other player. The equilibria are the outcomes in which each player gets at least his value.

Assuming that a player chooses his best expansion, that is, he considers himself as expanding first, for one outcome to be meta-rational for him it only has to be greater than the minmax. This is an easy consequence of the foregoing combination of min max min, etc., (that is, his critical level would be higher). This argument holds if every player considers himself as expanding first. Therefore if an outcome has values that are greater than the minmax for every player, it is meta-rational in any complete expansion. Thus we do not need to know the order in which the players are expanding their game, but this outcome would be viewed as an equilibrium as long as the players conceive of themselves as having policies, that is, they think of meta-games.

If we wish to apply meta-game theory to mixed strategies we expand the normal form so that each player has all combinations of his strategies listed separately and meta-game theory is then applied to the resulting normal form. M. Dresher of the RAND Corporation has proved that the probability of a solution of an N-person nonzero-sum game in pure Nash equilibrium strategies tends to $1 - e^{-1}$ as the number of strategies of the players tends to infinity. This result makes plausible a search for pure strategy solution in a game with a large number of strategies for each player and with a large number of players. A. J. Goldman [22a] shows that the probability of a saddle point in an n by m two-person, zero-sum game is $m!n!/(m + n - 1)!$ which tends to zero as $m, n \to \infty$.

3.7. APPLICATIONS OF META-GAMES TO NONPROLIFERATION AND TO VIETNAM

We now give an application of the general ideas appearing in Sections 3.6 and 2.5. The quantitative analysis is based on the tools of the theory of meta-games. From Section 2.5 we may translate admissible states to mean states which are preferred to the status quo; inadmissible states, those not preferred to the status quo; and equilibrium states those which consist of any state for which neither side has a state more preferred to it which he can move with impunity.

In the analysis of a specific conflict situation it is sufficient to list all fundamental options (that is, courses of action) available to the parties involved. Each option is assigned a value of 1 or 0, depending on whether it is to be taken or not. For simplicity, yes-no may suffice. There may be a complicated situation when yes-no is not enough, however. If different shades or values are available for an option, the basic option can be broken into several options, each of which is assigned a value of 1 or 0. Any certain fixed selection of values for all options to all parties is called an alternative. An example of an alternative is the status quo, in which the values of the options can be taken from real life as it is at the time the problem is formulated. The options of other countries may not be publicized, of course, and may require guessing. The idea is to compare all other alternatives with any single one (for example, the status quo), placing those less favored in one group and those more favored in another. The problem now is whether there is an alternative which is preferred by one of the parties and can be attained without the possibility of counter action (a sanction) by a second party, consisting of a change in the value of its options for that alternative, which would put the first party in a less desirable alternative than the status quo. The analysis of stability for a given alternative must be done several times—once for each party or country involved. This is the reason for the several tables and lists that follow. The status quo is unstable if there is an alternative that some country prefers and to which it can move without sanctions by another country. It is stable otherwise.

An example is given whose sole purpose is to serve as an illustration of the manipulations involved in analyzing a problem. It is concerned with nuclear proliferation as it affects West Germany. The issues are: (a) Defense against Soviet nuclear "confrontation" (attack or blackmail);

(b) European nuclear defense union; (c) Inspection. The participants are: West Germany, U.S.S.R., United States, and France. The options open to each party are:

	Status Quo
West Germany (four "yes/no" options)	
1. Develop nuclear arms	0
2. Nuclear confrontation directed against U.S.S.R.	0
3. Permit international inspection	0
4. Vote for joining France in a defense union	0
U.S.S.R. (three options)	
5. Permit inspection	0
6. Confront United States	0
7. Confront West Germany	0
U.S. (two options)	
8. Permit inspection	0
9. Confront U.S.S.R.	0
France (one option)	
10. Vote for union with West Germany	0

Meta-game theory can be applied to analyze the stability of this alternative (the status quo) if we can decide, for each other alternative, whether or not each country prefers it to the status quo.

The options appear in each alternative vector in the order in which they were just listed. Note that there are $2^{10} = 1024$ possible alternatives, many of which can be grouped in the same preference class because of slight difference in their effect. Thus, for example, the U.S.S.R. prefers the slight variation on the status quo given in the left columns, with the United States or West Germany permitting inspection. It does not prefer West German nuclear development or other actions, such as indicated by the right column of the following:

Preferred Alternatives		Status Quo	Not Preferred Alternatives	
0	0	0	1	1
0	0	0	0	1
1	0	0	0	0
0	0	0	0	0
0	0	0	0	0
0	0	0	0	1
0	0	0	0	0
0	0	0	0	1
0	1	0	0	0
0	0	0	0	0

The meta-game analysis of the status quo outcome will tell us: (1) Whether it is a possible equilibrium. (2) If it is, what are the policies that will keep it in equilibrium? (3) Whether it is dominated, that is, is there an outcome preferred by all? (4) Whether it is Kantian, that is, could it be the long-term, cooperative equilibrium? (See Tables 3.1–3.4.)

Table 3.1. West Germany and the Status Quo*

Preferred Alternatives					Status Quo	Not Preferred Alternatives					
–	–	1	0	0	0	1	1	0	0	–	–
1	0	0	0	0	0	0	0	0	0	–	–
0	–	–	0	0	0	–	–	1	0	–	–
0	–	1	–	–	0	–	0	–	–	–	–
–	–	–	1	0	0	–	–	–	0	–	–
0	0	0	0	0	0	0	0	0	0	–	1
0	0	0	0	0	0	0	0	0	0	1	0
0	1	0	0	0	0	0	0	0	0	–	–
0	–	–	–	0	0	–	–	–	1	–	–
0	–	1	–	–	0	0	1	–	–	–	–
No U.S.S.R. resistance to confrontation		Germany nuclear, defense union	U.S.S.R. inspected, Germany not	No inspection, offers to join		Germany nuclear, no defense union		No confrontation, Germany inspected	United States alone inspected	U.S.S.R. confronts Germany and/or U.S.	

* Dashes indicate that no matter what value (zero or one) is placed in that position, the preference of the alternative remains the same.

Although a country *A* would like to move to a more preferred position, it could be inhibited by the possibility that an adversary *B* may retaliate by selecting a not preferred alternative for *A* whose options have the same values for *A* but which has some different and preferred options for *B*. Note that for any alternative, *B* cannot change the values of *A*'s options but can change the values of his own options. After such action is taken by B, A can change values of its options in this not preferred alternative and perhaps obtain a preferred alternative for itself. This back and forth analysis between preferred and not preferred alternatives may end in an unpreferred position for A. If this were so for every country

Table 3.2. U.S.S.R. and the Status Quo

Preferred Alternatives				Status Quo	Not Preferred Alternatives					
–	–	0	0	0	0	1	0	0	–	–
0	0	0	0	0	0	0	0	0		1
–	–	1	0	0	–	–	0	0	–	–
–	–	–	–	0	–	–	1	0	–	–
–	–	0	0	0	1	–	0	0	–	–
1	0	0	0	0	0	0	0	0	–	–
–	1	0	0	0	0	0	0	0	–	–
0	0	0	0	0	0	0	0	0	1	0
–	–	–	1	0	–	–	0	0	–	–
–	–	–	–	0	–	–	–	1	–	–
U.S.S.R. confrontation, unopposed		United States and/or Germany inspected, U.S.S.R. not			No confrontation, U.S.S.R. inspected	No confrontation, nuclear Germany	Offers to join		U.S.S.R. confronted	

the status quo would be stable because no country could move freely to a preferred alternative. The United States, for example, has a preferred alternative as the second column from the left in the preferred category in Table 3.3, but the U.S.S.R. can change the 1 appearing in its option to a zero yielding the second alternative from the left, in the not preferred category. This action is an illustration of a sanction where the U.S.S.R. changes from permitting inspection to not permitting it. Thus for the moment the United States would not necessarily move to the preferred

Table 3.3. United States and the Status Quo

Preferred Alternatives			Status Quo	Not Preferred Alternatives							
0	1	0	0	1	1	0	0	–	–	–	–
0	0	0	0	0	0	0	0	–	–	–	1
–	1	1	0	0	1	0	–	–	–	–	–
–	–	–	0	–	–	–	–	–	–	–	–
1	1	0	0	–	0	0	0	–	–	–	–
0	0	0	0	0	0	0	0	1	0	0	0
0	0	0	0	0	0	0	0	–	1	0	0
0	0	0	0	0	0	0	0	–	–	1	0
–	–	0	0	–	–	0	1	–	–	–	–
–	–	–	0	–	–	–	–	–	–	–	–
No confrontation, U.S.S.R. inspected	Germany nuclear, U.S.S.R. and Germany inspected	Germany non-nuclear, inspected		Nuclear Germany, not inspected	Germany nuclear, inspected, U.S.S.R. not	No inspection, any offers to join	United States inspected, U.S.S.R. not	Any confrontation			

option unless it can guarantee by arms control agreements that the U.S.S.R. would adhere to permitting inspection.

The results of the general analysis of the example are: (a) The status quo is a possible equilibrium. (b) It is kept in equilibrium by these policies: (1) United States retaliation and/or German future retaliation discourages Soviet confrontation against the United States and/or Germany. (2) Soviet retaliation discourages Germany from nuclear development and confrontation against U.S.S.R. (3) French veto on European defense union discourages Germany from nuclear development without confrontation against U.S.S.R. (c) The status quo is undominated, that is, no alternative is better for all. But if Germany alone were

Table 3.4. France and the Status Quo

Preferred Alternatives		Status Quo	Not Preferred Alternatives					
0	0	0	1	0	–	–	–	–
0	0	0	0	0	–	1	0	0
–	–	0	–	–	–	–	–	–
1	0	0	–	1	–	–	–	–
–	–	0	–	–	–	–	–	–
0	0	0	0	0	–	–	1	0
0	0	0	0	0	1	0	0	0
0	0	0	0	0	–	–	–	1
–		0	–	–	–	–	–	–
0	–	0	–	1	–	–	–	–
No confrontations, Germany non-nuclear, Union, any inspection			No confrontation, Germany nuclear	No confrontation, Germany non-nuclear, Defense union	Any confrontation			

inspected and there were no European defense union, this would be better for the U.S.S.R., United States, and France. (d) The status quo is not Kantian, that is, it is not a fully cooperative equilibrium. Germany will always prefer that the United States confront the U.S.S.R. with no U.S.S.R. resistance (for example, Soviet Union gives up East Germany). France always prefers some inspection. These are the assumptions about preferences. We may try any assumptions that may be of interest. A computer may be used if the number of outcomes is large.

Note that meta-game theory may be considered normative when there is a single meta-equilibrium, or when the totality of equilibria is taken as the optimum set to consider. From this set a single equilibrium is then singled out as most desirable.

The theory may be applied recursively on a day to day basis in a negotiation process to determine the next move to be made.

The Requirements for a Stable Settlement in Vietnam

Here is another example of the application of meta-games carried out by a group of people interested in becoming familiar with applications. The validity of the conclusions of course can be no better than the quality of value judgments that went into the exercise. The individuals were not government experts who had access to privileged government information. Hence their conclusions are not necessarily those that would result if the tool were used by government experts. The explanation of technical details similar to those given for the above example are repeated in order to make the example self-contained.

This meta-game analysis seeks to determine whether a peaceful settlement of the Vietnam problem is possible, given certain assumptions about the preferences of the conflicting parties and the options open to them.

We take as a starting point the idea that a long-term settlement must be one that involves eventual withdrawal of United States troops. We therefore analyze a long-term peaceful settlement accompanied by United States withdrawal.

The analysis was performed considering only assumed preferences for the parties involved. No assumptions as to the United States' preferences, negotiating positions, and so on, were made. The results are therefore indicative only of the game-theoretic outcome if the United States exercises its options as noted below but does not imply that the United States should or will. If the assumptions are correct, however, the only stable solution other than continued escalation is given below and the methods by which the United States can reach it are limited.

The actual model, which is somewhat complex, is shown at the end of this section. There also we give the detailed assumptions concerning options and preferences. The main conclusions reached are the following (The reader is urged to study Tables 3.5–3.7; the following verbal analysis follows from the tables):

1. Any settlement must be preferred by *either* the North Vietnamese (N.V.N.) *or* the National Liberation Front (N.L.F.), to the prospects

they foresee from continued escalation of the conflict. If possibly the N.V.N. and N.L.F. *differ* in their views, it is sufficient that *one* of them sees better prospects from the settlement than from continued escalation; but at least one of them must prefer the settlement.

2. On the assumption that a settlement preferred by the N.V.N. or N.L.F. to continued escalation would *not* be preferred to this by the South Vietnamese (S.V.N.), we asked whether such a settlement would therefore be unstable. We found that it would *not* necessarily be unstable, provided the S.V.N. believed that the alternative to accepting the settlement was United States' *withdrawal* while they continued to fight alone against the N.V.N. and the N.L.F.

3. If U.S. withdrawal from South Vietnam were *not* to lead to the S.V.N. eventually having to fight alone against both the N.V.N. and the N.L.F.—if, on the contrary, it were to be accompanied by a settlement of the conflict between these parties that would be lasting—then the direct conclusion from our analysis was that a difficult condition had to be met. This was that either the N.V.N. or the N.L.F. (that is, one or both) must believe that if they started the conflict again, U.S. forces would return; and simultaneously the S.V.N. must believe that if *they* were to restart the conflict, U.S. forces *would not* return.

4. The following points are not a consequence of the mathematical analysis but constitute possible changes in the assumed preference orderings assigned to the participants that might mitigate the difficulty of achieving this outcome. In particular, the fact that the above condition seemed difficult to achieve led us to ask how it might realistically be softened. If the settlement accompanying U.S. withdrawal led to a reconciliation between the parties in Vietnam so that their preferences changed, we might have one of the following: (a) the S.V.N., even if they believed that renewed hostilities would lead to a return of the United States, might no longer prefer this to the settlement that had been achieved; (b) the N.V.N. or N.L.F., even if they believed that renewed hostilities would *not* lead to a U.S. return, might nevertheless come to prefer the settlement. Other possibilities that would make the "difficult" condition of (3) above unnecessary would be: (c) the effective "swallowing-up" of the S.V.N. by the N.V.N. and/or N.L.F.; (d) acceptance of U.S. aid, which the S.V.N. and the N.V.N. or N.L.F. would not wish to see discontinued as a result of a resumption of hostilities.

5. So far we have considered the requirements for a long-term settlement—meaning one that by definition entails withdrawal of U.S. forces. In the short term we find that a *cease-fire* (with no withdrawal of U.S. or N.V.N. forces) could be stable provided that either the N.V.N. or N.L.F. prefer it to continued escalation. However, as in the previous analysis of the difficulty of discontinuing the process of escalation, a cease-fire would

be difficult to maintain if not accompanied by reasonable prospects for a settlement. It would require knowledge by each side of the others' intentions and reactions in connection with military movements. This seems to imply a well-defined cease-fire line. Such a line would be hard to draw in the South Vietnamese countryside, where often each side claims a certain "percentage" of control over the same area. It seems that a cease-fire line would require both sides to "desert" large numbers of persons whose loyalty they now claim. In addition, on the assumption that the S.V.N. prefers continued escalation to a cease-fire, they (the S.V.N.) must believe if *they* break the cease-fire, U.S. forces will not be drawn into breaking it also.

6. The above points seem to suggest the following tentative scenario toward a settlement:

With the "negotiation" between the United States and N.V.N. of a complete bombing halt, further negotiations produce a touchy and unstable cease-fire (because of the virtual impossibility of drawing cease-fire lines). In this cease-fire situation real negotiations involving the United States, S.V.N., N.V.N., and N.L.F. begin. More or less working over the objections of the S.V.N., the other three blueprint a coalition government from the South, including the S.V.N. and N.L.F. The United States' attempts to represent the S.V.N.'s best interests here, but the S.V.N. is rather intransigent. Ultimately, the success of the negotiations depends on the creation of a structure that incorporates the vital interests of the N.L.F. as well as the S.V.N. Finally, when a coalition has been trilaterally negotiated, the S.V.N. bends (or breaks) enough to accept it. The S.V.N. is *forced* into this position by fear of a United States withdrawal if they do not accept it. The S.V.N. counter-threat to fight without the United States and, in effect, embarrass the United States by standing alone, however suicidal, is not believed and in fact does not occur; ultimately, the United States and N.V.N. withdraw, the S.V.N. and N.L.F. are left to chart their own future (probably including ultimate reconciliation with the North).

Alternative scenarios of very significant probability (unfortunately) involve a breakdown at any of the early negotiation stages or of the cease-fire, or involve the impossibility of negotiating a reasonable coalition because of intransigence on one side or the other. Then the situation may well revert to war at some significant level, from which it is difficult for the United States to withdraw, however much it may wish to do so.

The cease-fire may be so fragile that it would be better to avoid it, because its breakdown may be inevitable and carry with it disastrous consequences for negotiations. A simple policy of "no aggressive actions/

defense only" unilaterally enunciated on either side would be more stable (if perhaps more bloody).

The details of the above scenario may be constructed differently keeping the basic structure of achieving a negotiated settlement constant.

The following tables show the assumptions made about the problem. We assume that the United States has three options: cease bombing, cease-fire and withdraw. The other three parties have the options shown against their names. An *outcome* of the situation is shown by a column of 1's and 0's. A blank represents a possibility of either a 1 or a 0. A 1 means that the option is taken; a 0 that it is not. The central column between the two lines in Table 3.5*a* represents a cease-fire situation. The set of outcomes represented by columns to the left of the cease-fire column

Table 3.5. North Vietnamese Preferences

	Cease-Fire								Settlement						
	Preferred					Not Preferred			Preferred				Not Preferred		
United States															
Cease bombing	1*	1	–	1*	1*	–	–	–	1*	1*	–	1*	–	–	–
Cease-Fire	1	1	–	1	1	0	–	0	1*	1	–	1*	0	–	–
Withdraw	0	1	0	0	0	0*	0	0*	1	–	0	1	0*	0	–
S.V.N.															
Cease-fire	1	–	1	0	1	0	0	–	1	0	1	1*	0	–	0
Settlement	–	–	–	0*	0	0*	0*	–	–	0*	–	1	0*	–	0*
N.V.N.															
Cease-fire	0	0	0	0	1	–	–	–	0	0	0	1*	–	–	–
Withdraw	0*	0*	0*	0*	0	–	–	–	0*	0*	0*	1	–	–	–
N.L.F.															
Cease-fire	–	–	0	0	1	–	1	1	–	0	0	1*	–	1	1
Settlement	–	–	0*	0*	0	–	–	–	–	0*	0*	1	–	–	–
	(*a*)								(*b*)						

are assumed to be preferred by North Vietnam to the cease-fire. The outcomes to the right of the cease-fire column are assumed not preferred by the North Vietnamese. There are certain logical implications requiring that if one option is taken by the party another option must also be taken. For example we assume that if the United States ceases fire she must also cease bombing. This is indicated on the charts by an asterisk over an option that is *implied*, that is, has to be taken because some other option has been taken.

The arrow at the bottom of Table 3.5*a* shows how North Vietnam can improve its position from the cease-fire by unilateral action (assuming the

Table 3.6. National Liberation Front Preferences

	Cease-Fire						Settlement					
	Preferred				Not Preferred		Preferred				Not Preferred	
United States												
Cease bombing	1*	–	1*	1*	–	–	1*	–	1*	1*	–	–
Cease-fire	1*	–	1	1	–	0	1*	–	1	1*	–	0
Withdraw	1	0	0	0	0	0*	1	0	0	1	0	0*
S.V.N.												
Cease-fire	–	1	0	1	0	0	–	1	0	1*	0	0
Settlement	–	–	0*	0	0*	0*	–	–	0*	1	0*	0*
N.V.N.												
Cease-fire	–	–	–	1	1*	–	–	–	–	1*	1*	–
Withdraw	–	–	0	0	1	–	–	–	0	1	1	–
N.L.F.												
Cease-fire	0	0	0	1	–	–	0	0	0	1*	–	–
Settlement	0*	0*	0*	0	–	–	0*	0*	0*	1	–	–
			(*a*)						(*b*)			

Table 3.7. South Vietnamese Preference

	Cease-Fire						Settlement			
	Preferred				Not Preferred		Preferred			Not Preferred
United States										
Cease bombing	1*	–	1*	1*	1*	1*	–	–	1*	1*
Cease-fire	1	0	1	1	1	1*	–	–	1*	1*
Withdraw	0	0*	–	0	–	1	0	–	1	1
S.V.N.										
Cease-fire	0	0	0	1	–	–	0	0	1*	–
Settlement	0*	0*	0*	0	–	–	0*	0*	1	–
N.V.N.										
Cease-fire	0	–	1	1	0	0	–	1	1*	0
Withdraw	0*	–	–	0	0	0*	–	–	1	0*
N.L.F.										
Cease-fire	1	–	–	1	0	1	–	–	1*	–
Settlement	–	–	–	0	0*	–	–	–	1	–
			(*a*)					(*b*)		

other parties' options remain fixed). The second arrow shows how reactions of the other parties to such a move can place the North Vietnamese in such a position that they are again unable to improve their position to better than the cease-fire position. These reactions we call the *sanctions* that could lead the North Vietnamese to accept the cease-fire. Our assumptions suffice to establish that these are the only sanctions that could accomplish this. The same interpretation applies to the other charts.

For each country we consider the sanctions that make a cease-fire stable and also those that make a negotiated settlement stable.

As can be seen from the assumptions about N.V.N. and N.L.F. preferences, the settlement option is to be interpreted as S.V.N. or N.L.F. acceptance by the S.V.N. and or N.L.F. of a negotiated settlement that is preferred by the N.V.N. and the N.L.F. to continued escalation.

3.8. COMMENTS ON GAMES, SPORTS, AND SPORTSMANSHIP

How people differ in their bargaining methods may depend on thinking patterns cultivated in games and sports. These patterns are often derived from zero-sum games and applied to bargaining situations with incomplete information (which are nonzero-sum).

In his book "Test Ban and Disarmament" Arthur Dean [17] has made an interesting observation which we hope to examine in this section in a slightly more general way to provoke some thinking on the subject. He said that a

"Soviet diplomat, like a skilled chess player, does not expect his opposite number to give up something for nothing, not even a pawn. He puts in this category any attempt to split the difference between two positions as a basis for compromise. He would take advantage of an indiscretion or a mistake and will stretch or cut statements to fit his political bed of Procrustes as he wishes."

The Russians are known to be good chess players, whereas Americans are poker fans. In this light the Cuban missle crisis has been interpreted as follows: The Russians pushed their missiles into Cuba and said "queen my pawn"; the Americans replied "we call."

The games played by a country's people from a very early age on provide primitive patterns for characterizing and developing attitudes toward competition later in life. Conversely, cultural and moral conditioning may lead to the selection of certain types of sports and games for channeling drives. It is in the nature of countries that are dedicated to games (particularly sports) to develop a highly competitive attitude. Such a country looks at its relations with the outside world in terms of competition and has a high degree of sympathy for, and a tendency to cooperate with, those who are willing to give it an opportunity for extending its spirit of competition and sportsmanship. This attitude must be carefully distinguished from aggression. A nation that does not make this distinction between competition and aggression may confuse the two. It may see an abundance of competitive spirit from another nation as aggression directed toward itself.

Men analyze game and sport situations more rationally and with greater objectivity than they do conflicts in which they are involved, mainly because the game has a traditional form that is not alien. Some become angry, hostile, and unsportsmanlike in games and sports because they are unable to accommodate the abilities of the other side in proper perspective.

Some sports are decided by few scorings, for example, football and soccer; others, such as basketball, by a large number of scorings. Bridge is a discrete game, where each hand or each rubber requires a calculation of a limited number of moves. Its resolution is much quicker than chess, which has such a large number of alternatives that it almost requires a continuous (as opposed to discrete) outlook as a guide for selecting moves. In most games the object is to compete to win, and a loser's valiant effort rarely counts. Some games accumulate scores over a season of competition in order to give more credit to those who make progress throughout, rather than those who win by small margins.

Although chess is a game of strategy involving scheming and evasive tactics, all indicating flexibility and sacrifice for possible future gain, backgammon is an example of a game of blocking the opponent while the player himself makes progress. It does not provide as wide an opportunity for matching wits but still has its subtleties as the player decides when it is more advantageous to block and when it is better to move forward. In popularity, backgammon outranks most other games in certain parts of the world, particularly in the Middle East. Go is a game of Chinese origin, widely played in Japan also. It allows the occupation of territory with strategies of encirclement and blocking.

What can be said about the impact of games on attitudes in the international scene?

1. People have a tendency to perceive situations as zero-sum (that is, the gain to one side is the loss to the other) whether they are or not. The majority of competitive games are zero-sum games. A nation that emphasizes zero-sum games may have a cultivated attitude that makes negotiations that are rarely zero-sum difficult to carry through.

2. This competitive win-lose approach shapes the attitudes and emotions of people as if situations are all or nothing. Games are primitive representations of real life.

3. Sportsmanship involves a certain useful altruism and willingness to give a share to the other side. Some games teach a spirit of cooperation and expose the person to conditions in which flexibility is required. Football is an example of a game that is cooperative within the team and competitive between teams.

NEGOTIATIONS FOR AGREEMENTS

Chapter 4

NEGOTIATIONS, BALANCE OF POWER ANALYSIS, INCOMPLETE INFORMATION

4.1. INTRODUCTION: SOME OBSERVATIONS ON BARGAINING AND NEGOTIATIONS

Conflicts sometimes occur by design and sometimes by the natural shaping of events. In general the solution of a problem giving rise to friction cannot be achieved without compromises. To be able to compromise, the parties in a conflict must be willing to enter into bargaining to reconcile their differences. A decision is then made based on the agreements of the bargain and occasionally means are found to monitor the peaceful fulfillment of the agreement. This is the rational process to pursue whenever several interests are involved. The solution agreed upon may not be optimal and may or may not be an improvement of the existing situation.

One technique used today is to have sufficient power in the background in order to encourage the other side to negotiate by giving him a strong hint of the futility of fighting. Power also ensures that the other side will conform to the bargain.

Still another technique for resolving conflicts is actually to fight. This technique is used mainly because the parties involved cannot foresee the outcome. Each party depends on a combination of luck and capability on its side, or accident and loss of control on the other side, to give it victory through battle. "War is an extension of diplomacy," Clausewitz maintained.

To enter into negotiations requires an attachment to the cause being served and an ability to see the problem from the opposite party's viewpoint. An interesting example of this ability is seen in labor conflicts. Both owner and worker have a vested interest in the continuation of the operation. A conflict may develop from within or from outside pressures (such as the rise of the cost-of-living index). Carefully organized techniques are developed to settle the conflict, perhaps including threats, but the responsible leaders of both sides must assume that there is a desire to continue a constructive exchange of views.

In the final analysis, little can be achieved by science in politics without the effective help of the negotiator who is familiar with policies and is aware that problems seen from divergent viewpoints cannot be solved without compromise.

In this framework we can distinguish between a diplomat and a politician. The former carefully studies the goals, objectives, and policies of his country and attempts to portray them successfully to other nations in order to make it easier for the two countries to come together in the solution of mutual problems. He may be able to show that the objectives of his country are not necessarily remote from those of another country. He should be able to distinguish between the natural long-term and the temporary objectives both of his country and of other countries. Little compromise can be made on natural objectives of national integrity, economic security, etc. They are independent of the government in power. They derive from the national character and the position of that country in the world. Temporary objectives may be related to dealing with powers and alliances which develop in various times of history.

A politician, on the other hand, presents himself as a person who is capable of understanding the objectives and goals of a group of people whom he wishes to represent. He then sets out to serve as a representative of these interests, attempting to attain the goals to the extent that he is able (or feels that in the national interest he should). A politician becomes a diplomat when he is successful in bringing the representatives of divergent interests together.

Both politicians and diplomats must be knowledgeable and able at the art of bargaining, otherwise they would lose advantage to their competitors who are also attempting to maximize for themselves within the conditions provided by the bargain. The approach would be to convince the other side of the mutual benefit that might result from compromising.

A politician is not bound by policy, hence is freer (within the constraint of wanting to be re-elected) to represent his group than a diplomat, who must interpret all his actions within the policy of his country. A major role of diplomats is to interpret the possible policies and actions of other nations in order to make the policies of their own country more effective. A politician attempts to shape policies by guiding the fulfillment of internal needs of the country. The two tasks are complementary.

Arthur Dean in his interesting book [17] makes several pointed comments on the art of negotiation. It has been observed, for example, that diplomats of some countries truly expect dogmatic hostility and nefarious purpose from their counterparts. Some diplomats, unaccustomed to unilateral concessions, become suspicious of the motives and reasons behind such an approach when it is followed by the other side. Some have been known to conclude that a concession is a weakness. On occasion diplomats of some countries have indicated a desire for agreement if a controversial part of a problem is withheld at that time by their opposite number, then later argued that the act of accepting to withhold the item is equivalent to withdrawing it from serious consideration.

Informal private contacts between negotiators facilitate the exchange of views, and provide an opportunity for each to inform the other more clearly regarding the positions of their governments and to indicate in general terms where successful agreement is most likely to be reached.

A diplomat must approach his negotiation projects without time pressures so that he will not feel impelled to make concessions to hasten an agreement.

It is a popular belief that bluffing is advantageous in diplomacy. Bluff, however, is accompanied by the danger of considerable loss in prestige and credibility resulting from making threats that are challenged and then not carried out. Diplomacy, as Dean points out, requires patience, persistence, calmness, tough-mindedness, imperviousness to insults, constant resourcefulness, and an unwillingness to be discouraged. A negotiator's arguments should be well thought out and he should be alert in negotiation so that essentials are not sacrificed.

The process of negotiation involves several steps starting with research and coordination within the framework of national policy on the issue to be negotiated and including estimates of the other parties possible positions (before formulating one's own positions), formulation of own positions, estimate of possible outcomes (which may be arranged according to desirability, feasibility, enforceability, good intentions, or intransigence), selection of initial strategy or position, confrontation, and settlement [31].

We have already mentioned in Chapter 3 that when maximizing the objectives of a single individual, the larger the set of possible choices, the larger the maximum value (or it may remain the same). In game theory this need not be the case. By restricting the set of strategies available to a player it is possible that he could obtain a more favorable solution.

Here are a few observations on negotiations influenced by Schelling [59]:

1. The power to constrain an adversary to accept a bargain may depend on the power to bind oneself and to convince the other side that one is not authorized to alter commitments.

2. Whatever position is adopted must appear credible to the other side. A man who knocks on a door and threatens to stab himself unless he gets $10, for example, is more likely to get his demand if his eyes are bloodshot.
3. The threat of mutual destruction would not work with an adversary who is unintelligent.
4. The ability to bluff the other side into thinking that the offer made is the maximum is useful. Deception may be an outright distortion of facts or a tactical maneuver to make him believe something you may not necessarily intend to adhere to.
5. An advantage may result to the one who is known to be unavailable to receive a bargaining message since he cannot be threatened.
6. An indispensable ability in negotiations is to be able to communicate the strength of commitment persuasively. To this end it is useful to instruct a bargaining agent that no changes are possible. He is then more convincing. Both sides may do this. The resolve may not necessarily be equal, however. If it is, an immovable position may result.
7. A large organization, for the sake of prestige and credibility, must carry out its threats or induce the other side to negotiate.
8. To maintain cooperation, penalties may be essential.
9. Threats require the ability to commit oneself to action and to convey a convincing intention to carry out the action.

Parties in negotiations often use the preservation of the status quo or the development of a new status quo in which they maintain the same relative positions, as a criterion for the balance of power. A mathematical model follows whose purpose is to define and analyze the notion of balance of power, which plays a significant role in negotiations.

4.2. AN ANALYSIS OF THE BALANCE OF POWER

In the case of negotiation with variable threat, the threat phase is competitive. Balance of power is the negotiation of threats. We use zero-sum game theory as a means to determine which threats are rational. Thus balance of power analysis defines the amount of concession that one can obtain from others. To develop the ideas further the following additional explanation of the importance of the concept of balance of power [27] is presented.

It is often argued that arms control and disarmament proposals (called "ACD proposals") will have little chance of mutual acceptance by two rival powers or power groups unless they tend to preserve the relative balance of power between the two sides, since neither side will voluntarily agree to proposals that would shift the existing balance of power to its own disadvantage. This makes it desirable

1. to find a precise theoretical definition for the notion of "preserving the existing balance and power," and
2. to investigate the policy implications of such a definition.

Of course, any definition, however precise it may be on an abstract theoretical level, will always be subject to considerable margins of error when applied to the real world, because of our incomplete information about the relevant variables and the imperfect fit of the theoretical model itself. In spite of this, however, it may provide valuable qualitative insights for the policy maker.

Game-theory provides a very suitable analytical model for finding the definition mentioned above, viz., Nash's theory of two-person cooperative games [35b].

Using Nash's theory we obtain the following definition. For each country i ($i = 1, 2$) let v_i denote its total peace-time military expenditure. Let w_i denote its total war-time military expenditure after the outbreak of hostilities. Let a_i be the total economic and noneconomic (for example, in terms of human life and happiness) damage that country i will suffer in a war. All these variables are assumed to be measured in utility units (although money measures may possibly be used as approximations in the case of purely economic costs). Then each country's war damage a_i will be an increasing function of the opponent's pre-war and war-time military expenditures v_j and w_j, and will be a decreasing function of its own pre-war and war-time military expenditures v_i and w_i. Thus

$$a_i = A_i(v_i, w_i; v_j, w_j), \quad i, j = 1, 2 \qquad j \neq i \tag{1}$$

but

$$\frac{\partial a_i}{\partial v_i} < 0 \quad \text{and} \quad \frac{\partial a_i}{\partial w_i} < 0 \tag{2}$$

$$\frac{\partial a_i}{\partial v_j} > 0 \quad \text{and} \quad \frac{\partial a_i}{\partial w_j} > 0 \tag{3}$$

Moreover, each country's total war costs will be

$$\eta_i = w_i + a_i = w_i + A_i(v_i, w_i; v_j, w_j). \tag{4}$$

That is, they will consist of the country's own war-time military expenditure w_i and the damage suffered from enemy action a_i. (We do not include the country's pre-war military expenditure v_i, since in war time this will be a matter of past history and no longer subject to present policy choices.)

Nash's theory says that a given country's relative power position (that is, its ability to obtain favorable settlements in outstanding international issues as a result of its military strength) will depend on the ratio of the total costs η_i the country itself would suffer in a war, to the total costs η_j the other side would suffer. Suppose the two countries agree to reduce their peace-time military expenditures v_i and v_j by some specified amounts Δv_i and Δv_j respectively. Then this agreement will preserve the two countries' relative power position if and only if it will leave the ratio

$$\eta_1/\eta_2 \tag{5}$$

unchanged. If the agreed changes $\Delta v_i = dv_i$ and $\Delta v_j = dv_j$ are sufficiently small, this is equivalent to the requirement that

$$d\eta_1/\eta_1 = d\eta_2/\eta_2 \tag{5}$$

This, in turn, is equivalent to requiring that

$$\left(\frac{\partial \eta_1}{\partial v_1} dv_1 + \frac{\partial \eta_1}{\partial v_2} dv_2\right) \Big/ \eta_1 = \left(\frac{\partial \eta_2}{\partial v_1} dv_1 + \frac{\partial \eta_2}{\partial v_2} dv_2\right) \Big/ \eta_2 \tag{7}$$

which can be written as

$$\left(\frac{\partial a_1}{\partial v_1} dv_1 + \frac{\partial a_1}{\partial v_2} dv_2\right) \Big/ (w_1 + a_1) = \left(\frac{\partial a_2}{\partial v_1} dv_1 + \frac{\partial a_2}{\partial v_2} dv_2\right) \Big/ (w_2 + a_2).$$

This requirement has the following intuitive interpretation. The relative balance of power between the two countries will be preserved if the ACD measures agreed on tend to change the costs of a war for both countries in the same proportion (for instance, if they reduce both countries' war costs by 10 per cent in utility terms).

This change in any given country's war costs, however, will itself be the resultant of two opposite forces. Any agreed-on decrease in the opponent's peace-time military expenditure v_j will tend to weaken the opponent's offensive capabilities and therefore will decrease the damages the country would suffer in a war. (That is, $\partial a_i/\partial v_j$, $i \neq j$ is always positive, and since dv_j is assumed to be negative, the whole term containing $\partial a_i/\partial v_j$ will be negative.) On the other hand, any agreed upon decrease in the country's own peace-time military expenditure v_i will tend to weaken its own defensive capabilities, and so will tend to increase the damages the country would suffer in a war. (That is, $\partial a_i/\partial v_i$ is always negative, and since dv_i is assumed to be negative, the whole term containing $\partial a_i/\partial v_i$ is positive.) In most cases, however, probably the first (favorable) effect will predominate.

We briefly summarize the policy implications of this model. The previous discussion shows that, at least in theory, the concept of "preserving the existing balance of power" can be given a reasonably precise mathematical meaning. But it is equally clear that in real life it will usually be very hard to predict how any given ACD agreement would affect the balance of power between the two parties (because it is very hard to predict how it would shift the costs of a war for each side). Thus any prediction—however careful, intelligent, and well informed—is always subject to considerable uncertainty.

This uncertainty seems to be the main obstacle to fast progress in the ACD field, because all major powers seem to have a strongly decreasing marginal utility for increases in their relative power. (In decision theory this type of utility function is called a utility function with strong aversion to risk.) In other words, any given country will tend to assign very high negative utility to the fact that a given ACD proposal might shift the balance of power to its own disadvantage, even if the probability of this is very small. On the other hand, it will tend to assign a relatively low positive utility to the fact that the same ACD proposal might equally well have the opposite effect and might actually shift the balance of power to its own advantage. The possibility of a favorable shift will not compensate for the possibility of an unfavorable shift, unless the magnitude and/or the probability of the former are much larger than the magnitude and the probability of the latter.

These considerations suggest that in order to improve the chances for ACD agreements it would be important to reduce the uncertainty about the likely effects of such measures on the two sides' relative power positions. It also would be very helpful to reduce the uncertainty about the two sides' true utility functions (that is, the importance they attach to alternative policy objectives, for example, to a higher standard of living for their own population as compared with military adventures). Any changes in the international situation that would reduce the importance of military power would decrease the significance of the uncertainty about the likely effects of ACD agreements on the two sides' power positions.

4.3. REVEALING INFORMATION IN NEGOTIATIONS

The problems of arms control may be studied through the analysis of the factors that contribute to the stability of arms races, the reduction of the probability of conflict, and the minimization of damage if conflict occurs. To produce such stability certain measures of agreement must be taken through negotiations leading to treaties. This process of negotiation is influenced by a number of factors among which two are significant: (a) the amount of information available to each side regarding what the other side wants; (b) the utilization of threats and counter threats to derive greater advantage.

Many situations in real life in which people face conflicting interests are not games treated by classical game theory, because usually the parties do not possess enough information either of their own or of their opponents' actual utility payoffs which result from the various choices of strategies. In addition, each may not know the amount of information available to the other.

We define a game with incomplete information as a game in which some or all players are ignorant about the other players' true payoff functions or about some other parameters of the game situation. Games with "incomplete" information must be sharply distinguished from games with "imperfect" information. In the latter the players are ignorant about some previous moves in the game but may be fully informed about all parameters characterizing the game situation at the beginning of the game before any moves have taken place.

One of the major difficulties in ACD negotiations is precisely the incomplete information the various participants have about one another's utility functions, true military strength and technological knowledge, information and assessment of the situation, and so on. Therefore games with incomplete information play a very essential rôle in the analysis of arms control and disarmament problems, and progress in the theory of these games is essential for better understanding of ACD problems.

It is a case of incomplete information for almost any conflict in which weapon systems are involved, because military secrets are highly guarded. Thus any consideration of gradual disarmament treaties should take into account the possibility that the course taken in performing the terms of a treaty may reveal highly safeguarded military secrets.

Suppose, for example, that a gradual disarmament procedure is being proposed, under which both the United States and the Soviet Union desire the gradual destruction of a given collection of weapons. One way of doing so is to let each country divide its own remaining collection each year into, for instance, ten parts and to let the other country choose which part should be destroyed. Clearly, a "naive" way of choosing may reveal secret military preferences and advantage can be taken of this when the remainder is to be divided.

In order to better grasp the intricacies that may govern the choice of action on each side, think of the following "simple" situation involving two brothers, Tom and Dick, who must divide between them a cake with a cherry. Suppose Tom is indifferent to cherries and does not care whether there is a cherry in his part or not; and suppose that Tom knows that Dick likes cake but also knows that Dick loves cherries. Using the foregoing procedure he would then divide the cake into unequal portions, leaving the cherry in the smaller part, knowing that his brother would select this part, leaving him with the greater portion of the cake. How small the portion with the cherry should be depends on Tom's knowledge of the amount of cake that Dick would be willing to sacrifice for the cherry. Clearly, it is advantageous for Dick to hide his preference for cherries, or at least to give the impression that such a preference is small.

Consider a case in which Dick knows that Tom is indifferent to cherries, whereas, unknown to Tom, but suspected by him, Dick loves cherries. In addition, Dick knows that Tom is not certain of his preference. Suppose, however, that both brothers also know that they will have to divide a cake every day for many days. It is logical to suppose that Tom should test his brother's preferences by cutting the cake into different sizes the first few days and checking which part Dick chooses. If Dick always selects the part he really prefers, he will reveal in a few days his trading price, and henceforth Tom will be able to take full advantage of the knowledge thus acquired.

How should Dick act? Should he act as if he does not love cherries? Should he choose the smallest portion in a random way, according to a fixed probability? Or should he act in yet another way?

In the terminology of game theory, these examples are situations in which the players are to play a game at several, or even an infinite number of, stages, where at least one of the players is not quite sure about the true payoffs, and where the moves (but not the partial payoffs) chosen by the players at each stage become known after this stage and before the next one.

By saying that a player is not quite sure about the true payoffs, we mean that the player has a certain probability distribution over all the possibilities, and the other player may be "not quite sure" about the nature of this probability distribution.

We emphasize that this is one of the simplest examples of such games. Some results of a general nature can be stated for these examples and for games that are slightly more complicated.

The traditional approach to games with incomplete information has been to analyze them in terms of the players' reciprocal expectations. Thus, for instance, in a two-person game player I will form some expectation about the nature of player II's payoff function U_2 whereas player II will form some expectation about the nature of player I's payoff function U_1; these may be called the two players' first-order expectations. Then each player may form some estimate of the other player's first-order expectation and this estimate may be called his second-order expectation.

Player I's second-order expectation is what he believes player II thinks of his own payoff function U_1. Then each player may form some third-order expectation about the other player's second-order expectation, and so on ad infinitum. It is easy to see that this approach does not lead to an analytically tractable mathematical model.

Two instances of games with incomplete information are studied here. The first is an infinite-stage zero-sum game in which the opponent is known but the payoff matrix is not known. The second example is a one-shot game, which need not be zero-sum, in which the game, that is, the payoff, corresponding to each opponent is known, but the opponent himself is unknown. Thus there is a probability distribution over the payoffs of the opponents.

4.4. MODELS OF GAMES WITH INCOMPLETE INFORMATION [2]

Consider a two-person, constant-sum game which is played repeatedly. Assume first that player I knows exactly the payoff matrix of this game, but player II knows only that this game is one of several m by n constant-sum matrix games $G_1, G_2, \ldots, G_\alpha$ of which he knows the payoffs, called stage games. On the other hand, player II has a probability distribution $(\bar{p}_1, \bar{p}_2, \ldots, \bar{p}_\alpha) \equiv \bar{p}$ $(\bar{p}_i \geq 0, i = 1, \ldots, \alpha, \Sigma\bar{p}_i = 1)$ over the corresponding matrices and this distribution is assumed to be known to player I. It is also assumed that the situation repeats itself indefinitely using the same G_i and p_i, $i = 1, \ldots, \alpha$. As the play of a stage game is completed, the strategies chosen are announced. The payoffs are not disclosed to player II, however, but are credited to each player's account. Player I can, of course, observe them at the end of the play. Let $\Gamma_\infty(\bar{p})$ denote this game with incomplete information and let its value, if it exists, be denoted by $v_\infty(\bar{p})$. The object of each player is to maximize the expected average payoffs that he receives at each stage. We also denote by Γ_n, $n = 1, 2, \ldots$, the game that results if the players play in stages.

To analyze this game consider a related game $\Delta(p)$ with payoff $u(p)$, which is played only once and in which it is assumed that neither player is informed about the actual payoff matrix and that both have the same probability distribution given by $(p_1, \ldots, p_\alpha)$ over the stage games $G_1, \ldots, G_\alpha$. It has been proved by Aumann and Maschler [2] that $v_\infty(\bar{p})$ exists and $v_\infty(\bar{p}) = \underset{0 \leq p \leq 1}{\text{cav}}\ u(p)$ at $p = \bar{p}$. The concavification (or least concave majorant) of $u(p)$, that is, cav $u(p)$ is the smallest concave function that is not less than $u(p)$. (A function $f(x)$ is concave if for any two values x and y, $f(\lambda x + (1 - \lambda)y) \geq \lambda f(x) + (1 - \lambda)f(y)$, $0 \leq \lambda \leq 1$, i.e., it looks like the rainbow curve as seen from beneath.) Thus, for example, if $\alpha = 2$:

$$v_\infty(\bar{p}) = \max_{p^L \le \bar{p} \le p^R} [\lambda u(p^L) + (1 - \lambda)u(p^R)]$$

where λ is chosen so that $0 \le \lambda \le 1$ and $\lambda p^L + (1 - \lambda)p^R = \bar{p}$ (see Figure 21). Consequently, the problem has been reduced to the computation of $u(p)$ for all values of p. Before giving a description of the optimal strategies of each player, look at the three examples in Table 4.1. In each example the stage game is given and its corresponding one-shot game and the payoff for the zero-sum game are obtained in the usual way. Finally, a plot of the payoff and its concavification is given.

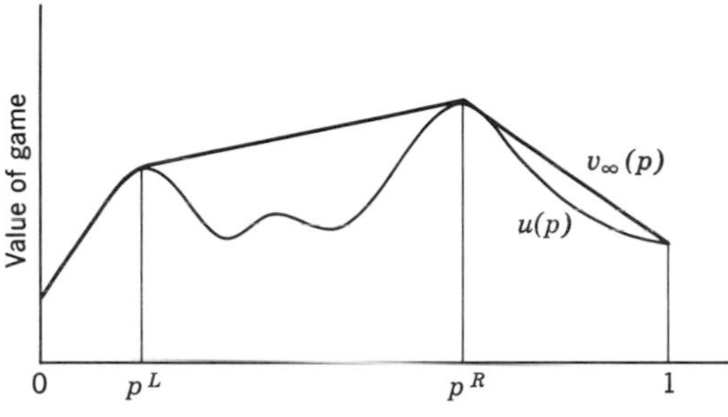

Figure 21

Consider the first game. In Γ_1, player I, who knows which of the two payoff matrices is the one being played, chooses the first row if G_1 is being played and the second row in the opposite case. Player II (to make his decision he will have to multiply each matrix by its probability, add all matrices, and look at the resulting matrix) should choose the first column if $p < \frac{1}{2}$ and the second if $p > \frac{1}{2}$. He expects to pay player I, $v_1 \equiv \min(p, 1 - p)$. Player I cannot continue to play the same strategy if the players replay the game on to Γ_∞, for then player II will discover whether it is G_1 or G_2 and he will select an appropriate column which guarantees him paying zero at each stage. If player I acts as if he himself also does not know which of the two games is being played, we obtain the one-shot game. If he does this at every stage, then the payoff used for the one-shot game would apply at every stage. As can be seen from that game, player I can expect $u(p) = p(1 - p)$ (calculated as the payoff of a zero-sum, two-person game) at every stage, which is an improvement on getting zero.

Remark. When Γ_n is being considered, we refer each time to the expectations from the point of view of player II, that is, his average

Table 4.1

	Stage Game	One-Shot Game, $\Delta(p)$	Expected Payoff $u(p)$ of $\Delta(p)$	Concavification from Geometry; Value of the Game
(1) Player I	Player II G_1: $\begin{array}{c\|cc} & B_1 & B_2 \\ \hline A_1 & 1 & 0 \\ A_2 & 0 & 0 \end{array}$ p G_2: $\begin{array}{c\|cc} & B_1 & B_2 \\ \hline A_1 & 0 & 0 \\ A_2 & 0 & 1 \end{array}$ $1 - p$ Repetition of the same game an ∞ number of times	$\begin{array}{c\|cc} & B_1 & B_2 \\ \hline A_1 & p & 0 \\ A_2 & 0 & 1-p \end{array}$	$p(1 - p)$	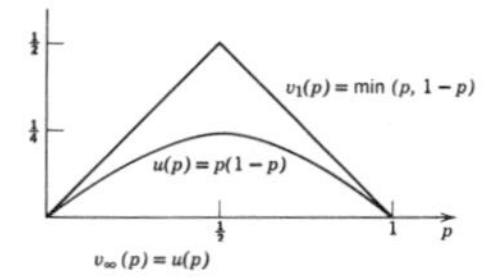
(2) Player I	Player II G_1: $\begin{array}{c\|cc} & B_1 & B_2 \\ \hline A_1 & -1 & 0 \\ A_2 & 0 & 0 \end{array}$ p G_2: $\begin{array}{c\|cc} & B_1 & B_2 \\ \hline A_1 & 0 & 0 \\ A_2 & 0 & -1 \end{array}$ $1 - p$ Repetition of the same game an ∞ number of times	$\begin{array}{c\|cc} & B_1 & B_2 \\ \hline A_1 & -p & 0 \\ A_2 & 0 & -(1-p) \end{array}$	$-p(1 - p)$	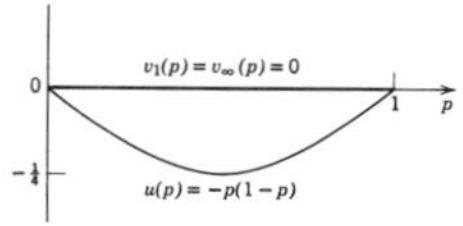
(3) Player I	Player II G_1: $\begin{array}{c\|cc} & B_1 & B_2 \\ \hline A_1 & 1 & 0 \\ A_2 & 0 & 2 \end{array}$ p G_2: $\begin{array}{c\|cc} & B_1 & B_2 \\ \hline A_1 & -2 & 0 \\ A_2 & 0 & -1 \end{array}$ $1 - p$ Repetition of the same game an ∞ number of times	$\begin{array}{c\|cc} & B_1 & B_2 \\ \hline A_1 & 3p-2 & 0 \\ A_2 & 0 & 3p-1 \end{array}$	$\left.\begin{array}{ll} \dfrac{(3p-1)(3p-2)}{3(2p-1)}, & \begin{array}{l} 0 \le p \le \frac{1}{3} \\ \frac{2}{3} \le p \le 1 \end{array} \\ 0 & \frac{1}{3} \le p \le \frac{2}{3} \end{array}\right.$	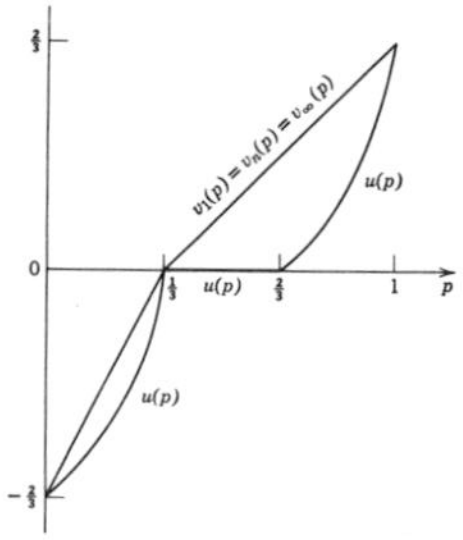

expected payment to player I. The average expected payoff that player I expects to get depends on the actual game which is being played at each stage.

If the players play optimally in Γ_1, for example, player I will receive zero if G_1 is being played and $p > \frac{1}{2}$, and he will receive 1 if G_1 is being played and $p < \frac{1}{2}$. Both numbers are different in general from min $(p, 1 - p)$. If G_2 is being played he will receive 1 if $p > \frac{1}{2}$ and 0 if $p < \frac{1}{2}$. It can be shown, however, that regardless of which game is taking place at the various stages, player I can do better than to use a min-max strategy against player II's interests.

It is reasonable to expect that player I should do better. In fact it can be proved that for any finite number of stages he can do better, but in the long run, that is, in Γ_∞, for this particular game he can only assure himself $u(p)$, that is, $v_\infty(p) = u(p)$ and thus the extra knowledge is not helpful.

If the payoff is that of the second example, player I should, at every stage, choose the second row if G_1 is being played and the first in the contrary case. Thus $v_1(p) = v_n(p) = v_\infty(p) = 0$, $n = 2, 3, \ldots$; however, $u(p) = -p(1 - p)$. In this case the knowledge player I has would be helpful, and revealing this knowledge to his opponent would not harm him.

In the third example player I can force player II to pay more than $u(p)$ except when $p = 0, \frac{1}{3}$, or 1. If he plays optimally in Γ_n, he can force player II to pay him an expected average amount which is equal to $v_1(p)$ given by

$$v_1(p) = \begin{cases} -\frac{2}{3}(1 - 3p) & 0 \le p \le \frac{1}{3} \\ \frac{1}{3}(3p - 1) & \frac{1}{3} \le p \le 1 \end{cases}.$$

In this case, player I should play at each stage as if he were playing optimally in a one-shot game whose payoff is $v_1(p_i)$. Here, p_i, $i = 1, 2, \ldots$ is the conditional probability that game G_1 is actually being played as computed by a player who knows p, and who knows that player I is playing according to the one-shot game strategy, and what player I's choices were at stages $1, 2, \ldots, i - 1$.

If this strategy is used, the probability of eventually discovering the actual game which is being played is less than 1 (in general, it is equal to $\frac{1}{4}$ when $p = \frac{1}{2}$). Thus this strategy can be said to partially reveal the actual game. Here $v_\infty(p) = v_1(p) = v_n(p)$. In general, it is not true that $v_\infty(p)$ is equal to $v_1(p)$ or to $u(p)$. However, we have $u(p) \le v_1(p)$.

Theorem. The value of $\Gamma_\infty(p)$ exists and is the concavification of $u(p)$, the value of $\Delta(p)$ in which neither player knows which is the true alternative but both have the same probability distribution p over the alternatives.

In the analysis of strategies, we first describe how player I should choose his optimal strategies. Suppose that $\alpha = 2$ (there are two payoff matrices G_1 and G_2) and note, as previously shown, that $\bar{p}$ determines p^L and p^R, which are the maxima of $u(p)$ at the two extremes of the graph. Player I should act so that if player II discovers this strategy he finds that the probability distribution is either p^L or p^R. If $\bar{\lambda}$ and $1 - \bar{\lambda}$ are the probabilities of these two events, since $\bar{p}$ is the a priori distribution, we have

$$\bar{\lambda}p^L + (1 - \bar{\lambda})p^R = \bar{p}.$$

After this act on the first play of the game, player I will henceforth play at each stage as if he himself is facing $u(p^L)$ or $u(p^R)$. One method of effecting such a strategy follows:

Let the numbers s and t satisfy $0 \leq s, t \leq 1$ and

$$\frac{\bar{p}_1 s}{\bar{p}_1 s + \bar{p}_2 t} = p_1{}^L \qquad \frac{\bar{p}_1(1 - s)}{\bar{p}_1(1 - s) + \bar{p}_2(1 - t)} = p_1{}^R$$

where

$$\bar{p} = (\bar{p}_1, \bar{p}_2),\ p^L = (p_1{}^L, p_2{}^L),\ p^R = (p_1{}^R, p_2{}^R).$$

Player I should have two coins, the first with probability s of turning a head and the second with probability t of turning a head. He flips the first coin if G_1 is being played and the second in the opposite instance. If heads appear, the conditional probability can be shown to be p^L; if tails appear, this probability is p^R. By observing the coins without knowing which is which, player II can deduce this new probability distribution to be used by player I.

Player II's strategy essentially consists of mixing his choices at each stage (this mixture is too complicated to give here) so that he is acting more against those a priori stage games in which he is worse off, up to the stage for which he is considering the strategy.

The idea of a stage game may be viewed as a simplified first step in analyzing gradual reduction in arms, for example. The reductions are to be made over each year (corresponding to a stage of the game) and each country has alternatives regarding which weapons to destroy. The model just given assumes the same payoffs, however, and we must consider a game whose payoffs change from stage to stage.

In addition, the payoffs in the real case need not be zero-sum and this is being investigated. Finally, the game need not be repeated indefinitely but only over a small number of stages. The assumption that one side knows the nature of a situation and the other does not has a number of realistic justifications. It also enables each side to look at the unfavorable aspects of negotiation situations in which it has no knowledge about what the other side's policy is. We shall soon turn to the more frequently encountered phenomenon in which neither side knows the exact payoff matrix. There is always the problem of how to estimate the payoffs, but however they are estimated, which is done implicitly in practice, the theory gives some general useful suggestions and conclusions arising out of the novel context in which it is formulated. For a person concerned with the utility problem (recall the cake-cutting example), this line of approach seems to be an excellent and promising alternative.

In real life, in the absence of complete information one attempts to place a probability distribution on the available possible alternatives through analysis and evaluation made by experts. This probability distribution will generally change when more facts regarding the actions of the opposite side become available. In conducting negotiations, the value of an exchange of ideas is to provide better estimates of the other side's intentions even when agreements are not readily reached. It is important to note, however, that this is a two-way process that also reveals information to the other side, some of which it may not be desirable to disclose.

If this approach is developed to the extent that it is closer to the real life situation, it would be possible to say precisely what degree of information should be revealed or withheld. We have now learned that *any attempt to make use of information not available to a wise opponent results in partially revealing this information to him.*

The strategies of player I just described involve partial and systematic utilization of this information. In fact, the model indicates that if player I is a negotiator, it may be advantageous to his country if he is not given all the information available so that he will not be faced with deciding how much of it he should reveal in his discussions.

Certain games, as in the first example, show that the player who has the information cannot benefit by using it and thus he proceeds to play as in the one-shot game. There are other cases where only a partial and determinate amount of the information should be used. In fact, this is the type of strategy sometimes used where information is released only partially by subjecting it to rumors and a variety of interpretations in order to let the other side grasp only a part of it. The present approach underlines the importance of this technique and emphatically shows that *putting all cards on the table may be a great disadvantage* and has the tendency to create a feeling of expecting to gain more where, in fact, one would end up gaining less. The most important object is to keep both sides interested in negotiations so they can approach each other; no negotiations, no stage games.

4.5. LACK OF INFORMATION ON BOTH SIDES

If both players have only partial knowledge of the true payoffs then two possibilities may occur:

1. The beliefs are consistent with a joint probability distribution (the consistent case).
2. The beliefs are inconsistent.

Example. Suppose the true game is one of four games arranged in a square:

	II_A	II_B
I_A	G_1	G_2
I_B	G_3	G_1

and assume that player I is told in which row the true game is located. Suppose also that player II is told in which column the true game is located. We shall say that player I is of type A if he is told that the game is located in the first row and that he is of type B if he is told that the game is located in the second row. Similarly, we shall call player II type A or B according to his information. To make things more complicated, we shall assume that each type of player may differ from the other type of the same player by his evaluation of the situation; that is, his beliefs on the type of his opponent. Thus the information on the beliefs can be summarized in the following two matrices:

Player I's belief

	II_A	II_B
I_A	$\frac{1}{2}$	$\frac{1}{2}$
I_B	$\frac{1}{3}$	$\frac{2}{3}$

Player II's belief

	II_A	II_B
I_A	$\frac{3}{5}$	$\frac{3}{7}$
I_B	$\frac{2}{5}$	$\frac{4}{7}$

which, for example, express the following facts: Player I type A believes that the probabilities that his opponent is of type A or B are equal (and therefore he thinks he plays either G_1 or G_2 with equal probabilities). Player II type B thinks that his opponent is of type A with probability $\frac{3}{7}$, and so on. Finally, we assume that the foregoing matrices are known to both players, as is the foregoing description.

This is an example of consistent beliefs, because the matrices could be drawn from a joint probability distribution

$$\begin{pmatrix} \frac{1}{4} & \frac{1}{4} \\ \frac{1}{6} & \frac{1}{3} \end{pmatrix}$$

where the entries represent an a priori probability distribution on which of the games G_1, G_2, G_3, G_4 is the true game. To compute this matrix we consider the general form of a matrix of a joint probability distribution

$$\begin{pmatrix} a & b \\ c & d \end{pmatrix}.$$

From player I's matrix we must have

$$\frac{a}{a+b} = \frac{1}{2}, \frac{b}{a+b} = \frac{1}{2}, \frac{c}{c+d} = \frac{1}{3}, \frac{d}{c+d} = \frac{2}{3}.$$

We must also have from player II's matrix

$$\frac{a}{a+c} = \frac{3}{5}, \frac{c}{a+c} = \frac{2}{5}, \frac{b}{b+d} = \frac{3}{7}, \frac{d}{b+d} = \frac{4}{7}.$$

We have consistency if we get the same values for a, b, c, d in both cases.

If, however, the players' beliefs are given by

	II_A	II_B
I_A	$\frac{1}{3}$	$\frac{2}{3}$
I_B	$\frac{1}{3}$	$\frac{2}{3}$

	II_A	II_B
I_A	$\frac{3}{5}$	$\frac{3}{7}$
I_B	$\frac{2}{5}$	$\frac{4}{7}$

then it is easy to check that no probability matrix

$$\begin{pmatrix} a & b \\ c & d \end{pmatrix}$$

exists with

$$\frac{a}{a+c} = \frac{3}{5}, \frac{b}{b+d} = \frac{3}{7}, \frac{a}{a+b} = \frac{1}{3}, \frac{c}{c+d} = \frac{1}{3}.$$

This would be an example of an inconsistent case.

At present very little can be said about the inconsistent case. All that is known is that it can be reduced to a repeated two-person, *nonconstant-sum* game in the following sense.

For each repeated game Γ_∞ with inconsistent matrices of beliefs, with a stage game which is either constant-sum or nonconstant-sum, there corresponds a repeated, in general, nonconstant-sum game Γ_∞^* (whose structure is completely known) so that each equilibrium strategy-tuple (if such exists) for Γ_∞^* is essentially an equilibrium strategy-tuple for Γ_∞.

For the consistent case, the full answer is known. First, each consistent game essentially can be reduced to a game in which the joint probability distribution is a distribution of independent events. The events are to be player I of types A or B and to be player II of types A or B. The matrix

$$\begin{pmatrix} \frac{1}{4} & \frac{1}{4} \\ \frac{1}{6} & \frac{1}{3} \end{pmatrix}$$

does not represent independent events; but the matrix

$$\begin{array}{c|cc} & \frac{1}{4} & \frac{3}{4} \\ \hline \frac{1}{3} & \frac{1}{12} & \frac{1}{4} \\ \frac{2}{3} & \frac{1}{6} & \frac{1}{2} \end{array}$$

does.

The way to achieve an equivalent presentation with a joint matrix of independent events is simply to choose such a matrix and then change the payoffs in the stage games in such a way that in terms of expectations the final payoff remains the same.

The discussion may therefore be restricted to the consistent-independent case, where it is meaningful to speak of the probability p of player I to be of type A, and the probability q of player II to be of type A. For simplicity, we discuss the case in which each player can only be one of two types. The result can be immediately generalized if more types exist. Therefore we speak of the one-shot game Δ in which nature decides with probabilities p and q whether players I and II will be of type A (making independent lotteries) and both players are not told what the decision was. Let $u(p, q)$ be the value of Δ as a function of p and q. It has been shown that by strategies similar to those just stated, player I can guarantee to receive in $\Gamma_\infty(\bar{p}, \bar{q})$ at least

$$v_\infty(\bar{p}, \bar{q}) \equiv \operatorname*{cav}_p \operatorname*{vex}_q u(p, q) \qquad \text{at} \quad (p, q) = (\bar{p}, \bar{q}),$$

where vex $f(x)$ is the largest convex function (reverse the inequality in the definition of a concave function given previously) which is not greater than $f(x)$, $0 \leq x \leq 1$. Similarly, player II can guarantee for himself not to pay more than

$$\bar{v}_\infty(\bar{p}, \bar{q}) \equiv \operatorname*{vex}_q \operatorname*{cav}_p u(p, q) \qquad \text{at} \quad (p, q) = (\bar{p}, \bar{q}).$$

Thus, if $v_\infty(\bar{p}, \bar{q}) = \bar{v}_\infty(\bar{p}, \bar{q})$, the repeated game has a value and we also know the optimal strategies for both players.

We know that $u(p, q)$ is a surface lying above the unit square. Obviously, many such surfaces exist for which vex cav = cav vex. R. Stearns and J. Aumann also constructed games whose $u(p, q)$ surface has this property [2, 68]. For some time the question remained open regarding whether such a game has a value.

An important achievement of Stearns [68] was proving that there is no strategy for player I which guarantees him more than the foregoing cav vex and there is no strategy for player II which guarantees him more than vex cav. Therefore such games have no value.

So far we have assumed that after each stage the actions of the players are being revealed. This may be an unrealistic assumption in many real life situations. Replacing the matrix representation of a stage game by a tree we can represent various information patterns that become known at the end of each stage (including the case of no information on the actions). All the preceding theorems remain true with slight modification in this general set-up. Moreover, it is not necessary to assume that the same stage game remains unchanged from stage to stage. The results hold true if the stage games "look the same" to each player and many moves that do not enter the information sets of such player are different from one stage to another.

It has been mentioned that the time element plays an important role in real life.

Games with Discount Factor [44a]

The payoff matrices of a repeated game may be discounted from stage to stage using the same constant factor $0 \leq r \leq 1$. Thus every element of the matrices is multiplied by r for the second stage, by r^2 for the third, and so on. We now examine this type of game and underline its practical importance.

A serious disadvantage of undiscounted infinite-stage games is that no finite number of stages makes any difference in the payoff, because we are looking at the long-run average. Thus what one does in any particular stage does not matter because the criterion is the infinitely long-run average. Therefore undiscounted games never tell what strategy to play at present but only in the long run. When a game is a two-sided, incomplete information game the undiscounted case does not even tell the long-run strategy because rational play is undefined. There are two ways of considering that game: defensively and offensively. Unlike the situation for finite zero-sum games, these solutions are different.

If there are timing problems, for example, when to make a threat or how valuable it is to win first, then those problems can be taken into account as discounted games. Solutions to such games always exist in the sense that a strategy can be computed (although this is difficult in practice) for each player which will dictate his actions in each stage. The existence and uniqueness applies to the bilateral incomplete information case, although finding the solution is more difficult than in the unilateral case. When the discount rate is $r = 0$ the discounted game is equivalent to the one-shot game; when $r = 1$ the discounted game is equivalent to the infinite-stage undiscounted game. For values of r in $0 < r < 1$, we have discounted games. The problem for this last case is to strike a good balance (which can be expressed algebraically but is difficult to give here) between the immediate benefit of the present payoff and the long-run benefit of concealing information. The information that one might try to conceal in the infinite-stage game will be entirely revealed in the discounted game over a large number of stages.

For a small discount rate, that is, when the emphasis is largely on the immediate future, the payoff function can be computed by a simple recursion, so that a simple number-theoretic computation will permit us to get the result for any rational value of the probability. However, because the one-shot payoff function has a corner—a point of discontinuity for the derivative—the payoff function for r has a corner too. In fact, it has infinitely many corners because it has a discontinuous derivative wherever p is rational. On the other hand, when the discount factor is larger (in this example, when $r \geq \frac{1}{3}$) the optimal behavior on the part of player I is always to play a mixed strategy, whichever stage game alternative is chosen in the random move. Under these circumstances, the maximum over the dummy parameter in the recursion equation always occurs in the interior of its interval, and it appears that the payoff function will be differentiable, except at a finite number of points.

Aumann and Maschler [2] have discovered the complete conditions for equilibrium point solutions of the two-person nonzero-sum repeated and undiscounted game of incomplete information in which only one side has information on his opponent. A basic principle is that the uninformed player's estimate of the other player's type must be consistent with the actions revealed by the other player's strategies. This says that at any time this player has received information that he can process by observing the other player's play. The results are generally not unique and conditions for uniqueness are not known. As yet nothing is known about convergence.

The case of incomplete information for both sides appears very difficult. The characterization suggests the use of signaling in bargaining. Dropping hints is an example of signaling. It allows the correlation of bargaining strategies. An interesting lesson learned is that the relation, repetition with the use of threads implies cooperation, which holds under complete information does not hold here.

4.6. THE TYPE OF OPPONENT

Under a wide range of conditions any game with incomplete information can be represented by a model of the following form. Each player i ($i = 1, \ldots, n$) may belong to any one of k_i possible attribute classes or "types," differing in their psychological characteristics (for example, in their utility functions); in the economic, military, and other resources available to them; in the amount of information they have about the other players; etc. Each player knows his own type but generally is ignorant about the other players' types. All players know the joint probabilities of all possible type combinations for the n players, however.

More formally, the true payoff function of each player i is of the form:

$$x_i = U_i(s_1, \ldots, s_i, \ldots, s_n) \tag{1}$$

where $s_1, \ldots, s_i, \ldots, s_n$ are the strategies of players $1, \ldots, i, \ldots, n$. The function U_i, however, will generally be unknown to players $1, \ldots, i-1, i+1, \ldots, n$ (and may be unknown even to player i himself). But we can write player i's payoff function in the form:

$$\begin{aligned} x_i &= U_i(s_1, \ldots, s_i, \ldots, s_n) \\ &= V_i(s_1, \ldots, s_i, \ldots, s_n; c_1, \ldots, c_i, \ldots, c_n) \end{aligned} \tag{2}$$

where $c_1, \ldots, c_i, \ldots, c_n$ are vectors consisting of those parameters of the game situation which are known only to player $1, \ldots$, or to player $i, \ldots$, or to player n respectively, whereas the function V_i itself is known to all n players. (This last assumption is permissible because all those parameters of the payoff function U_i which are not known to all n players are incorporated into the vectors $c_1, \ldots, c_i, \ldots, c_n$.)

For each player i the vector c_i summarizes the special information that player i has about the game, and so may be called player i's information vector. Alternatively, this vector c_i can also be interpreted as representing player i's "type," that is, his personal attributes unknown to the other players, and so may be called his attribute vector or type vector.

Although each player i will know only his own type vector (or attribute vector or information vector) c_i, all players will know the joint probability distribution $R^* \equiv R^*(c_1, \ldots, c_n)$ of these type vectors $c_1, \ldots, c_n$ for all n players. Since each player i will know his own type vector c_i, however, he will actually assess the probability that the other $(n-1)$ players will belong to some specific combination of types $c_1, \ldots, c_{i-1}, c_{i+1}, \ldots, c_n$, not in terms of the probability distribution R^* itself, but rather in terms of the corresponding conditional probability distribution

$$R_i^* = R^*(c_1, \ldots, c_{i-1}, c_{i+1}, \ldots, c_n|c_i) \tag{3}$$

Using this model as a start, Harsanyi has defined solution concepts for various classes of games with incomplete information. For example, for two-person bargaining games with incomplete information the appropriate solution concept is a certain generalization of Nash's solution for two-person bargaining games (which itself originally has been defined on the assumption of complete information).

Nash's original solution concept is defined as follows. Let P be the set of all feasible payoff vectors $u = (u_1, u_2)$ in the game. Let $t = (t_1, t_2)$ be the conflict payoff vector specifying the conflict payoffs t_1 and t_2 that the two players would obtain if they could not agree on any feasible payoff vector $u \in P$ as the outcome of the game. Then the Nash solution will be that particular payoff vector $u = (u_1^*, u_2^*)$ which maximizes the Nash product

$$\pi = (u_1 - t_1) \cdot (u_2 - t_2) \tag{4}$$

subject to the constraints

$$u = (u_1, u_2) \epsilon P \tag{5}$$

and

$$u_1 \geq t_1, u_2 \geq t_2. \tag{6}$$

This solution concept can be generalized to two-person bargaining games with incomplete information as follows. Suppose that player I's type vector c_1 can take K different values, whereas player II's type vector c_2 can take M different values. We can write

$$c_1 = c_1{}^1, \ldots, c_1{}^k, \ldots, c_1{}^K \tag{7}$$

and

$$c_2 = c_2{}^1, \ldots, c_2{}^m, \ldots, c_2{}^M. \tag{8}$$

If the two players agree on any given joint strategy s chosen from the set of all feasible joint strategies $S = \{s\}$, then they will receive the payoffs

$$x_1 = V_1(s; c_1{}^k, c_2{}^m) \tag{9}$$

and

$$x_2 = V_2(s; c_1{}^k, c_2{}^m) \tag{10}$$

where $c_1 = c_1{}^k$ and $c_2 = c_2{}^m$ are the type vectors of player I and player II respectively.

Let

$$r_{km} = R^*(c_1 = c_1{}^k \quad \text{and} \quad c_2 = c_2{}^m) \tag{11}$$

be the joint probability density function corresponding to the probability distribution $R^*(c_1, c_2)$.

As player I will know only his own type vector $c_1 = c_1{}^k$ but will not know his opponent's type vector $c_2 = c_2{}^m$, he will not be able to predict the actual payoff x_1 he will receive if he and his opponent agree on some specific joint strategy $s \epsilon S$. All he will be able to compute will be his conditional payoff expectation

$$x_1^k = E(x_1|c_1 = c_1^k) = \frac{\sum_{m=1}^{M} r_{km} V_1(s;\ c_1^k,\ c_2^m)}{\sum_{m=1}^{M} r_{km}}. \tag{12}$$

Similarly, player II will be able to compute only his own conditional payoff expectation

$$x_2^m = E(x_2|c_2 = c_2^m) = \frac{\sum_{k=1}^{K} r_{km} V_2(s;\ c_1^k,\ c_2^m)}{\sum_{k=1}^{K} r_{km}}.$$

Thus the expected outcome of using a given joint strategy s can be best described by specifying the two players' conditional payoff expectations $x_1^1, \ldots, x_1^k, \ldots, x_1^K$ and $x_2^1, \ldots, x_2^m, \ldots, x_2^M$ for all possible values $c_1 = c_1^1, \ldots, c_1^k, \ldots, c_1^K$ and $c_2 = c_2^1, \ldots, c_2^m, \ldots, c_2^M$ of the two players' type vectors c_1 and c_2. Let

$$x = (x_1^1, \ldots, x_1^k, \ldots, x_1^K;\ x_2^1, \ldots, x_2^m, \ldots, x_2^M) \tag{13}$$

be the $(K + M)$ vector formed from these conditional expectations. We shall call x the conditional payoff vector corresponding to this joint strategy s. Let $P = \{x\}$ be the set of all conditional payoff vectors x corresponding to feasible joint strategies $s \in S$.

Finally, let

$$t_1 = T_1(c_1^k, c_2^m) \tag{14}$$

and

$$t_2 = T_2(c_1^k, c_2^m) \tag{15}$$

be the conflict payoffs that the two players would receive if they could not agree on any feasible joint strategy $s \in S$.

The corresponding conditional payoff expectations will be

$$t_1^k = \frac{\sum_{m=1}^{M} r_{km} T_1(c_1^k,\ c_2^m)}{\sum_{m=1}^{M} r_{km}} \tag{16}$$

and

$$t_2^m = \frac{\sum_{k=1}^{K} r_{km} T_2(c_1^k, c_2^m)}{\sum_{k=1}^{K} r_{km}} \tag{17}$$

the quantities t_1^k and t_2^m may be called the conflict-payoff expectations of the two players. The conditional payoff vector

$$t = (t_1^1, \ldots, t_1^k, \ldots, t_1^K; t_2^1, \ldots, t_2^m, \ldots, t_2^M) \tag{18}$$

will be called the conflict-payoff vector of the game.

We also introduce the marginal probability r_k^* associated with any given c_1 value $c_1 = c_1^k$, and define it as

$$r_k^* = \sum_{m=1}^{M} r_{km}. \tag{19}$$

Similarly, the marginal probability r_m^{**} associated with any given c_2 value $c_2 = c_2^m$ is defined as

$$r_m^{**} = \sum_{k=1}^{K} r_{km}. \tag{20}$$

Now the generalized Nash solution for this two-person cooperative game with incomplete information is defined as the conditional payoff vector $x = \bar{x} = (\bar{x}_1^1, \ldots, \bar{x}_1^K; \bar{x}_2^1, \ldots, \bar{x}_2^M)$ maximizing the generalized Nash product

$$\bar{\pi} = \prod_{k=1}^{K} (x_1^k - t_1^k)^{r_k^*} \prod_{m=1}^{M} (x_2^m - t_2^m)^{r_m^{**}} \tag{21}$$

subject to the constraints

$$x = (x_1^1, \ldots, x_1^K; x_2^1, \ldots, x_2^M) \epsilon P \tag{22}$$

and

$$x_1^k \geq t_1^k, \; x_2^m \geq t_2^m, \text{ for } k = 1, \ldots, K \quad m = 1, \ldots, M \tag{23}$$

As a numerical example, consider a two-person bargaining game where two players have to divide \$100 between them. If they cannot agree, then they receive only some specified conflict payoffs t_1 and t_2. More specifically, we shall assume that both players have to name some payoff demands y_1 and y_2. If the payoff vector $y = (y_1, y_2)$ corresponding to these payoff demands is feasible, that is, if

$$y_1 + y_2 \leq 100 \tag{24}$$

then they will receive the payoffs demanded by them, that is, they will receive the payoffs

$$x_1 = y_1 \quad \text{and} \quad x_2 = y_2. \tag{25}$$

Otherwise they will receive the conflict payoffs

$$x_1 = t_1 \quad \text{and} \quad x_2 = t_2. \tag{26}$$

It is assumed that both players have linear utility functions for money so that their utility payoffs can be taken to be the same as their money payoffs.

The only parameter about which the players have incomplete information is the other player's conflict payoff. Each player's type vector can have only two possible values. Thus

$$c_1 = c_1{}^1 \quad \text{or} \quad c_1{}^2 \tag{27}$$

and

$$c_2 = c_2{}^1 \quad \text{or} \quad c_2{}^2. \tag{28}$$

If $c_i = c_i{}^1$, $i = 1, 2$, then player i's conflict payoff will be

$$c_i = 0, \tag{29}$$

whereas if $c_i = c_i{}^2$ then his conflict payoff will be

$$c_i = a \quad \text{where} \quad 0 \leq a \leq 50. \tag{30}$$

Intuitively, if $c_i = c_i{}^1$ then player i will have a weak bargaining position, whereas if $c_i = c_i{}^2$, he will have a strong bargaining position.

We shall assume that the four possible type vector combinations $(c_1{}^1, c_2{}^1)$, $(c_1{}^1, c_2{}^2)$, $(c_1{}^2, c_2{}^1)$ and $(c_1{}^2, c_2{}^2)$ are equally likely so that

$$r_{11} = r_{12} = r_{21} = r_{22} = \tfrac{1}{4}. \tag{31}$$

Any possible (normalized) strategy s_i^* of a given player i will be of the form

$$s_i^* = (y_i{}^1, y_i{}^2) \tag{32}$$

where $y_i = y_i{}^1$ is the payoff demand that player i will make in the case $c_i = c_i{}^1$, whereas $y_i = y_i{}^2$ is the payoff demand that player i will make in the case $c_i = c_i{}^2$.

The generalized Nash solution leads to the following optimal strategies s_i^* for the two players. If $a \leq \bar{a} = \sqrt{80{,}000} - 250 = 32.84$, then both players should use the strategies $s_i^* = (50, 50)$. That is, regardless of whether they are in a strong position or a weak position, they should choose the payoff demands $y_1 = y_2 = 50$.

If $a \geq \bar{a} = 32.84$, however, both players should use the strategies

$$s^* = (y_i^1, y_i^2)$$

where

$$y_i^1 = 25 - \frac{a}{2} \tag{33}$$

and

$$y_i^2 = 75 + \frac{a}{2}. \tag{34}$$

Thus each player, if he is in a strong position, should choose the payoff demand $y_i = 75 + a/2$.

This result has the interesting implication that, even if both players act rationally, their behavior will give rise to a conflict with probability $r_{22} = \frac{1}{4}$. If both players happen to be in a strong position, that is, in the case (c_1^2, c_2^2), both will put forward the payoff demand $y_1 = y_2 = 75 + a/2$, which will make their payoff demands impossible to satisfy simultaneously since $y_1 + y_2 = 150 + a > 100$. But this will happen only if the parameter a takes a large enough value to make it worthwhile for each player to put forward a very high payoff demand if he happens to be in a strong position, even if this means risking a conflict with probability $r_{22}/(r_{21} + r_{22}) = r_{22}/(r_{12} + r_{22}) = \frac{1}{2}$.

The solution concept just described applies to the fixed-threats case. For its generalization to the variable-threats case, see Part II of the paper mentioned in Reference 25a.

Using these solution concepts J. Harsanyi and R. Selten are now working on the problem of optimal information disclosure in two-person cooperative games, which is perhaps the most interesting problem in this area from the point of view of arms control and disarmament. The preliminary results suggest the following interesting generalizations.

If lying is impossible, the players will often be forced to disclose much more information than they wish to disclose. For instance, any player who is in a strong bargaining position for any reason whatever will usually find it advantageous to disclose this fact because this will enable him to obtain better terms from the other player. Therefore if a given player refuses to disclose the relevant information, the other player will be able to infer at once that the first player is in a weak bargaining position.

In contrast, if lying is possible then the amount of information the players can effectively communicate to each other will tend to be much less than they wish to communicate, because the two players will tend to give very little credence to any information coming from the other player.

Part III

APPLICATION OF AGREEMENTS AND THEIR ENFORCEMENT: THE EFFECTIVENESS OF ACTIONS

Chapter 5

MODELS OF VIOLATION INSPECTION PHENOMENA

5.1. INTRODUCTION

The purpose of inspection is to guard against violations of an arms control treaty. There are a number of problems associated with inspection. A country may not wish foreign inspectors to roam freely in its territory or to prolong their stay in one of its regions. It may feel that a limited quota of inspections is necessary to inhibit intrusion. But with a limited number of inspections the country may decide that it is possible to clandestinely violate the agreement. It may even be able to simulate the signs of a violation in order to waste the other side's periodic inspection efforts and carry on more hidden violations. Tamperproof mechanical devices (called black boxes), when perfected for the purpose, may be used as substitutes for human inspectors, thus removing the necessity of frequent intrusions.

The purpose of a theory of inspection is to provide, under various assumptions, optimum strategies for an inspector which would maximize his probability of detecting a violation by an evader whenever it occurs [36]. Probability is an integral component of the theory because of uncertainty in interpreting evidence. To detect clandestine production of arms, probabilities must also be used to make inferences. Here violations are detected by employing sampling methods to keep a record of the production and flow of strategic materials and point out unusual activities.

5.2. TWO ELEMENTARY MODELS

A Confidence Model

Suppose that there are altogether N detected disturbances among which n are violations and suppose that $m < n$ inspections are allowed. Let p be the probability of correctly identifying a violation. Then the probability that M or more violations are detected is

$$p(M, n, m, N) = \sum_{i=M}^{n} \left[\binom{n}{i} \binom{N-n}{m-i} \Big/ \binom{N}{m} \right] \sum_{j=M}^{i} \binom{i}{j} p^j (1-p)^{i-j}.$$

If m inspections reveal no violations, then the expression

$$1 - \sum_{i=0}^{n} \left[\binom{n}{i} \binom{N-n}{m-i} \Big/ \binom{N}{m} \right] (1-p)^i$$

gives the probability (or degree of confidence) that there are less than n violations.

A Prior-Free Model

In the case of d detections with probability p that a violation is detected, we give the probability that there have been exactly k violations. Observe that the first $d - 1$ detections can arise from among the first $k - 1$ violations followed by a violation which is detected. This gives the negative binomial distribution

$$\binom{k-1}{d-1} p^d (1-p)^{k-d}.$$

This type of approach leads to what is known as a prior-free distribution. A more accurate estimate of the probability of a violation is obtained by combining this negative binomial distribution with a probability distribution (for example, the binomial distribution) of noise, that is, by taking into consideration the fact that a signal of apparent violation may be due to causes other than an actual violation.

For a more useful model for decision-making purposes, and in order to decide whether to inspect or not, Bayes' approach may be used.

5.3. A MODEL BASED ON BAYES' THEOREM [55a]

Ordinarily, we estimate the probability of effects given the probability of causes. Bayes' theorem, however, enables us to do the opposite in certain cases. Suppose a cause B consists of a number of factors B_i, $i = 1, 2, 3, \ldots$, that is, causes any of which may bring about an effect A.

Then the probability that the cause B occurs is $P(B) = \sum_{i=1}^{\infty} P(B_i) = 1$. Let $P(B_i)$ be the a priori probability of the occurrence of the cause B_i and $P(A|B_i)$ be the conditional probability that A occurs as a consequence of the cause B_i. Given that A occurs, what is the a posteriori probability $P(B_iA)$ that it is a consequence of B_i? We have

$$P(B_iA) = P(B_i)P(A|B_i) = P(A)P(B_i|A).$$

From this we obtain the probability that B_i was the cause of A:

$$P(B_i|A) = \frac{P(B_i)P(A|B_i)}{P(A)}.$$

Now since we must assume that A could have occurred as a consequence of any of the causes B_i we have

$$\begin{aligned} P(A) = P(BA) &= P(\Sigma B_iA) = \Sigma P(B_iA) \\ &= \Sigma P(B_i)P(A|B_i) \end{aligned}$$

and we have Bayes' theorem:

$$P(B_i|A) = \frac{P(B_i)P(A|B_i)}{\Sigma P(B_i)P(A|B_i)}$$

Attempts have been made to utilize this approach in inspecting nuclear test-ban violations when the number of inspections is limited. A seismograph detects and registers a shock, an effect. It can be due to several causes: an earthquake, a false signal, or an actual test. Can anything be said about the likelihood of its being an actual test, given a certain number of detections and having an estimate of the prior probability that it is a test?

One of the most important functions of an inspection system is to provide assurance that an arms control treaty is being kept. Bayes' theorem gives a quantitative measure of this assurance. Suppose that there are N factories capable of missile production. Suppose also that inspectors are entitled to choose n factories at random and search them for missiles being manufactured in violation of a treaty. If no missiles are found in the n factory sample, there is a degree of assurance that the treaty is being observed. To establish a numerical measure of our assurance we offer the following model. Let our uncertainty about the number of factories manufacturing contraband missiles, an uncertainty felt before receiving inspection reports, be represented by the following prior distribution:

Number of Violating Factories	Prior Probability
0	$\frac{1}{2}$
1	$\frac{1}{2}N$
2	$\frac{1}{2}N$
.	.
.	.
.	.
N	$\frac{1}{2}N$

This prior distribution gives a weight of $\frac{1}{2}$ to compliance and a weight of $\frac{1}{2}$ to violation to represent a state of mind in which one is as ready as not to suspect the adversary of violation.

We shall prove that after the inspection data has been received, the a posteriori probability of compliance has the value

$$\frac{n+1}{n+2-\dfrac{n}{N}}.$$

Thus uncertainty is replaced by a degree of assurance measured by Bayes' theorem. If the sample shows a violation it is known that there was no compliance. If the sample shows no violation, however, confidence in compliance increases according to the sample size n. If $n = 0$ the assurance is $\frac{1}{2}$, if $n = 1$ it is $2N/(3N - 1)$, and so on. To increase assurance of compliance the inspection effort must be intensified, which is also intuitively obvious.

Proof. Let V be the number of violating factories among the N factories and let v be the number of violations found in the sample of size n. Let $P(V)$ be the prior distribution of violations as given in the table. We want $Pr(V = 0|v = 0)$, which gives the probability of compliance. By Bayes' theorem:

$$Pr(V = 0|v = 0) = \frac{Pr(V = 0)Pr(v = 0|V = 0)}{Pr(V = 0)Pr(v = 0|V = 0) + \sum_{V=1}^{N} P(V)Pr(v = 0|V)}.$$

$$Pr(v = 0|V) = \binom{V}{0}\binom{N - V}{n}\Big/\binom{N}{n}$$

and from the table $P(V = 0) = \frac{1}{2}$. Clearly $Pr(v = 0|V = 0) = 1$.

Therefore

$$Pr(V = 0|v = 0) = \frac{\frac{1}{2}}{\dfrac{1}{2} + \displaystyle\sum_{V=1}^{N} \frac{\binom{V}{0}\binom{N-V}{n}}{2N\binom{N}{n}}}$$

It is shown in "Theory of Probability" by Jeffreys (second edition, Section 3.2) that

$$\sum_{V=0}^{N} \binom{V}{0}\binom{N-V}{n} = \binom{N+1}{n+1}.$$

Hence

$$\sum_{V=1}^{N} \binom{V}{0}\binom{N-V}{n} = \binom{N+1}{n+1} - \binom{N}{n}.$$

Thus

$$Pr(V = 0|v = 0) = \frac{\frac{1}{2}}{\dfrac{1}{2} + \dfrac{\binom{N+1}{n+1} - \binom{N}{n}}{2N\binom{N}{n}}}$$

$$= \frac{1}{1 + \dfrac{\binom{N+1}{n+1}}{N\binom{N}{n}} - \dfrac{1}{N}}$$

$$= \frac{1}{1 - \dfrac{1}{N} + \dfrac{\dfrac{(N+1)!}{(n+1)!(N-n)!}}{N\dfrac{N!}{n!(N-n)!}}}$$

$$= \frac{1}{1 - \dfrac{1}{N} + \dfrac{N+1}{N(n+1)}}$$

$$= \frac{1}{1 + \dfrac{N-n}{N(n+1)}} = \frac{n+1}{n+2-\dfrac{n}{N}}.$$

Let us take a more realistic approach to the a priori probabilities and assume that we expect violations to occur in 1, 2, or 3 factories. Then we have $P(0) = \frac{1}{2}$, $P(1) = \frac{1}{6}$, $P(2) = \frac{1}{6}$, $P(3) = \frac{1}{6}$, $P(k) = 0$ for $4 \leq k \leq N$.

$$Pr(V = 0|v = 0) = \frac{\frac{1}{2}}{\frac{1}{2} + \frac{N-n}{6N} \frac{2N^2 + n^2 - 3nN - 6N + 5n + 4}{N^2 - 3N + 2}}.$$

For small values of n this may be approximated by

$$\frac{3}{5\left(1 - \frac{n}{N}\right)}.$$

We may work out yet another realistic example in which the $P(V)$ are weighted in some order so that their sum is $\frac{1}{2}$.

5.4. DECISION THEORETIC MODEL

Consider the following model, which utilizes a decision parameter C denoting the complexity of a signal received at a recording instrument. Complexity is a measure of the rate of energy arrival in the short P-wave part of the record [20a]. A signal may contain additional information besides complexity, but we will only use complexity here. Let q be the average annual number of earthquakes and let e be the average annual number of test explosions. A signal whose complexity x satisfies $x < C$ is identified as an explosion, whereas if $x \geq C$, it is identified as an earthquake. Let $f(x)$ and $g(x)$ be the density functions of earthquakes and explosions respectively as functions of the complexity x. Let $F(C)$ and $1 - F(C)$ be the respective probabilities that an earthquake is identified as an explosion or as an earthquake. Let $G(C)$ and $1 - G(C)$ be the respective probabilities that an explosion is identified as an explosion or as an earthquake. The average number of signals identified annually as earthquakes is

$$q[1 - F(C)] + e[(1 - G(C)]$$

and the average number of signals identified annually as explosions is

$$qF(C) + eG(C).$$

Let A be the probability that an explosion whose complexity exceeds C is classified as a suspicious event. Let B be the probability that the site of that suspicious event is chosen for on-site inspection (that is, B is the proportion of suspicious events to be inspected) and let M be the probability that the inspection proves it to have been an explosion. This leads to

$$A = 1 - [1 - MBG(C)]^e.$$

Let us take this value as the smallest value of A for which it is possible to decide that an explosion has, in fact, taken place and let us denote it by $\bar{A}$. The average number of inspections I is given by

$$I = B[qF(C) + eG(C)]$$

and upon solving for B in the previous expression and substituting here we have

$$I = \frac{1}{MG(C)}[1 - (1 - \bar{A})^{1/e}][qF(C) + eG(C)].$$

C can be chosen to minimize I subject to the fact that $0 < B(C) \leq 1$. Note from either expression that B can be expressed as a function of C.

The probability $\bar{A}$ may be taken at a low percentage level, for example, 10%. To determine the minimum number of inspections that would catch a violation at this level for $\bar{A}$ we first write

$$I = \frac{1}{M}[1 - (1 - \bar{A})^{1/e}]\left[e + q\frac{F(C)}{G(C)}\right].$$

If we assume that $G(C) = 0.50$ at $C = 300$ (see the following) and take $e = 3$, $q = 200$, and $M = 0.5$, we have for the fraction of suspicious events to be inspected $B = .138$. Note that the only dependence of I on C appears in the fraction $F(C)/G(C)$. Suppose from experimental data we find that this ratio attains a minimum value of .09 at $C = 300$. Then I min $\simeq 1.4$ inspections.

5.5. A TREATY ADHERENCE, INSPECTIONS, AND BLACK BOXES

Here we shall see that poor inspectors may be preferred by a country to the use of highly reliable black boxes. This depends on the policies of the country and of its opponent.

Consider the problem of signing a test-ban treaty between the United States and the U.S.S.R. Each country has three alternatives: (a) not signing, (b) signing but not abiding (not abiding may be replaced by being completely prepared to resume testing if necessary), and, finally, (c) signing and abiding. We also suppose that we have the following payoff matrices (based on examination of the literature of political statements to determine preferences) whose entries are ordinal utilities which only indicate preference ordering [43]:

Payoffs to United States

		U.S.S.R. strategies		
		N.S.	S.N.A.	S.A.
	N.S.	-100	-100	-100
U.S. strategies	S.N.A.	-100	-120	-110
	S.A.	-100	-130	100

Payoffs to U.S.S.R.

		U.S.S.R. strategies		
		N.S.	S.N.A.	S.A.
	N.S.	-80	-80	-80
U.S. strategies	S.N.A.	-80	155	130
	S.A.	-80	160	150

One need not agree with the values assigned by the author of this paper for illustrative purposes in order to appreciate the use of the analysis.

Because of the dominance of the middle column in the payoff to the U.S.S.R., it is clear that the latter will prefer to sign but not abide and the best response to this strategy is for the United States not to sign.

Suppose that an inspection system is introducted involving on-site inspection where the probability of detecting a violation is 5%. Suppose that the detection of a violation will lead to cancellation of the treaty with payoff -98 to the United States, and -90 to the U.S.S.R. What is the effect of this inspection scheme? We compute from the U.S.S.R. payoff matrix as follows: if there is a violation and it is detected (with probability .05), the treaty will be canceled. On the other hand it may not be detected (with probability .95). The expected payoff to the U.S.S.R., assuming that it uses S.N.A. while the United States uses S.A., is

$$.05(-90) + .95(160) \approx 147\tfrac{1}{2} < 150.$$

From this we see that the U.S.S.R. would do better to sign and abide. A method of improving this payoff is to reduce the size of the tests, that is, decrease .05. If the size of the tests is reduced enough, their frequency can be appropriately increased with net detection probability below .05.

When the inspection team identifies a violation, the probability that it is an earthquake is $\delta = 0$.

Consider now a black box that can identify a violation. Assume it reports a violation that does not occur simultaneously with an earthquake with probability $\gamma = 1$, that is, 100% certainty, and reports an earthquake as a violation with probability $\delta = .0196$. Assume that the a priori probability of conducting a test simultaneously with an earthquake is $\eta = .10$.

The probability that a given report of the black box is in fact a violation is

$$\beta = \frac{\gamma\eta}{\gamma\eta + (1 - \eta)\delta} = .85.$$

In this case the United States decides by computing its expected payoff

$$.85(-130) + .15(100) > -98$$

not to cancel the treaty. Thus even with a very good black box the United States will not cancel the treaty in spite of possible violation. The U.S.S.R. will conduct its tests without fear of cancellation. Thus, from the standpoint of the United States, inspection teams are preferred, whereas the U.S.S.R. would prefer black boxes.

In general if the payoff matrix is given by

		U.S.S.R		
		N.S.	S.N.A.	S.A.
	N.S.	a, b	a, b	a, b
United States	S.N.A.	a, b	e, f	p, q
	S.A.	a, b	r, s	c, d

with $r < e < p < a < c$, $b < q < f < s$, $f < d < s$ or $q < d < f$ and if a^* and b^* are the payoffs to the United States and to the U.S.S.R. due to cancellation, suppose that a^* is slightly larger than a, and b^* is slightly less than β. If $\beta < (c - a^*/c - r)$ the United States will not cancel the treaty as a result of U.S.S.R. violations. We assume that the quantity on the right is near unity.

If the opposite inequality holds, as with on-site inspection, the U.S.S.R. loses by not changing policy if $\gamma > (s - d)/(s - b^*)$, the right side of which is assumed to be near zero.

The conclusion is that on-site inspection puts great limitations on a potential violator.

5.6. A GAME-THEORETIC MODEL

Consider the case of two parties who have agreed to ban all tests of nuclear explosions. One of the parties plans to conduct n clandestine tests over a period of time, whereas the other party has m inspections available with which he hopes to discover violations. There are l stages in this process where l may indicate the number of days in the period of agreement.

The number of tests n is guessed by the inspecting party. At each stage an inspector is faced with deciding whether a certain signal is due to an earthquake, is a test, or whether it is of doubtful nature. A signal of doubtful nature that is actually an earthquake occurs with probability p. If it is clearly an earthquake, however, its probability is $1 - p$. A test produces a signal that is doubtful with probability q. The probability is $1 - q$ that a test signal is correctly interpreted as a test. At each stage an inspector may or may not inspect. If he inspects, he finds a violation with probability r provided that at that stage a violation really occurred. The inspector is allowed m inspections and the violator must test n times. In this game the payoff is 1 if a violation is detected and 0 if it is not. The value of the game $V(l, m, n)$ can be interpreted as a probability that at least one test is discovered. The object is to analyze the game. Although optimum strategies are hard to derive, nevertheless, we can give the problem an interesting structure and attempt deriving some conclusions by specializing the parameters. The game can be solved recursively as a two by two matrix game, with the following matrix:

		Violator	
		Test	No test
Inspector	Inspects	$q(1 - r)V(l - 1, m - 1, n - 1) + qr + (1 - q)$	$pV((l - 1, m - 1, n) + (1 - p)V(l - 1, m, n)$
	Does not Inspect	$qV(l - 1, m, n - 1) + (1 - q)$	$V(l - 1, m, n)$

This matrix assumes that the inspector knows that the violator has run a test even if he has not found this out by inspection.

If only a single violation is allowed it is possible to obtain explicit solutions for the value of the game. If $p = q = \frac{1}{2}$ and $r = 1$, for example, then

$$V(l, 1, 1) = \tfrac{1}{2}[1 - \tfrac{1}{2}(\tfrac{2}{3})^{l-1}]^{-1}$$

More generally, we can show that

$$\lim_{l \to \infty} V(l, m, 1) = \tfrac{1}{2}$$

for $p = q = \frac{1}{2}$, $r = 1$.

Let $V(l, m)$ be the minmax value of the game with l events and m inspections. We have the additional conditions for $l \geq m \geq 1$,

$$V(1, 1) = 1 \qquad \text{for} \quad l \geq 1$$

and

$$V(1, 0) = 0 \qquad \text{for} \quad l \geq 0. \tag{1}$$

Then the following matrix provides the inductive determination of $V(l, m)$ when $l > m \geq 1$.

	Test	Do not test
Inspect	1	$pV(l-1, m-1) + (1-p)V(l-1, m).$
Do not inspect	0	$V(l-1, m)$

This matrix game has a dominant main diagonal. Thus to solve it we must solve the recurrence relation

$$V(l, m) = \frac{V(l-1, m)}{1 + p[V(l-1, m) - V(l-1, m-1)]},$$

which must hold for all integers $l > m \geq 1$ and satisfy (1). To solve this system, we introduce the functions $F(l, m)$ defined by $F(l, l) = 1$ for $l \geq 1$, $F(l, 0) = 0$ for $l \geq 0$, and

$$F(l, m) = \sum_{k=0}^{m-1} \binom{l-m+k-1}{k} p^k$$

for $l > m \geq 1$. Then for all $l \geq m \geq 0$

$$V(l, m) = \frac{F(l, m)}{F(l+1, m+1)}.$$

This result can be cast in terms of the negative binomial distribution.

To explain the model, note that if one has a certain number of suspicious events and the same number of inspections, the probability of finding a single test is one. But if the number of inspections is equal to the expected number of suspicious events, the probability of finding a single test is less than one.

5.7. BRIEF COMMENTS ON SAMPLING IN ARMS CONTROL

We have already stated that a major purpose of inspection is to verify whether the inspected party is abiding by the terms of an arms control treaty. The verification can be done through checking on the production and storage of military materials, the movement of materiel-carrying vehicles, the amount of arms maintained at a particular military establishment, and the presence or absence of hidden military establishments. In the case of nuclear or other types of tests prohibited by the treaty the inspector must look for certain types of evidence to assist in the interpretation of suspicious signals [1*b*].

It would be absurd and impossible to study the entire suspect population to find out whether a treaty is being adhered to. Industrial producers have learned from experience that to control the quality of their products they need only check occasional samples, rather than every item. The cost of inspection samples may be sufficiently high that even then one looks for improved methods of controlling quality.

Sampling methods may differ in complexity when applied to arms control problems, but basically the ideas and techniques so useful in studying population characteristics are applicable and worthy of exploration.

We need not go into the details of various types of sampling methods such as random, stratified, cluster, sequential, and others. Nor do we need to mention various methods of inference which utilize correlation and regression, estimation and testing of hypotheses. These basic concepts and their uses are to be found in standard texts on statistics and its applications. We try to portray here the type of control situation encountered by an inspection team in which sampling methods may be used effectively to check the compliance of parties with an arms control treaty.

The problems of sampling take two theoretical turns. The first is to determine the size of the sample and the type of sampling procedure appropriate for a specific arms control situation, and the second is to make inferences from the sample about the entire population. Both these aspects of sampling must be done in such a way as to satisfy the conditions imposed by a disarmament treaty and to cope with other conditions not under the control of the inspection team. The sampling results must then be evaluated in terms useful to the decision makers of a country.

An area in which sampling may be useful for arms control purposes is in the analysis of accounting record systems which keep information on the flow and production of materials. Apart from the costliness of the utilization of such records for inspection purposes, it may not be feasible to obtain access to these records through negotiations. If such records could be made available by agreement, however, their purpose must be kept in mind. Accounting control has the purpose of establishing and maintaining a system of records and transactions, assets and liabilities to prevent dissipation and loss through careless actions, or, if losses occur, to discover them and prevent their recurrence.

There are a number of unusual problems which occur in the sampling of nonphysical facilities such as the inspection of records. One of these is the relevance of the records kept to the real figures. Another involves the consistency of the records.

If the present level of activities controlled by a treaty are declared in a listing by the parties involved, an inspection team has something to use as a basis to look for declarable activities which have not been declared. On the other hand, to obtain an estimate of whether a certain declared activity is expanding beyond the level prescribed by the treaty is more difficult, because the flow of materials is not a simple black and white matter but involves all shades of gray. This requires considerable diligence and clue-hunting by the inspection team. Naturally, small-scale violations would not benefit a violator and arms build-up for substantial military activity would involve a comprehensive plan of violation.

We believe that these are the methods that will apply in the final phases of disarmament. They are the tools that will be used in the everyday business of enforcing arms control treaties. But long before that point is reached, the philosophy underlying the material of the first five chapters of this book will play an important role in producing actual arms cut measures.

A brief description of problems encountered in sampling for inspection in arms control follows. Sampling procedures are of little use in estimating a property that is not widespread in the population. If only a few members among many have this property, for example, one in ten thousand, then unless the sample size is very large (a costly operation) the estimates are likely to be incorrect. For example, if a small sample reveals the presence of the desired property the estimate for the entire population will be far higher than it actually is. No sampling procedure can resolve this difficulty, and care must be exercised in what is chosen for sampling. This applies to searching for violation in producing industrial parts for a few units of a weapon. It is like looking for a needle in a haystack.

Suppose that it is desired to inspect a factory that produces parts for machinery used in agriculture but could produce an excess amount also suitable for military equipment. Suppose also that the amount of machinery used for peaceful purposes is not known and hence it is not known how many units of a specific part are destined for this purpose. How would we find out if an excess amount is being produced?

We may have to set up standards for the longevity of this item and the longevity of the agricultural machine using the item. An estimate of the number of new machines is also needed by observing the factories that produce them. Using random samples from the population of machinery we can obtain an estimate of the population size and its demand for this item. Now we have an estimate of the number of units needed to build new machines and to serve as replacements in old ones. By observing the rate of production of the given item, and by estimating the maximum that can be produced, we can confirm or deny a suspicion that clandestine use is being made of the item in constructing weapons.

Statistics provides tools for measuring the effectiveness of actions which are followed in carrying out a policy. These measures or indices serve as criteria for indicating how closely the objectives are being fulfilled. Percentages and averages, for example, are frequently used to show how much of an operation has been completed. Sometimes we may use visual inspection to assess the degree of satisfaction of the objectives. If a large number of inspections must be made to examine many areas, however, statistical methods are needed for obtaining an overall index of fulfillment. An action may be considered effective to the extent that it satisfies the objectives pursued through a given policy. Thus in addition to developing consistent objectives and stable policies, actions (as expressions of policies) must be taken which are effective in fulfilling the objectives.

It sometimes happens that there is no effective action that can be used to carry out a policy. Such is the case between two nations that block each other's actions. When a nation cannot act in pursuit of its objectives it is frustrated. Chapter 6 is concerned with general concepts of frustration, aggression, and factors that influence the resolution of conflicts.

Part IV

INTERMEDIATE AND LONG-RANGE PROBLEMS OF ARMS CONTROL—ANALYSIS OF THE GROWTH OF CONFLICTS: IDEAS AND PERSPECTIVES

Chapter 6

SOME RESEARCH ON CONFLICTS

6.1. INTRODUCTION

In this final chapter ideas relevant to the causes and elements of conflict will be examined. We shall first describe some research done on escalation as it occurs in laboratory type conflicts and give examples of factors affecting these escalations. An example of the analysis of a number of nations for stability follows, based on various types of events occurring in these nations over a period of five years.

Conflict is associated with frustration and frustration with the lack of satisfaction of needs maintains one school of thought [20b] which we have chosen as an example. War and peace as expressions of repeated frustration and resolution are briefly described. Other schools of thought [55b], some of which are briefly mentioned, attribute the causes of war to aggressive instinct; hatred; boredom; misunderstanding; cultural differences; a desire to unify a divided country by finding a common enemy; increasing scientific discovery; stimulating sluggish economies by creating an "artificial" demand; extending markets; survival of the fittest; spreading dynamic civilization; aggrandizement of the elites in the military-industrial complex and so forth. Whatever the cause of conflict may be, the theory of Section 2.4 gives a rationale for deciding whether or not to engage in conflict. A look at the present situation can be discouraging. Hence a broad look is given to the future, which shows adequate opportunity for peace if we manage to survive the present. The final section outlines some areas of research and action for the present (and near future) that should aid in peacefully resolving conflicts.

6.2. EXPERIMENTS ON THE ESCALATION OF CONFLICT

We are sometimes led to the premature conclusion that if nations realized the dangers of nuclear weapons, they would rationally resolve open conflicts, at worst through wars waged by conventional means. There would be a natural tendency, however, for the losing side to resort to nuclear threats to deter its defeat and even to re-establish its position. This could end in disaster. In addition there are nations that do not wish to conform to our traditional definition of rationality, particularly if they have little to lose materially. Until escalation processes and their methods of control are adequately understood, there is little hope for assuming a controlled form of conventional war. Such understanding and control would considerably enhance the hope of limiting the damages of war in case there is an outbreak of hostilities. It should also have applications to conventional war, providing indicators for the direction the war would go if certain actions were taken. Such actions sometimes are intended to cause eventual deescalation by inhibiting the enemy, but in fact the conflict gradually intensifies.

In the last few years the Arms Control and Disarmament Agency has undertaken a study with the Operations Research Center of the University of Pennsylvania whose concern is to identify conditions under which conflicts escalate or deescalate and to determine the possibility of affecting the rates of escalation and deescalation through control of the conditions in interaction between the conflicting parties. The study has been based on (a) the analysis of selected historical conflicts and the literature derived from them, (b) the conduct of experiments to determine the effect of interactions among variables, and (c) the development of a theory applicable to the experimental work and its extension to the real world.

The outcome of the analysis of the literature was a set of hypotheses concerning escalation and deescalation which is being tested in experimental situations for (a) generality and (b) identification of the critical variables. Examples of hypotheses are: (a) In the absense of communications, escalation is more likely to take place. (b) The stronger the ideological components, the more likely is escalation. (c) Escalation depends on economic development. (d) Escalation is more likely if conflict can take place in small steps. (e) Escalation is more likely in the presence of multilateral commanders [47].

A relatively complex experimental situation called "artificial reality" (or "rich game") was constructed which, nevertheless, was the simplest that could be constructed to satisfy the following conditions:

1. It is "rich" enough to test a large number of hypotheses that have been formulated about the real phenomena under study; in this case, the dynamics of large-scale social conflict. (Clearly, such tests cannot confirm any hypotheses about reality, but they can define limits on the generality of hypotheses or show how they should or can be generalized). The purpose underlying this condition is to assure an experimental situation that is realistic enough so that most assertions made about real conflicts are applicable to it.

2. There must be an explicit formulation of the variables and the scales used in measuring them, along with simplification of reality (for example, holding a variable constant). This makes it possible to design successively enriched experimental situations by the addition of complexities one at a time or in controlled combination.

3. The relevant behavior in the experimental situation must be describable in quantitative terms.

4. The situation must be decomposable into a set of simpler experimental situations, and, when possible, these simpler situations should be ones that have already been experimented on or closely resemble situations that have been analyzed.

The experimental situation that satisfies these conditions is not used as a model of reality but rather is regarded as a first step in developing quantitative models of the real situation; hence its name, "artificial reality." It is used to generate a history that is to be explained by the first theory to be constructed. The history is generated by experimentation—by placing the rich game—which is designed to test systematically hypotheses about real conflict that have been translated into operational and quantitative terms so as to apply to this artificial world.

Remarks on the Development of the Artificial Reality

The present artificial reality consists of two symmetric games played simultaneously. One is a positive-sum "Prisoner's Dilemma" game somewhat representative of an international (two-nation) economy. The other is a negative-sum game called "Chicken" with similarities to internation warfare in which nations take a head-on collision course in the hope of forcing one another to make concessions.

The parties (Red and Blue) can invest various amounts of resources in either game, and the marginal returns to their investments are as follows:

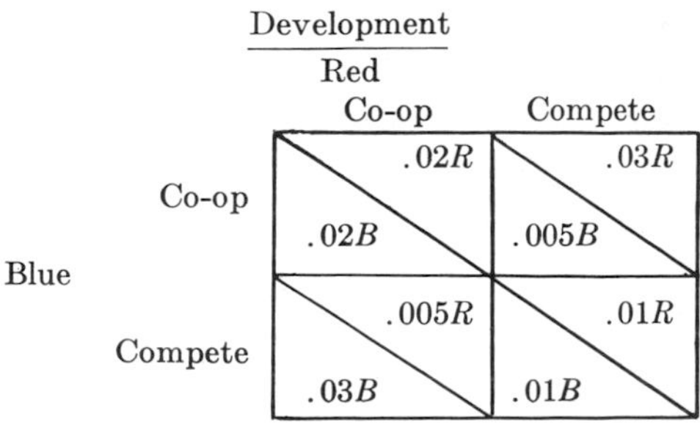

Arms

Red

Blue		Defense	Offense
	Defense	$-.05B$ (Blue); $-.05R$ (Red)	$B - 1.2R$ (Blue); $1.2R - B$ (Red)
	Offense	$1.2B - R$ (Blue); $R - 1.2B$ (Red)	$-1.2R$ (Blue); $-1.2B$ (Red)

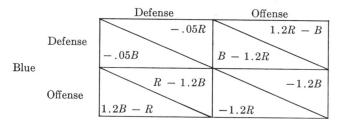

B = Amount of Blue's resources invested in the particular row.
R = Amount of Red's resources invested in the particular column.

The only basic restriction on the play of a game is a limit on the amount that can be invested in arms. This limit is 20% of the largest resource level among all of the players. This limit prevents the immediate annihilation of any one party and provides the opportunity to investigate the stability of the various equilibria. The game is played by offering each player a sum of money to invest in one of the sectors over several plays. After each investment, payoffs, as indicated, are made to the players. Between plays, the players may negotiate or they may not. Several other factors which condition the game will be discussed below. Escalation here will mean increasing investment in the arms area, particularly in offense.

Study of the artificial reality helps in the development of the theory in two ways. First, it provides intuitive ideas to be formalized in the theory and tested in specially designed experiments. Second, it provides an opportunity to gain insight into the difficulties that can occur in applying the theory to real life situations. Its contribution to deescalation will come in the gradual isolation of factors having direct bearing on intensifying or "cooling off" a conflict situation.

Conversely, theoretical analysis has helped in the study of the artificial reality by pointing to certain ways of analyzing the data.

The history of the artificial reality is examined by means of statistical tests designed to find the effect upon this data of variations in the conditions under which the artificial reality games are conducted. Such conditions and their effects (summarized for brevity) are

1. Communication (unilateral, that is, only one person can communicate, bilateral, or none). *It has been found that unrestricted communication tends to reduce the probability of escalation.*

2. Relative levels of "technological" effectiveness to inflict damage (equal or unequal). *In this case whether equal or not the probability of escalation is roughly the same.*

3. Relative levels of initial resources (equal and high, equal and low, or unequal). *It appears that this factor has no effect on escalation.*

4. Number of sides (2 or 3). *Experiments show that the greater the number of independent parties, the more likely is escalation.*

5. Size of sides (1 or 3). *Teams tend to react more defensively than individuals.*

6. Spying (receiving information about other side's current move; yes or no). *No correlation has been found between spying and the propensity to escalate. When combined with incomplete information about the opponent's payoff, however, spying tends to generate aggression.*

7. Player expertise (naive or experienced—in the sense of having participated before). *The more experienced a player is, the less likely is escalation.*

8. Personalities of players (for example, cooperative or aggressive as evidence by past play and/or psychological tests). *This is being investigated.*

9. Variations in payoff (with or without a lump sum payoff at the end to the person with the larger resources). *This appears to have no effect on escalation.*

10. Preconditioning. *A hostile preconditioning has the effect of enhancing cooperation provided the communication channels are open. If the channels are closed one cannot simply make this statement.*

Artificial reality is now being used to construct a theory about the characteristics of the players, for example, their attitude toward each other as well as toward the game.

6.3. AGGRESSION AND POLITICAL STABILITY

Let us now examine some of the findings of an interesting study concerned with the causes of aggression and the elements conducive to the stability of a country.

I. K. Feierabend and R. L. Feierabend [20b] have studied political aggressive behavior for 84 countries for the period 1948–1962. In their study political stability is defined as the degree or the amount of aggression directed by individuals or groups within the political system against other groups or against the complex of officeholders and individuals and groups associated with them.

For the purpose of the study, data on internal conflict behavior in these 84 nations were collected. A scale ranging from 0 (denoting extreme stability) through 6 (denoting extreme instability) was used. The rationale for the division is given in terms of specific events representing differing degrees of stability or instability. For example, a general election is associated with a 0 position; resignation of a cabinet official falls into the 1 position on the scale; peaceful demonstrations into the 2 position; assassination of a significant political figure into the 3 position; mass arrests into the 4 position; coup d'etat into the 5 position; and civil war into the 6 position.

To validate this scheme, judges were asked to sort the same type of events along the same continuum, and close agreement was obtained. Similarly, two independent efforts of assigning items to the scale involving data from 84 countries for a seven-year time period yielded close agreement.

Underlying this type of analysis is a postulate from frustration-aggression theory—"aggression is always the result of frustration." Because aggressive behavior is sometimes inhibited through punishment, it may lead to constructive solutions to problems.

Generally, political instability results from unrelieved socially experienced frustration, that is, high and prolonged expectations unmatched by equal satisfaction levels. We have the following relation:

$$\frac{\text{social want satisfaction}}{\text{social want formation}} = \text{systemic frustration.}$$

Ideally, in the absence of systemic frustration, we can expect political stability. With it, political stability may still occur, if (a) in the society, politically relevant strata capable of organized action are largely lacking; or (b) it is a society in which constructive solutions to frustrating situations are available or anticipated (the effectiveness of government and also the legitimacy of regimes will be relevant factors); or (c) there is a sufficiently coercive government capable of preventing overt acts of hostility against itself; or (d) as a result of the coerciveness of government, the aggressive impulse is vented or displaced in aggression against minority groups and/or against other nations; or (e) individual acts of aggression are sufficiently abundant to provide an outlet.

Following the allotment to groups, a sum total of each country's stability ratings was calculated. Countries were then rank-ordered within groups on the basis of this frequency.

Note that the distribution is skewed toward instability, a condition more prevalent than stability within the sample of nations and during the period for which the data are analyzed.

Another approach to the ordering of internal conflict was based upon the frequency of occurrence of 30 types of internal conflict determined for the 84 countries for the time period, 1948–1962. This analysis was used in three different ways.

Table 6.1. Frequency Distribution of Countries in Terms of Their Degree of Relative Political Stability, 1955–1961 (Stability Score Shown for Each Country)

0 Stability	1	2	3	4	5	6 Instability
N. Zea. 000	Norway 104	W. Germany 217	Tunisia 328	France 499	India 599	Indonesia 699
	Netherlands 104	Czech. 212	Gr. Britain 325	U. of S. Africa 495	Argentina 599	Cuba 699
	Cambodia 104	Finland 211	Portugal 323	Haiti 478	Korea 596	Colombia 681
	Sweden 103	Romania 206	Uruguay 318	Poland 465	Venezuela 584	Laos 652
	Saudi Ar. 103	Ireland 202	Israel 317	Spain 463	Turkey 583	Hungary 652
	Iceland 103	Costa Rica 202	Canada 317	Dom. Rep. 463	Lebanon 581	
	Philippines 101		U. S. 316	Iran 459	Iraq 579	
	Luxembourg 101		Taiwan 314	Ceylon 454	Bolivia 556	
			Libya 309	Japan 453	Syria 554	
			Austria 309	Thailand 451	Peru 552	
			E. Germany 307	Mexico 451	Gutemala 546	
			Ethiopia 307	Ghana 451	Brazil 541	
			Denmark 306	Jordan 448	Honduras 535	
			Australia 306	Sudan 445	Cyprus 526	
			Switzer. 303	Morocco 443		
				Egypt 438		
				Pakistan 437		
				Italy 433		
				Belgium 432		
				Paraguay 431		
				USSR 430		
				Nicaragua 430		
				Chile 427		
				Burma 427		
				Yugoslavia 422		
				Panama 422		
				Ecuador 422		
				China 422		
				El Salvador 421		
				Liberia 415		
				Malaya 413		
				Albania 412		
				Greece 409		
				Bulgaria 407		
				Afghanistan 404		

A global instability profile for all types of events, for all countries, was drawn to show changes in the world level of instability during the time period under study. As seen in Figure 22, instability has been on the increase in recent years, reaching one peak in the late 1950s and an even higher level in the 1960s.

Frequencies of particular types of instability behavior were compared for the entire sample of countries. The range of frequencies was from 18 (execution of significant persons) to 403 (acquisition of office). When

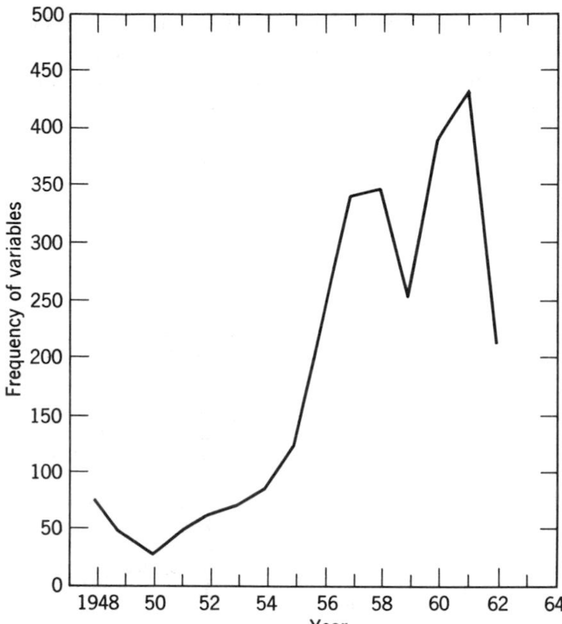

Figure 22. Frequency of variables by year, 1948–1962.

the events were rank-ordered in terms of frequency of occurrence and the rank-ordering divided into quartiles, the first quartile, with the highest frequency of occurrence (1555 occurrences), included events denoting routine governmental change (such as acquisition of office, vacation of office, elections, and significant changes of laws). The second quartile (704 occurrences) appeared to be one of unrest, including such events as large-scale demonstrations, general strikes, arrests, and martial law. The third quartile (333 occurrences) indicated serious societal disturbance in the form of coups d'etat, terrorism and sabotage, guerrilla warfare, and exile. And the fourth quartile (150 occurrences) consisted primarily of events connoting violence: executions, severe riots, civil war. Thus an inverse relationship was revealed between the frequency of occurrence of an event and the intensity of violence which it denotes.

Finally, countries were compared for the relative frequency of occurrence of all 30 instability behaviors during this time period. The range was from 136 events (France) to one event (Switzerland). The median of this distribution was represented by Laos and Burma, with 28 and 26 events respectively.

The following is given as an indication of the level of frustration in terms of social want and its satisfaction levels:

$$\frac{\text{want satisfaction low}}{\text{want formation high}} = \text{high frustration},$$

$$\frac{\text{want satisfaction low}}{\text{want formation low}} = \text{low frustration},$$

$$\frac{\text{want satisfaction high}}{\text{want formation high}} = \text{low frustration}.$$

From these empirical thresholds the authors provide a composite picture of the stable country. It is a society which is 90% or more literate; with 65 or more radios and 120 or more copies of newspapers per 1000 population; with 2% or more of the population having telephones; with 2525 or more calories per day per person; with not more than 1900 persons per physician, with a GNP of 300 dollars or more per person per year; and with 45% or more of the population living in urban centers. If all of these threshold values are attained by a society, there is an extremely high probability that the country will achieve relative political stability. Conversely, in terms of threshold values, the more they fail to meet these levels, the greater the likelihood of political instability.

Thus the hypothesis promulgated in this study is that *the faster (the slower) the rate of change in the moderization process within any given society, the higher (the lower) the level of political instability within that society.* This may seem contrary to the previous conclusion, but it is concerned with rates and not with terminal values. At present, that is, in the late sixties, the picture looks somewhat different. The level of aspiration has been raised. No development, or very slow development also causes instability and hence at any given time there is a level of development which is optimal for a given country.

The countries with the lowest rate of change are predominantly stable, as measured both by a low level of yearly fluctuations in instability and by a lack of any worsening trend toward instability over time. Conversely, the countries with the highest rate of change on the ecological variables are beset by instability, as measured both by yearly fluctuations in instability levels and the absence of evidence of any improvement in trend toward stability over time. Furthermore, countries experiencing intermediate rates of change toward modernization are also intermediate in instability, showing some conflicting combination of fluctuation and trend over time.

6.4. NONSCIENTIFIC SPECULATIONS

The War and Peace Sequence

A look at history and at the world around us suffices to convince us that the phenomenon "war" has accompanied all forms of human society since prehistoric times. It has been a recurrent expression. The hopeful optimist who considers war an illness also assumes that peace is the healthful, normal state of affairs. It is somewhat difficult to consider as pathological a sociological situation that has been ever present since the dawn of society.

War has been defined as an impasse to peace. Through violence, man evades the problems of peace. Peace, war, peace, war . . . is an infinite progression of two elements closely tied together in a back-and-forth flow of tides of aggression and ebbs of tranquillity. It reminds one of a well-known mathematical sequence $1, -1, 1, -1 \ldots$ for which one cannot discern a unique limit toward which the elements converge because it has two limits 1 and -1. When there is no unique answer, we need to work to achieve the preferred answer. Will we converge to war, to peace, or to neither?

Perhaps not all the elements of this sequence have had universal impact on history (for example, some wars have not been significant), but the existence of this chain is a powerful expression from generations of humanity. When peace has been attained, rather than considering it a state at hand to be nurtured and cherished, as new problems arise people begin to look to war in order to resolve international discords and internal frustrations. Gradually a state of war casts its shadow over peace; combustibility is heightened.

War appears to be a social institution that performs a definite function for parts of humanity. Some have seen it as the only means to ameliorate disequilibrium and cope with economic, geographic, political, population, and other problems arising in human affairs [9, 10, 39a]. Nations have been known to fight solely to purge themselves from internal frustration. The great wars may be regarded as periodic disequilibria among nations. They are cruel ways of spasmodic relaxation and re-equilibrium. War has also been a source of inspiration and greater striving for peace. Both the League of Nations and the United Nations came on the heels of great wars. Perhaps without the threat of war, our logical edifice of constructing social and international order and our dialectic as to why we should help the developing countries would topple. Editorials say, "A world in which the gap between the developed and the underdeveloped world is steadily widening is a world that threatens the safety and the security of the American people, if it does not affront their humanity."

As society operates today, the military establishment and its concern about war have a stimulating effect on the economy (even though wasteful of the world's scarce resources) through large expenditures on weapon industry, the use of elaborate technology, and the employment of considerable manpower. Because weapons are not consumer items, this component of the economy is largely independent of the domestic economic cycle and can be used by a government to prime and control the economy. In this sense weapon production is regarded by many as beneficial rather than wasteful. In a permanently peaceful environment a substitute for this powerful economic "wasteful" force is needed, perhaps through space and oceanic projects or other similar activities that cannot in a few decades be absorbed into the consumer economy, so that they can continue to exercise the desired independent effect on the economic market. As another alternative it has been argued that in case of total disarmament inspection could become such an intensive effort that its expenditures could become a partial substitute for military activity. This alternative does not appear very feasible because if nations halt weapon production there will be little left to inspect.

In politics the threat of war has often served as an integrating force to keep a government in power and bring the divisive forces of a nation together to face an external menance. Sociologically, the war system serves as a cohesive force that brings together or simply drafts dissident elements to work for the common good of national defense. It engages the aggressive energies of various members of society. By channeling energies in this manner war contributes to maintaining internal order. In a state of permanent peace this function could be replaced by sufficiently menacing natural or contrived forces. Pollution and other social ills of long duration may serve as surrogates.

An erroneous thought persists that war provides a logical framework and an integrating force for intensified intellectual activity. For example, it is claimed to heighten the intensity of expression in the arts (Goya, Delacroix, war poets), literature (Hemingway), social ethics, and calls for efforts to rejuvenate human nature.

Although the period of the Rennaissance involved some wars, it has not been argued that the upsurge of creative genius in the arts, in metaphysics and in social and natural philosophy derived mainly from wars. Rather the patronage of artists by princes, intellectual freedom at universities, and reaction to established values are among the factors leading to an upsurge of progress in cognitive and in aesthetic order. The French impressionist period in the arts is far more impressive in its accomplishments than any movement the arts derived from war.

To define peace as the total absence of war is to do injustice to the cause of peace. Coexistence, for example, is a form of peace involving societies with limited hostilities toward one another. It is essential to redefine peace not as it manifests itself in the variable form as it occurs between wars but rather as it relates to the deep roots of collective aggression.

Some have based their search for peace on the conscientious good will of man. Others have taken a fatalistic attitude of the inevitability of war. There is a spectrum of attitudes between these two extremes, ranging from those who maintain with Clausewitz that war is intentional as an arm of policy to those who feel that aggressive expression of frustration in society has inevitably manifested itself in war.

Concerning methods of improving security in the face of international frustration, there are two schools of thought. One school argues that the presence of arms has a deterrent and stabilizing effect on the expression of hostility. Saving the peace is essentially conceived in the maxim, "If you want peace, prepare for war." The other school argues that in the presence of very powerful weapons, small conflicts can quickly enlarge to a level of mutual destruction and that the presence of such a possibility should encourage less reliance on weapons and more on negotiations.

In the year 1966–1967, world expenditures for armaments have been estimated at $136 billion, $58 billion of which was spent by the U.S. and $35 billion by the Soviet Union [28a]. Since the year 1963–1964 American and Soviet expenditures for armaments, in aggregate, have grown by 27.8%, a sum which is equivalent to the total spent in 1964 (for which information is available at present) by Canada, West Germany, Red China, France, Great Britain, Indonesia, and Italy for the purpose. The defense expenditures of the seven states mentioned have also grown considerably since that year. The world's armaments expenditures in 1964 represented 6.5 to 7.1% of its gross social product. Differences in statistical methods of estimating the foregoing figures are insignificant in relation to the magnitude of the costs discussed.

Are these expenditures buying peace for the world, or are they preparing us for war? Where should we go from here? The most pertinent conclusion to be reached from the foregoing is that those nations that possess security and power should set an example of persistent willingness to negotiate and bargain. They need to concentrate their energies on resolving problems peacefully, at the same time letting their actions show other nations the value of such an approach. Perhaps this is our best course as we toil laboriously toward our ultimate goal of a world in which the use of force has been subordinated to the rule of law.

In an unpublished paper, Heller who is also the author of reference 27a, has advanced the idea that in order to speed up cooperation between nations toward peaceful existence and international security, it is of essence to establish an organization or system of government elected by the world's citizens in direct popular vote. He gives a feasible method for doing this. Such a government would serve the exclusive function of maintaining world peace, without impinging on any of the other functions of the national governments.

The United Nations would conceivably form a part (a consultative body) of such a government, which could be complete with legislative, judiciary, and executive branches. The initial steps to create such a government could consist of the convening of a provisional committee of outstanding world citizens that would prepare the convocation of a world constitutional assembly selected among the leaders of various cultural and professional organization. This assembly designs an adequate form and election procedures of the government.

By receiving worldwide publicity and disseminating information, such a government could help create an atmosphere of greater understanding. It would influence the thinking of the national governments in the direction of international cooperation and bring about the transfer of their defense functions to the central government.

Speculations on the Future

In search of peace humanity is often seen, in the words of Valery, to be marching backwards into the future.

Peace is not likely to burst upon the earth by a sudden change of human nature. There is not likely to be a unity of human purpose by spontaneous generation unless perhaps it is brought about by a modern war of large dimensions which will break our spirit. Otherwise, peace must be sought, gradually, diligently, and by a cumulative, intensified, integrated, and continuous effort. It seems reasonable to postulate that if peace is going to be achieved it will happen as an evolutionary process involving trial and error. Trial and error is a painful way to learn. The appreciation for what peace might do for society collectively and for people individually needs to develop in a world free of doubt, fear, and oppression. We must try to approximate such a world before we can presume that a change will take place in human nature.

In varying degrees the elements of peace are embedded in every human being as he learns to live with others. But how to achieve international peace is a responsibility of society, and no single individual has in him the solution to that problem. As people unite and mesh together the fulfillment of their aspirations they must find the means to live in harmony. This too is a process of evolution. Living in society induces and expedites the process whereby most individuals learn early to control their excessive aggression. It is likely that the solution to the problem of peace may be found in both empiric and theoretical models of social phenomena.

If peace is attainable in our society, we need to diagnose and pull together those elements of society which would make peace possible. Our inadequately developed consciousness about what the ultimately desired society should be like blurs our vision of those elements that would accelerate our understanding and practice of peaceful living. Collectively man is more aware today of the consequences and futility of conflict.

Two books written by scientists in a speculative tone point to the increasing social unity of man. The first is *Instinct of the Herd in Peace and War* by Trotter [70] and the second is *The Phenomenon of Man* by Teilhard de Chardin [13]. They point out that man has been implicitly guided by nature to higher and higher forms of altruistic gregariousness. According to Chardin, social aggregation, keeping the utmost value of each individual, is a complex form toward which life is evolving just as multicellular organisms evolved from the single cell. In this view the consciousness of man as an individual is a major evolutionary step above physical evolution. Social aggregation is yet another step in evolution with a higher level of consciousness in which humans fulfill their individual consciousness.

The gregariousness of man is expressed by a mixture of wolf-pack aggressiveness, sheep flock, and swarm-of-bees social tendencies. The danger is that an excess of aggressiveness may cause the destruction of this higher form of life.

Gregariousness alone is insufficient for the formation of stability of a social unit [80a]. In addition to a search for security and self-protection, man has developed the rudiments of an altruistic capacity to assimilate the interests of others and see their problems as his own. The stability of the herd depends on this quality of altruism, which obviously is most effectively developed through intercommunication. If altruism and empathy predominate, a utopian social organism may develop with substantial power for achievement. In it quarrels will be regarded simply as disease.

Modern communication and transportation are gradually leading to homogeneous human habits, increasing the awareness of a single race of people. A conscious move working toward human unity was started in modern times by forming the League of Nations, later followed by the United Nations. A world court for arbitrating on international issues presides at the Hague. Thought has also been given to an international police force and even to world government.

Our limited capacity for looking into the extended future is one reason why we have a natural tendency to be tied to the present with its technological and scientific contexts around which life seems to gravitate. However attractive technology and its conquest of nature may seem today, it is likely to be a passing phase in human development from which the essentials have been extracted and saved. There have been many great visions of future societies in the past. Their intensity was perhaps no less than ours. Some examples of other visions of future society are the following.

1. Primarily technological and economic progress; conquest of the cosmos as objective.

   a. 1984, Orwell
   b. Communism, Marx
   c. Brave New Worlds, Huxley
   d. Profiles of the Future, A. C. Clarke.

2. An intellectually and morally oriented society realizing the fulfillment of what man's nature and evolution reveal.

   a. The Republic, Plato
   b. Utopia, Thomas More
   c. Altruistic Society, Trotter.

3. A spiritual world in which physical being is reduced to small dimensions.

   a. Christianity, *New Testament*
   b. Cosmogenesis, de Chardin
   c. Evolving spirituality, Buddha.

Some go so far as to consider anarchism as the way of the future. Another extreme available to our society is to eliminate the future. Such awareness of the past and its visions coupled with our own view should help us maintain a balanced outlook as we move ahead.

6.5. FURTHER DEVELOPMENTS IN SCIENCE FOR ARMS CONTROL

We must ultimately feed, educate, and appropriately employ (or occupy) every member of the human race so that he feels as adequate and satisfied as human nature permits. He can then be creative and vigorous because he will have no reasons for permanent frustration.

Operations research can make a significant contribution by developing estimates of how much of our resources and those of other nations should go into defense, and how much should be used to aid less-developed nations to maximize the likelihood of peace.

Based on these studies, the rich countries might take on a phased projected plan for developing the rest of the world. Any blueprint for such an attempt would require the participation of the whole world.

The widening disparity between the rich countries and the poor countries is one major cause of conflict in our time and will continue to be so in the foreseeable future. Myrdal [47a], urges an underdeveloped country to attempt any and all measures that can be taken to enhance its own economic welfare, at the same time avoiding self-defeating policies arising out of resentment, which would lead to barriers against the rich world's culture and values.

Naturally, there are other causes of conflict in the world besides the economic one; for example, that illustrated by the exercise of power politics in World War I. The outlook for solving conflicts of this nature is not as encouraging. One of the extrapolations from limited experimentation is that early contacts and communication, negotiation, talking it over, and letting the other side hear the opponent's views face-to-face is the most effective means known today for checking escalation in a conflict situation. Nuclear power seems to have taught a lesson of restraint so that great powers are not easily provoked into precipitous action over small incidents but limit their response. Noneconomic conflicts are fairly common, hence research on their resolution requires at least as much attention as that given to economic problems which we understand better.

Let us now look at projected scientific application into three areas of arms control. Given that in the future wars may still have to be fought, perhaps the protagonists will fight them mathematically on computers with full ingenuity and precision rather than on the battlefield with actual weapons. This would not halt the development of weapons but would halt destruction. If man continues to use his present philosophy on wars, weapons would still be necessary to deter any real action by either side. There could be a number of computer runs, maybe thousands of them, to vary any nuances that occur to the generals and leaders of the participating countries. The type of computer and program used would be agreed on in advance. So far, computer models need precise information. It is almost certain that in some areas not all the information needed can be translated from experience to a scale of measurement, but we have given examples in this book in which ordinal utilities would suffice and seem to have a wide applicability. Thus there is hope of circumventing this problem. The possibility that the winner on the computer may proceed to dictate to the loser may discourage the loser from going to the computer; hence the entire idea needs careful planning and the use of controls perhaps through world courts. This approach involves a certain amount of good will among men even though they continue to be aggressive-

paralleling competitive games. There is considerable hope that increased cooperation would obviate the necessity of substituting wars on computers. The computer idea here is a simplification of the notion that in order to resolve a conflict, the parties need to work together rather than separately and that they would use their best judgements and intentions in this approach even at the "risk" of helping each other.

Another use has been contemplated whereby information about ideas, policies, and statements corresponding to various issues of current interest is stored on a computer. A policy maker can check the declared positions of other governments and the gamut of new developments in a short time period.

A third computer application concerns the analysis of a problem with a large number of options to determine stable policies. A computer would serve as the organizer and interrogator when used by decision makers who would supply value judgments. This process computerizes the manipulations of Section 3.7.

Undoubtedly one of the major obstacles to progress in international affairs is the little knowledge available on multi-interest competitive situations. The theory of games has assumed general responsibility for this area and progress of a theoretical nature has been made. The present formulations of game theory, however, do not take specific account of questions of ethical behavior. Ethics are subverted to rationality.

There are sufficient instances to show that ethical behavior is not necessarily rational—in the sense of being optimum for a side's best interests—and therefore may lead to loss of advantage in a world of propaganda. Rational behavior is defined to be the strategy most likely to lead to the satisfaction of objectives. Game theory is not a theory about ethics. Its recommendations for rational behavior to a decision maker, a complex entity of rationality and ethics, may go against his beliefs.

Rational decision making as applied to problems of conflict derives its tools from nonzero-sum games. The attitudes of players do not matter in zero-sum games because they are normative, giving best strategies regardless of attitude. In nonzero-sum games no satisfactory normative theory exists, particularly for noncooperative games. For example, the Prisoner's Dilemma game of Chapter 3 is a nonzero-sum game that can be used to explain behavior. Without considering attitudes we have a Nash-type equilibrium dominated by a meta-game equilibrium derived by considering attitudes. Meta-game theory is a recent development which shows promise for making game theory more useful in application.

Physics has not yet solved the problem of more than two bodies occurring in a dynamic configuration. It is not possible to give the general solution describing the trajectory of each of the bodies with respect to the entire system of several bodies. So far game theory has not found it easy to tackle the problem of optimally relating the interests of more than two individuals coexisting in a competitive framework. Ordinary game theory takes a time-static look at optimal strategies; differential game theory determines strategies as functions of time.

An operations research study on risk of boat collisions in a narrow channel between Denmark and Sweden concluded that the hazards of increased traffic, consisting mostly of ocean-going liners and of ferry boats, and threatening to double in the next few years, would lead to an eightfold increase in three boats being too close together and possibly some of them would collide. The rules and knowledge of navigation were clear and specific in the case of two, but not more than two, boats approaching each other. Not having a solution to the multiple-boat problem, the possibility of building a bridge over the channel to reduce the ferry traffic was suggested as a solution to the problem. A useful lesson learned from this imaginative approach can be applied in solving N-person problems, where intuition is not much help and knowledge is feeble—in a clash of multiple interests it may be advisable to consider alternative and radically different solutions rather than to force a "solution" in the existing framework.

An important problem in negotiating a lasting disarmament agreement is the uncertainty about future developments. As world power configurations continue to change, there is a shift in the balance of power, of the equilibrium of forces and coalitions. Uncertainty also derives from the difficulty of predicting the intentions and relations of nations toward each other and the resulting effect on a third country. These are some of the problems to be pursued through N-person games.

So far arms control agreements have proceeded by proscribing nonuse, nondevelopment, nontesting, nonproduction, and nonproliferation of weapons. As previously mentioned, disarmament proposals which place a percentage on the amount of weapons to be traded off would be impractical unless they take into consideration the strongly nonlinear effects of weapons cuts. Reduction of a force can bring it to a threshold at which what remains would be ineffective in fulfilling its missions. Since military posture is a function of time, a country with a small number of weapons may not wish to decrease its capability below a certain minimum because it must be prepared in case of an outbreak of hostilities. For example, a country with three airplanes may not wish to give up 30% of this force because two airplanes may be virtually useless, whereas three may provide adequate defense. A country with 100 airplanes may be very willing to give up 30% of its airplanes, however.

In order to preserve a comparable strength, a 30% cut in the weapons of one country may in the balance justify only a 20% cut in another's (in numbers, payload, etc.). Such a percentage approach has tended to arrange its steps so that if trouble develops each side can still annihilate the other by keeping an "umbrella" of minimum forces to accomplish the task.

Lack of agreement on a percentage scale may be due to the absence of a good measurement of nonlinear effects. The effectiveness of a combination of two weapon systems is not obtained simply by adding their separate capabilities. People are accustomed to thinking in terms of linear scales when dealing with numbers and have a willingness to use them because of their simplicity. People's experiences are often nonlinear, however, hence these experiences give rise to feelings that contradict the rational commitment to linear arguments. It would be simpler for harmony of thought and experience to study weapon effects from the start with nonlinear mathematics.

A consequence from the foregoing areas of research may be the growth to maturity of mathematics of politics. It is a beginning about which we can be optimistic. The need is for a model that increases understanding of moves and concessions to be made to prevent a conflict situation from escalating to a major crisis. We may reasonably expect that research on escalation and the nature of conflict will develop criteria for indicating to feuding nations the nature of their quarrels. The criteria can be tested on historical examples analyzed in the framework of a model within which stable solutions can be sought. Research on classifying games for stability and associating with each class a number of significant historical examples has been started. With each class and type of stability, a set of feasible solutions may be associated. This is a scientific attempt in preparation for the intermediate problems of arms control.

REFERENCES

[1] Ackoff, R., See Reference 47.

[1a] Alker, H. R., *Mathematics and Politics*. Macmillan, New York (1965).

[1b] Anscomb, F. J., Principles of Sampling as Applied to Disarmament Agreement, Contract No. ACDA/ST-37 with *Mathematica*, Princeton, New Jersey (1965).

[2] Aumann, R. J., and M. Maschler, Game Theoretic Aspects of Gradual Disarmament in "Development of Utility Theory for Arms Control and Disarmament," Contract No. ACDA/ST-80 and 116 with *Mathematica*, Princeton, New Jersey (1966).

[3] Basore, Bennett L., Private communication.

[4] Beaufre, A., *Strategy of Action*. Praeger, New York (1967).

[5] Beaufre, A., *Deterrence and Strategy*. Faber (1967).

[6] Bendix Corporation, A Report of Verification Requirements for Restrictions on Strategic Nuclear Delivery Vehicles" (1964).

[7] Boulding, Kenneth E., *Conflict and Defense*. Harper & Row, Boston (1961).

[8] Bouthoul, Gaston, *La Guerre*, *"Que Sais-je?"* Presses Universitaires, Paris (1953).

[9] Bouthoul, Gaston, *Sauver La Guerre*. Grasset, Paris (1963).

[10] Bouthoul, Gaston, *Avoir La Paix*. Grasset, Paris (1967).

[10a] Brody, Richard, A., and John Vesecky, *Soviet Responsiveness: A Critical Evaluation of Certain Hypotheses About Soviet Foreign Policy Behavior*. Stanford University (December 1965).

[11] Brown, R. H., "A Stochastic Analysis of Lanchester's Theory of Combat," *Operations Research Office Technical Memorandum*, ORO T-323 (1955).

[12] Buchanan, J. M., and G. Tullock, *The Calculus of Consent: Logical Foundations of Constitutional Democracy*. University of Michigan Press, Ann Arbor (1962).

[13] Chardin, Teilhard, *The Phenomenon of Man*. Harper & Row, New York (1959).

[14] Charlesworth, J. C., ed., *Mathematics and the Social Sciences*. American Academy of Political and Social Science, Philadelphia (1963).

[15] Cohen, B., *Conflict and Conformity*. M.I.T. Press, Cambridge (1963).

[16] Criswell, J. H., H. Solomon, and P. Suppes, eds., *Mathematical Methods in Small Group Process*. Stanford University Press, Stanford (1962).

[17] Dean, Arthur H., *Test Ban and Disarmament, The Path of Negotiation*. Harper & Row, New York (1966).

[18] Debreu, Gerard, *Theory of Value*. Wiley, New York (1959).

[19] Dresher, Melvin, *Games of Strategy; Theory and Applications*. Prentice-Hall, Englewood Cliffs, New Jersey (1961).

[20] Dresher, M., A. W. Tucker, and P. Wolfe, *Contributions to the Theory of Games, Vol. III*. Princeton University Press, Princeton, New Jersey (1957).

[20a] Ericsson, U., "Approaches To Some Test Ban Control Problems, *Försvarets Forskningsanstalt Avdelning*, **4**, Stockholm (February 1967).

[20b] Feierabend, Ivo. K., and Rosalind L. Feierabend, "Aggressive Behaviors within

Polities 1948–1962: A Cross-National Study," *J. Conflict Resolution,* **X**:*3* (1966), 249–271.

[21] Galtung, Johan, "A Structural Theory of Aggression," *J. Peace Research, 2* (1964), 95–119.

[22] Galtung, Johan, "Summit Meetings and International Relations," *J. Peace Research, 1* (1964), 36–54.

[22a] Goldman, A. J., "The Probability of A Saddlepoint," *American Math. Monthly* (Dec. 1957).

[23] Guetzkow, H., C. F. Alger, R. A. Brody, R. C. Noel, and R. C. Snyder, *Simulation in International Relations: Developments for Research and Teaching.* Prentice-Hall, Englewood Cliffs, New Jersey (1963).

[24] Harsanyi, J. C., "Bargaining and Conflict Situations in the Light of a New Approach to Game Theory," *The American Economic Review,* **55**:*2* (May 1965), 447–457.

[25] Harsanyi, John C., "A General Theory of Rational Behavior in Game Situations," *Econometrica* (March 1964).

[25a] Harsanyi, J. C., "A Generalized Nash Solution for Two-Person Cooperative Games with Incomplete Information," prepared under *Mathematica,* Contract No. ACDA/ST-116 (September 1966). Part I of this paper is based on joint work by Reinhard Selten and J. C. Harsanyi. Part II is by J. C. Harsanyi.

[26] Harsanyi, J. C., Games with Incomplete Information, Part I. The Basic Model, Working Paper No. 157, Part II, Bayesian Equilibrium Points, Working Paper No. 158, Part III, The Basic Probability Distribution of the Game, Working Paper No. 159, Center for Research in Management Science, University of California, Berkeley (February 1966).

[27] Harsanyi, J. C., A Game-Theoretical Analysis of Arms Control and Disarmament Problems in "Development of Utility Theory for Arms Control and Disarmament," Contract No. ACDA/ST-80 with *Mathematica,* Princeton, New Jersey.

[27a] Heller, I., A Conceptual Frame for the Study of International Relations for Arms Control and Disarmament Purposes, Part I, Static Deterministic Formulations (October 1967).

[28] Helmer, O., "The Game-Theoretical Approach to Organization Theory," *Synthese,* **15,** Reidel, Dordrecht, Holland (1963), 245–253.

[28a] Hennig, Eike, "Die Rüstungsgesellschaft und ihre Kosten," [Armament society and its costs] *Atomzeitalter, 6* (June 1967), 296–308.

[29] Howard, Nigel, "The Theory of Meta-Games," Management Science Center, University of Pennsylvania (May 1966).

29a] Intriligator, Michael D., Strategy In A Missile War: Targets and Rates of Fire; Security Studies Paper Number 10, University of California, Los Angeles (1967).

[29b] Intriligator, Michael D., Arms Races and War Initiation; The Effect of Strategic Choices. Department of Economics, University of California, Los Angeles (1968).

[30] Isaacs, Rufus, *Differential Games.* Wiley, New York (1965).

[31] Johnston, John M., and Paul A. Bornstein, A Game Theoretic Approach to the Negotiation Problem, M. A. Thesis, U.S. Naval Postgraduate School (1964).

[32] Joxe, Alain, The Logic of Preference Relation in a Power System with a Finite Number of Elements (French), G.E.M. P.P.S., Doc. No. 7E (1964).

[33] Karlin, Samuel, *Mathematical Methods and Theory in Games, Programming, and Economics, Vols. I and II.* Addison-Wesley, Reading, Massachusetts (1959).

[34] Khan, H., *On Thermonuclear War.* Princeton University Press, Princeton, New Jersey (1960).

[35] Khan, H., *Thinking the Unthinkable.* Horizon, New York (1962).

[36] Kuhn, H., Recursive Inspection Games in "Application of Statistical Methodology to Arms Control," *Mathematica,* ACDA/ST-3, Princeton (1963).

[37] Kuhn, H. W., and A. W. Tucker, *Contributions to the Theory of Games, Vol. I.* Princeton University Press, Princeton, New Jersey (1950).

[38] Lanchester, F., *Aircraft in Warfare, the Dawn of the Fourth Arm.* Constable, London (1916).

[39] Lazersfeld, P. F., ed., *Mathematical Thinking in the Social Sciences.* Free Press, New York (1954).

[39a] Lewin, Leonard C., *Report From Iron Mountain; On The Possibility and Desirability of Peace.* The Dial Press, Inc., New York (1967).

[40] Long, F. A., "Research for Disarmament," *International Science and Technology,* Conover-Mast, New York (August 1962), 52–59.

[41] Lotka, A., *Elements of Mathematical Biology.* Dover, New York (1956).

[42] Luce, R. Duncan, and Howard Raiffa, *Games and Decisions.* Wiley, New York (1957).

[43] Maschler, M., A Non-Zero-Sum Game Related to a Test Ban Treaty, Paper in "Applications of Statistical Methodology To Arms Control," *Mathematica,* ACDA/ST-3, Princeton (1963).

[44] Mayberry, J. P., The Notion of "Threat" and Its Relation to Bargaining Theory, Chapter I in "Models of Gradual Reduction of Arms," *Mathematica* Study ACDA/ST-116 for the Arms Control Agency, (1967).

[44a] Mayberry, J. P., Discounted Repeated Games with Incomplete Information, Chapter V in "Models of Gradual Reduction of Arms," *Mathematica* Study ACDA/ST-116 for the Arms Control Agency (1967).

[45] McGuire, Martin C., "Secrecy and the Arms Race," *A Theory of the Accumulation of Strategic Weapons and how Secrecy Affects It,* **CXXV,** Harvard University Press, Cambridge, Massachusetts (1965).

[46] McKinsey, J. C. C., *Introduction to the Theory of Games.* McGraw-Hill, New York (1952).

[46a] Midgaard, Knut, "Co-ordination in 'Tacit' Games: Some New Concepts," *Cooperation and Conflict: Nordic J. International Politics, 2* (1965).

[46b] Midgaard, Knut, "On Auxiliary Games and the Modes of a Game," *Cooperation and Conflict: Nordic J. International Politics, 1* (1966).

[47] Model Study of Escalation, Management Science Center, University of Pennsylvania **I, II** and **III** (1965).

[47a] Myrdal, Gunnar, *Rich Lands and Poor; the road to world prosperity,* Harper, New York (1957).

[48] Nilsen, S. S., "Political Equilibrium," *J. Conflict Resolution,* **3** (1959), 41–87.

[49] Nash, John, "Non-Cooperative Games," *Ann. Math.,* **54**:*2* (September 1951).

[50] Nash, John, "Two-Person Cooperative Games," *Econometrica,* **21** (1953), 128–140.

[51] Patterson, R. L., and W. Richardson, "A Decision Theoretic Model for Determining Verification Requirements," *J. Conflict Resolution,* **1**:*4* (September 1963) 602–607, and *J. Arms Control,* **1**:*4* (October 1963), 697–701.

[52] Rapoport, A., *Fights, Games and Debates.* University of Michigan Press, Ann Arbor (1960).

[52a] Rapoport, A., and Chammah, A. M., *Prisoner's Dilemma: A Study of Conflict and Cooperation.* The University of Michigan Press, Ann Arbor (1965).

[53] Rapoport, A., *Two-Person Game Theory, The Essential Ideas.* The University of Michigan Press, Ann Arbor (1966).
[54] Richardson, L. F., *Statistics of Deadly Quarrels.* Quadrangle, Chicago (1960).
[55] Richardson, L. F., *Arms and Insecurity.* Boxwood, Pittsburgh (1960).
[55a] Richardson, Wyman, Private communication (1967).
[55b] Rosen, S., "The Ideal Type of War," Dept. of Political Science, Univ. of Pittsburg, (1968).
[56] Saaty, Thomas L. *Mathematical Methods of Operations Research.* McGraw-Hill (1959).
[57] Saaty, Thomas L., and Joseph Bram, *Nonlinear Mathematics.* McGraw-Hill (1964).
[58] Saaty, Thomas L., "A Model for the Control of Arms," *Operations Research,* **12**:4 (July–August 1964), 586–609.
[58a] Saaty, Thomas L., Mathematical Structure in Politics: Mathematics Magazine, (to appear) November (1968).
[58b] Saaty, Thomas L., and P. J. Long, "Mathematical Foundation of the Stability of Deterrence," Arms Control and Disarmament Agency Study (1968).
[58c] Saaty, Thomas L., "An Application of Decision Theory; The Development of Additional Tools," Proceedings Decision Theory Symposium, Aix-en-Provence, (1967).
[59] Schelling, T. C., "An Essay on Bargaining," *The American Economic Review,* **46**:3 (June 1956), 281–306.
[60] Schelling, T. C., *The Strategy of Conflict.* Harvard University Press, Cambridge (1960).
[61] Shubik, Martin, *Game Theory and Related Approaches to Social Behavior.* Wiley, New York (1964).
[61a] Shubik, Martin, On the Strategy of Disarmament and Escalation, Chapter VI in "Development of Utility Theory for Arms Control and Disarmament," final report by *Mathematica* to the Arms Control and Disarmament Agency, Contract ACDA/ST-80 (1966).
[61b] Shubik, Martin, *Strategy and Market Structure.* Wiley, New York (1959).
[62] Siegel, S., and L. E. Fouraker, *Bargaining and Group Decision Making.* McGraw-Hill, New York (1960).
[62a] Singer, J. David (editor), *Quantitative International Politics: Insights and Evidence.* The Free Press, New York (1968).
[63] Smoker, Paul, A Pilot Study of the Present Arms Race, Peace Research Center, Lancaster, England, (May 1963).
[64] Smoker, Paul, "Fear in the Arms Race: A Mathematical Study," *J. Peace Research, 1* (1964), 55–64.
[65] Smoker, Paul, "Sino-Indian Relations: A Study of Trade, Communication and Defence," *J. Peace Research, 2* (1964), 65–76.
[66] Smoker, Paul, "A Wave Model of the Arms Race," Typescript, Lancaster, England (1964).
[67] Snyder, R. C., and J. A. Robinson, *National and International Decision Making.* The Institute for International Order (1962).
[68] Stearns, R., A Formal Information Concept for Games with Incomplete Information, Chapter IV in "Models of Gradual Reduction of Arms," Vol. II, *Mathematica* Study ACDA/ST-116 for the Arms Control Agency (1967).
[69] Thurstone, L. L., *The Measurement of Values,* University of Chicago Press, Chicago (1959).

[70] Trotter, Wilfred, *Instincts of the Herd in Peace and War.* Unwin, 1916.

[71] Tucker, A. W., and R. D. Luce, *Contributions to the Theory of Games,* **IV**:*40*, Princeton University Press, Princeton, New Jersey (1959).

[72] Ulmer, S. S., *Introductory Readings in Political Behavior.* Rand McNally, Chicago (1961).

[73] Vajda, S., *Mathematical Programming.* Addison-Wesley, Reading, Massachusetts (1961).

[74] Vajda, S., *The Theory of Games and Linear Programming.* Methuen, London; Wiley, New York (1956).

[75] Ventzel, E. S., *Lectures on Game Theory, Vol. VI.* Gordon and Breach, New York (1961).

[76] Voeglin, Eric, *The New Science of Politics.* University of Chicago Press, Chicago (1952).

[77] Volterra, V., *Lecon sur la théorie mathématique de la lutte pour la vie.* Gauthier-Villars et Cie, Editeurs, Paris (1963).

[78] von Neumann, John, and Oskar Morgenstern, *Theory of Games and Economic Behavior.* Princeton University Press, Princeton,New Jersey (1944).

[79] Williams, J. D., *The Compleat Strategyst.* McGraw-Hill, New York (1954).

[80] Westwick, Roy, W. A. McWorter, and Donald Quiring, "Games with a Winning Strategy," *Am. Math. Monthly,* P604 (May 1967).

[80a] Wharton, John F., What Nature Reveals About Peacemaking, *Saturday Review* (May 27, 1967), 11 10.

[81] Wiesner, Jerome B., "A Strategy for Arms Control," *Saturday Review,* (March 4, 1967), 17–20.

INDEX